T0185732

Mastering Structured Data on the Semantic Web

From HTML5 Microdata to
Linked Open Data

Leslie F. Sikos, Ph.D.

Apress®

Mastering Structured Data on the Semantic Web: From HTML5 Microdata to Linked Open Data

ISBN-13 (pbk): 978-1-4842-1050-5

ISBN-13 (electronic): 978-1-4842-1049-9

Managing Director: Welmoed Spahr
Lead Editor: Ben Renow-Clarke
Technical Reviewer: Maria Maleshkova
Editorial Board: Steve Anglin, Mark Beckner, Gary Cornell, Louise Corrigan, Jim DeWolf,
    Jonathan Gennick, Robert Hutchinson, Michelle Lowman, James Markham, Susan McDermott,
    Matthew Moodie, Jeffrey Pepper, Douglas Pundick, Ben Renow-Clarke, Gwenan Spearing,
    Matt Wade, Steve Weiss
Coordinating Editors: Melissa Maldonado and Christine Ricketts
Copy Editor: Michael G. Laraque
Compositor: SPi Global
Indexer: SPi Global
Artist: SPi Global

Distributed to the book trade worldwide by Springer Science+Business Media New York, 233 Spring Street, 6th Floor, New York, NY 10013. Phone 1-800-SPRINGER, fax (201) 348-4505, e-mail orders-ny@springer-sbm.com, or visit www.springeronline.com. Apress Media, LLC is a California LLC and the sole member (owner) is Springer Science+Business Media Finance Inc (SSBM Finance Inc). SSBM Finance Inc is a Delaware corporation.

For information on translations, please e-mail rights@apress.com, or visit www.apress.com.

Apress and friends of ED books may be purchased in bulk for academic, corporate, or promotional use. eBook versions and licenses are also available for most titles. For more information, reference our Special Bulk Sales–eBook Licensing web page at www.apress.com/bulk-sales.

Any source code or other supplementary material referenced by the author in this text is available to readers at www.apress.com and on the author's site at www.lesliesikos.com. For detailed information about how to locate your book's source code, go to www.apress.com/source-code/.

Contents at a Glance

Contents

About the Author

Leslie F. Sikos, Ph.D., is a Semantic Web researcher at Flinders University, South Australia, specializing in semantic video annotations, ontology engineering, and natural language processing using Linguistic Linked Open Data. On the cutting edge of Internet technologies, he is a member of industry-leading organizations, such as the World Wide Web Consortium, the Internet Engineering Task Force, and the Internet Society. He is an invited editor and journal reviewer actively contributing to the development of open standards. Dr. Sikos is the author of 15 textbooks covering a wide range of topics from computer networks to software engineering and web design. Devoted to lifelong learning, he holds multiple degrees in computer science and information technology, as well as professional certificates from the industry. Thanks to his hands-on skills, coupled with a pedagogical background, he can introduce technical terms and explain complex issues in plain English.

Dr. Sikos creates fully standard-compliant, mobile-friendly web sites with responsive web design—complemented by machine-readable annotations—and develops multimedia applications leveraging Semantic Web technologies. He works on the standardization of Linked Data implementations for the precise identification, description, and classification of multimedia fragments, advancing the traditional video annotation techniques. To solve syntactic interoperability, conceptual ambiguity, and implementation complexity problems of RDFS and OWL multimedia ontologies mapped from general-purpose XML Schema vocabularies, Dr. Sikos introduced a global video production and broadcasting ontology. Inspired by the creation and exploitation of rich Linked Open Data datasets, he proudly contributes to the Open Data and Open Knowledge initiatives. When he is not working, he enjoys reading, playing the organ, and cycling. For more information, visit `www.lesliesikos.com`.

About the Technical Reviewer

Maria Maleshkova, Ph.D., is a senior researcher at the Karlsruhe Institute of Technology (KIT), Germany. Her areas of expertise include Semantic Web services and web architectures, in particular focusing on the semantic description of Web APIs, RESTful services, and their joined use with Linked Data. In addition, she works on data integration with semantic technologies, domain modeling, and data annotation. She received a Ph.D. in computer science from the Knowledge Media Institute (KMi) at the Open University in Milton Keynes, England, where she worked on projects in the domain of service-oriented architecture and web services. Dr. Maleshkova has published more than 50 papers in conferences and international journals related to Semantic Web services, knowledge-based systems, knowledge engineering, and business process analysis. She is an active member of the Semantic Web community and has worked on several national and international research projects, involving both research and industrial partners.

Preface

With the evolution of the World Wide Web, more and more sophisticated web applications and services appear, making it possible not only to publish and search for information but also to share photos and videos, buy products online, chat with friends, book a hotel room, play games, and more. Many of these applications rely on file characteristics, metadata, tracking cookies, and data from user registrations, which makes it possible to provide customized services and to make offers of products or services the users might be interested in. However, because there is a huge gap between what the human mind understands and what computers can interpret, a large amount of data on the Internet cannot be processed efficiently with computer software. For example, a scanned table in an image file is unstructured and cannot be interpreted by computers. While optical character recognition programs can be used to convert images of printed text into machine-encoded text, such conversions cannot be done in real time and with 100% accuracy, rely on a relatively clear image in high resolution, and require different processing algorithms, depending on the image file format. More important, table headings and table data cells will all become plain text, with no correlation whatsoever. In other words, you lose the relationships between the data cells, including the table columns and rows, making data reusability very limited.

Beyond the lack of structure, much data are locked down in proprietary file formats that can be opened only in the commercial software they were created in. As well, related data are often stored in isolated data silos, making it impossible to automatically find new relations between seemingly unrelated data or make new discoveries based on the relation between data. Even if data is provided in a standardized, open-access format, software agents often cannot interpret the meaning of the represented information. HTML documents, which implement the core markup language of the Web, are semistructured but have limitations when it comes to machine-processability, because they are written primarily for humans. While they can be used to display data on a web site, software tools cannot "understand" the description of real-world persons and objects described in HTML, nor the relationships between them. For instance, on conventional web sites, a character sequence containing numbers can be a phone number, a date, an ISBN number of a book, or the age of a person, and there is no way for a computer program to interpret the meaning of such data. The situation can be improved by adding metadata annotations to the markup documents, but this won't make the entire document machine-interpretable, only small portions of it. Moreover, HTML documents use hyperlinks to link related web resources or parts of web documents to one another; however, there is no information about the type of these links. As a result, machines cannot interpret the relationships represented by hyperlinks, such as whether a link relates to additional information about a topic or the friendship between two people. Another popular format, XML, is used in structured documents that are both human- and machine-readable. XML is widely deployed from web site markup to configuration settings to web news feeds to office software tools; however, XML files are not machine-interpretable either.

Owing to the fact that the content of conventional web resources is primarily human-readable only, automatic processing is infeasible, and searching for related information is inefficient. This limitation can be addressed by organizing and publishing data using powerful formats that add structure and meaning to the content of web pages and link related data to one another. Computers can "understand" such data more easily and better, which can be used for task automation. The web sites and structured datasets that provide semantics (meaning) to software agents form the Semantic Web, the Artificial Intelligence extension of the conventional Web. On the Semantic Web, knowledge is represented in formal languages based on strict grammar, describing every resource and link in a machine-interpretable manner, most of the time with truly open access. This book is an example-driven tutorial for Semantic Web developers, Internet marketers, and researchers who want to unleash the potential of the Semantic Web. By bridging the gap between academia and the web design industry, this book will explain the core concepts as well as the mathematical background of the Semantic Web, based on graph theory and knowledge representation. You will learn how to annotate your web site markup with machine-readable metadata to boost your site's performance on next-generation Search Engine Result Pages. You will also understand how to reuse machine-readable definitions and how to describe your own concepts. By implementing best practices, you will be able to create typed links, so that computers can interpret a link, say, between two people who know each other, or a link between your web site and the machine-readable definition of topics you are interested in. Step-by-step guides will demonstrate the installation of integrated software development environments and the development of Semantic Web applications in Java.

These interlinked, machine-interpretable data can be used in task automation for web services, as well as for automatic knowledge discovery in research. The benefits of Semantic Web technologies have already been recognized by industrial giants such as Amazon.com, the BBC, Facebook, Flickr, Google, IBM, Thomson Reuters, New York Times, and Yahoo!, and the list is constantly growing. By implementing Semantic Web technologies to represent and connect structured data, you will reach a wider audience, encourage data reuse, and provide content that can be automatically processed with full certainty. As a result, your web sites will be integral parts of the next revolution of the Web.

CHAPTER 1

■ ■ ■

Introduction to the Semantic Web

The content of conventional web sites is human-readable only, which is unsuitable for automatic processing and inefficient when searching for related information. Web datasets can be considered as isolated data silos that are not linked to each other. This limitation can be addressed by organizing and publishing data, using powerful formats that add structure and meaning to the content of web pages and link related data to one another. Computers can "understand" such data better, which can be useful for task automation.

The Semantic Web

While binary files often contain machine-readable metadata, such as the shutter speed in a JPEG image[1] or the album title in an MP3 music file, the textual content of traditional web sites cannot be interpreted (that is, not understood) by automated software agents. The web sites that provide semantics (meaning) to software agents form the *Semantic Web*, an extension of the conventional Web [1] introduced in the early 2000s [2]. The Semantic Web is a major aspect of Web 2.0 [3] and Web 3.0 [4]. *Web 2.0* is an umbrella term used for a collection of technologies behind instant messaging, Voice over IP, wikis, blogs, forums, social media portals, and web syndication. The next generation of the Web is denoted as *Web 3.0*, which is an umbrella term for customization, semantic contents, and more sophisticated web applications toward artificial intelligence, including computer-generated contents (see Figure 1-1) .

■ **Caution**   The word *semantic* is used on the Web in other contexts as well. For example, in HTML5 there are semantic (in other words, meaningful) structuring elements, but this expression refers to the "meaning" of elements. In this context, the word *semantic* contrasts the "meaning" of elements, such as that of section (a thematic grouping), with the generic elements of older HTML versions, such as the "meaningless" div. The semantics of markup elements should not be confused with the semantics (in other words, machine-processability) of metadata annotations and web ontologies used on the Semantic Web. The latter can provide far more sophisticated data than the meaning of a markup element.

---

[1]Exif or XMP. For more information, see Leslie Sikos: *Web Standards: Mastering HTML5, CSS3, and XML* (New York, Apress, 2014).

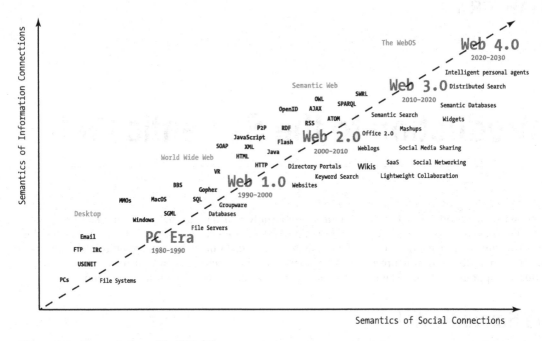

Figure 1-1. *The evolution of the Web [5]*

In contrast to the conventional Web (the "Web of documents"), the Semantic Web includes the "Web of Data" [6], which connects "things"[2] (representing real-world humans and objects) rather than documents meaningless to computers. The machine-readable datasets of the Semantic Web are used in a variety of web services [7], such as search engines, data integration, resource discovery and classification, cataloging, intelligent software agents, content rating, and intellectual property right descriptions [8], museum portals [9], community sites [10], podcasting [11], Big Data processing [12], business process modeling [13], and medical research. On the Semantic Web, data can be retrieved from seemingly unrelated fields automatically, in order to combine them, find relations, and make discoveries [14].

Structured Data

Conventional web sites rely on markup languages for document structure, style sheets for appearance, and scripts for behavior, but the content is human-readable only. When searching for "Jaguar" on the Web, for example, traditional search engine algorithms cannot always tell the difference between the British luxury car and the South American predator (Figure 1-2).

---

[2]The concept of "thing" is used in other contexts as well, such as in the "Internet of Things" (IoT), which is the network of physical objects embedded with electronics, software, and sensors, including smart objects such as wearable computers, all of which are connected to the manufacturer and/or the operator, and/or other devices.

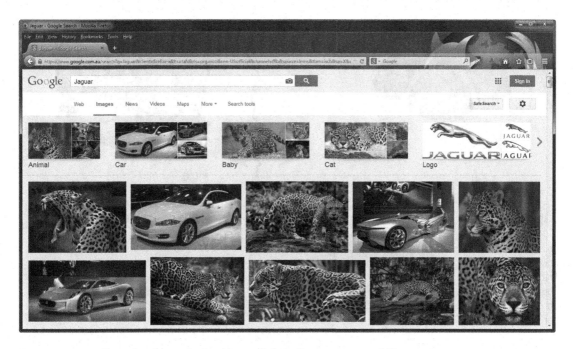

Figure 1-2. Traditional web search algorithms rely heavily on context and file names

A typical web page contains structuring elements, formatted text, and some even multimedia objects. By default, the headings, texts, links, and other web site components created by the web designer are meaningless to computers. While browsers can display web documents based on the markup, only the human mind can interpret the meaning of information, so there is a huge gap between what computers and humans understand (see Figure 1-3). Even if alternate text is specified for images (alt attribute with descriptive value on the img or figure[3] elements), the data is not structured or linked to related data, and human-readable words of conventional web page paragraphs are not associated with any particular software syntax or structure. Without context, the information provided by web sites can be ambiguous to search engines.

---

[3]This is only supported in (X)HTML5.

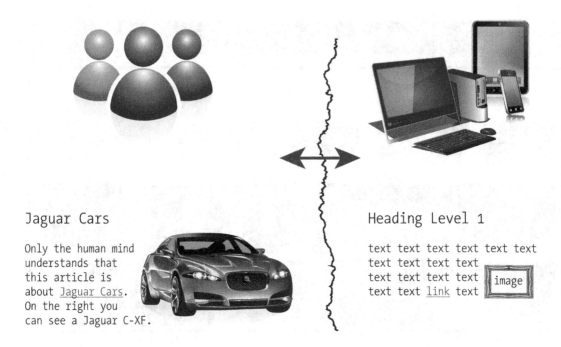

Figure 1-3. *Traditional web site contents are meaningless to computers*

The concept of machine-readable data is not new, and it is not limited to the Web. Think of the credit cards or barcodes, both of which contain human-readable and machine-readable data (Figure 1-4). One person or product, however, has more than one identifier, which can cause ambiguity.

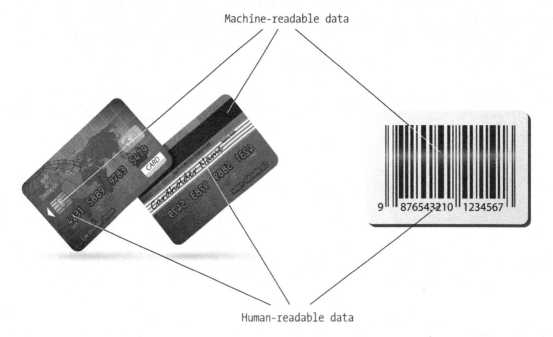

Figure 1-4. *Human-readable and machine-readable data*

Even the *well-formed XML* documents, which follow rigorous syntax rules, have serious limitations when it comes to machine-processability. For instance, if an XML entity is defined between `<SLR>` and `</SLR>`, what does *SLR* stand for? It can refer to a single-lens reflex camera, a self-loading rifle, a service-level report, system-level requirements, the Sri Lankan rupee, and so on.

Contents can be made machine-processable and unambiguous by adding organized (structured) data to the web sites, as markup annotations or as dedicated external metadata files, and linking them to other, related structured datasets. Among other benefits, structured data files support a much wider range of tasks than conventional web sites and are far more efficient to process. Structured data formats have been used for decades in computing, especially in Access and SQL relational databases, where queries can be performed to retrieve information efficiently. Because there are standards for direct mapping of relational databases to core Semantic Web technologies, databases that were publicly unavailable can now be shared on the Semantic Web [15]. Commercial database software packages powered by Semantic Web standards are also available on the market (5Store, AllegroGraph, BigData, Oracle, OWLIM, Talis Platform, Virtuoso, and so on) [16].

In contrast to relational databases, most data on the Web is stored in (X)HTML documents that contain *unstructured data* to be rendered in web browsers as formatted text, images, and multimedia objects. Publishing unstructured data works satisfactorily for general purposes; however, a large amount of data stored in, or associated with, traditional web documents cannot be processed this way. The data used to describe social connections between people is a good example, which should include the relationship type and multiple relationship directions inexpressible with the hyperlinks of the conventional Web [17].

The real benefit of semantic annotations is that humans can browse the conventional web documents, while Semantic Web crawlers can process the machine-readable annotations to classify data entities, discover logical links between entities, build indices, and create navigation and search pages.

Semantic Web Components

Structured data processing relies on technologies that provide a formal description of concepts, terms, and relationships within a knowledge domain (field of interest, discipline). *Knowledge Representation and Reasoning* is the field of Artificial Intelligence (AI) used to represent information in a machine-readable form that computer systems can utilize to solve complex tasks. *Taxonomies* or *controlled vocabularies* are structured collections of terms that can be used as metadata element values. For example, an events vocabulary can be used to describe concerts, lectures, and festivals in a machine-readable format, while an organization vocabulary is suitable for publishing machine-readable metadata about a school, a corporation, or a club. The controlled vocabularies are parts of conceptual data *schemas* (data models) that map concepts and their relationships.

The most widely adopted knowledge-management standards are the Resource Description Framework (RDF), the Web Ontology Language (OWL), and the Simple Knowledge Organization System (SKOS). *Knowledge Organization Systems* (*KOS*) are used for processing authority lists, classifications, thesauri, topic maps, ontologies, and so on. Web *ontologies* are formalized conceptual structures, in other words, complex knowledge representations of sets of concepts in a domain and the relationships between them. The *namespace* mechanism is used to reveal the meaning of tags and attributes by pointing to an external vocabulary that describes the concepts of the discipline in a machine-processable format, extending the vocabulary (set of elements and attributes) of markup languages. For example, a smartphone ontology defines all features of smartphones and the relationships between those features in a machine-processable format, so that software agents can "understand" the meaning of any of these features used to annotate a word on a web page by pointing to the ontology file. Web ontologies make it possible to describe complex statements in any topic in a machine-readable format. The architecture of the Semantic Web is illustrated by the "Semantic Web Stack," which shows the hierarchy of standards in which each layer relies on the layers below (see Figure 1-5).

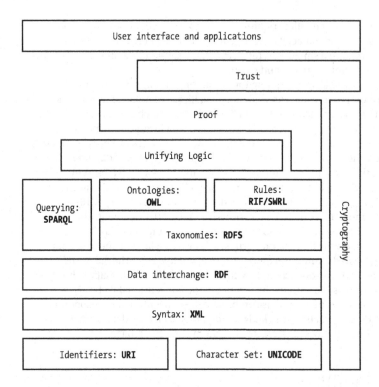

Figure 1-5. *The Semantic Web Stack*

While the preceding data formats are primarily machine-readable, they can be linked from human-readable web pages or integrated into human-readable web pages as *semantic annotations* such as microformats, RDFa, or HTML5 microdata.

Ontologies

The word *ontology* was originally introduced in philosophy to study the nature of existence. In computer science, ontology refers to conceptualization through a data model for describing a piece of our world, such as an organization, a research project, a historical event, our colleagues, friends, etc., in a machine-readable manner, by formally defining a set of classes (concepts), properties (attributes), relationship types, and entities (individuals, instances). The most advanced ontology languages (such as OWL) support the following components:

- *Classes*: Abstract groups, sets or collections of objects, object types. Classes usually represent groups or classes whose members share common properties. The hierarchy of classes is expressed as higher-level (superclass or parent class) and lower-level classes (subclass or child class). For example, a company can be represented as a class with subclasses such as departments and employees.

- *Attributes*: Aspects, properties, characteristics, or parameters that feature objects and classes

- *Individuals*: Instances or objects. For example, if our domain covers companies, each employee is an individual.

- *Relations*: The logical bond between classes, between individuals, between an individual and a class, between a single object and a collection, or between collections

- *Function terms*: Complex structures formed from certain relations that can be used in place of an individual term in a statement

- *Restrictions*: Formally defined limitations or ranges of valid values

- *Rules*: If-then statements (antecedent-consequent sentence) defining the logical inferences

- *Axioms*: Assertions in a logical form that, together with rules, form the overall theory the ontology describes. Unlike the definition of axiom in generative grammar or formal logic, where axioms include only statements defined as a priori knowledge, the axioms of Semantic Web ontologies also include the theory derived from axiomatic statements. Axioms are used to impose constraints on the values of classes or instances, so axioms are generally expressed using logic-based languages. Axioms are suitable for verifying the consistency of the ontology.

- *Events*: Attribute or relationship changes

Ontology Engineering

Ontology engineering is a field of computer science that covers the methods and methodologies for building ontologies. The purpose of Semantic Web ontologies is to achieve a common and shared knowledge ready to be transmitted between applications, providing interoperability across organizations of different areas or different views of the same area. *Ontology transformation* is the development of a new ontology to deal with the new requirements of an existing ontology for a new purpose. Creating a new single coherent ontology from two or more ontologies of the same knowledge domain is known as *ontology merging*. *Ontology integration* is the creation of a new ontology from two or more source ontologies from different knowledge domains. *Ontology mapping* is a formal expression to define the semantic relationships between entities from different ontologies. *Ontology alignment* is the process of creating a consistent and coherent link between two or more ontologies where statements of the first ontology confirm the statements of the second ontology.

Inference

The automatic discovery of relationships between seemingly unrelated structured data is called *inference*. The automatically generated new relationships are based on the structured data and additional information defined in the vocabulary, as, for example, a set of rules. The new relationships are either explicitly declared or returned through queries. As an example, if we make the statement "Unforgiven is a western," while an ontology declares that "every western is a movie," Semantic Web agents can automatically infer the statement "Unforgiven is a movie," which was originally not declared.

Semantic Web Features

The Semantic Web has many distinctive features that are rarely seen or not used at all on traditional web sites. For example, a large share of the data is published with explicitly declared open license, allowing data sharing and distribution that is truly free. The formally defined data connections make automatic knowledge discovery possible, along with accurate statement verification. Each and every object and feature is associated with a web address, so that you can refer to virtually everything, from a table cell to an image or a friendship of two people.

Free, Open Access Data Repositories

Open data and content can be freely used, modified, and shared by anyone for any purpose

—OpenDefinition.org

Automation and data processing rely on data access, so "open data" is a fundamental feature of the Semantic Web. There are already hundreds of government organizations, enterprises, and individuals publishing machine-readable, structured data as open data (`https://data.cityofchicago.org`, `http://data.alberta.ca`, `http://data.gov.uk`, etc.), although not all of them provide an open license explicitly that makes data truly "open." Semantic Web applications also benefit from open APIs, open protocols, open data formats, and open source software tools to reuse, remix, and republish data. On the Semantic Web, the machine-readable data of persons, products, services, and objects of the world are open and accessible, without registering and paying membership or subscription fees, and software agents can access these data automatically on your behalf.

Adaptive Information

While on the conventional Web, each web document is edited by a single person or a team, Semantic Web documents are edited by groups of people through related documents as a "global database." As a result, datasets are more accurate, more connected, and more descriptive. Information is not just about pages, but, rather, about connected and reusable data. The classification, reorganization, and reuse of data is a fundamental concept of the Semantic Web.

Unique Web Resource Identifiers

Web resources can be located by unique IP addresses. However, they are hard to remember, and their number is limited. This is why *domain names* are used in most cases. Figure 1-6 shows the relationship between a domain name and a URL: `www.masteringhtml5css3.com` is a subdomain of the node `masteringhtml5css3.com`, which is the subdomain of the `com` (which stands for *commercial*) domain. The domain name syntax rules are defined by RFC 1035 [18], RFC 1123 [19], and RFC 2181 [20].

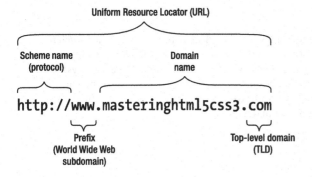

Figure 1-6. The domain within the URL

The tree of subdomains can contain a maximum of 127 levels. Each label may contain up to 63 characters. According to RFC 2181, the full length of a domain name is 253 characters. Conventional domain names cannot contain Latin alphabet–based characters with diacritics, non-Latin characters, or scripts. With the introduction of Internationalized Domain Names (IDN), it is possible to represent names and words in several languages in native alphabets and scripts.

A *Uniform Resource Identifier* (*URI*) is a character string that identifies a name or a resource on the Internet (RFC 2396 [21]). URIs can be classified as *Uniform Resource Locators* (*URLs*; RFC 1738 [22]), *Uniform Resource Names* (*URNs*), or both. A URN defines the identity of a resource, while the URL provides a method for finding it (including protocol and path). URIs are often used incorrectly as a synonym for URLs, although URI is a broader term (RFC 3305 [23]). Both the URN and the URL are subsets of the URI, but they are generally disjoint sets. The best-known examples of URLs are the web site addresses on the World Wide Web. Listing 1-1 shows the general URL syntax.

Listing 1-1. URL Syntax

```
protocol://domain:port/path?query_string#fragment_identifier
```

The *protocol* is followed by a colon. The other parts of URLs depend on the scheme being used. Usually, there is a domain name or an IP address, an optional port number, and an optional path to the resource or script. Programs such as PHP or CGI scripts might have a query string. The end of the URL can be an optional *fragment identifier*, which starts with the number sign (#), and in markup languages, it points to a section of the document available through the provided path. Fragment identifiers are widely used on the Semantic Web for distinguishing a file from the entity it represents (e.g., a person vs. the file that describes him/her or a book vs. the file that describes it). This use of fragment identifiers provides an unlimited number of unique identifiers, regardless of the restricted choice of domain names. Listing 1-2 shows an example, in which http is the protocol, www.masteringhtml5css3.com is the domain, and the URL identifies a book rather than the file webstandardsbook.rdf stored in the metadata directory.

Listing 1-2. A Typical URL with Fragment Identifier

```
http://www.masteringhtml5css3.com/metadata/webstandardsbook.rdf#book
```

Because many of the URL components are optional, one or more of them are often omitted.

To avoid the inconvenience of registering and renewing domain names and address the issue that not every user has his/her own domain name, web addresses can be redirected (typically using 302 HTTP redirection) to an intermediate and more persistent location on the Web, instead of the actual physical location of the file or directory. Such URLs are called *Persistent Uniform Resource Locators* (*PURLs*). Official PURLs are registered on https://purl.org. Many semantic vocabularies and ontologies use PURLs. Ontologies are listed under the ontology directory such as http://purl.org/ontology/vidont/.

Summary

In this chapter, you learned that a major limitation of conventional web sites is their unorganized and isolated contents, which is created mainly for human interpretation. You became familiar with the fundamental concepts of the Semantic Web, the main application areas, and the efficiency of structured data processing. You know the core Semantic Web components and understand that many standards rely on other technologies. You are familiar with distinctive Semantic Web features, such as open licensing, decentralized data storage with automatically inferred statements and knowledge discovery, and unique URI indentifiers associated with every bit of represented knowledge.

The next chapter will introduce you to knowledge representation and reasoning used to represent information with machine-processable standards.

References

1. Hausenblas, M., Adida, B., Herman, I. (2008) RDFa—Bridging the Web of Documents and the Web of Data. Joanneum Research, Creative Commons, World Wide Web Consortium. `www.w3.org/2008/Talks/1026-ISCW-RDFa/`. Accessed 18 January 2015.

2. Berners-Lee, T. (2001) Business Model for the Semantic Web. World Wide Web Consortium. `www.w3.org/DesignIssues/Business`. Accessed 18 January 2015.

3. Ankolekar, A., Krötzsch, M., Tran, T., Vrandečić, D. The Two Cultures: Mashing Up Web 2.0 and the Semantic Web. *Web Semantics: Science, Services and Agents on the World Wide Web* 2008, 6(1):70-75.

4. Shannon, V. (2006) A "more revolutionary" Web. *International Herald Tribune*. The New York Times Company. `www.nytimes.com/2006/05/23/technology/23iht-web.html?scp=1&sq=A+%27more+revolutionary%27+Web&st=nyt`. Accessed 18 January 2015.

5. Spivack, N. (2015) Web 3.0: The Third Generation Web Is Coming. `http://lifeboat.com/ex/web.3.0`. Accessed 16 March 2015.

6. Herman, I. (ed.) (2009) How would you define the main goals of the Semantic Web? In: W3C Semantic Web FAQ. World Wide Web Consortium. `www.w3.org/2001/sw/SW-FAQ#swgoals`. Accessed 18 January 2015.

7. Sbodio, L. M., Martin, D., Moulin, C. Discovering Semantic Web services using SPARQL and intelligent agents. Web Semantics: Science, Services and Agents on the World Wide Web 2010, 8(4): 310-328.

8. Herman, I. (2009) W3C Semantic Web Frequently Asked Questions. World Wide Web Consortium. `www.w3.org/RDF/FAQ`. Accessed 18 January 2015.

9. Hyvönen, E., Mäkelä, E., Salminen, M., Valo, A., Viljanen, K., Saarela, S., Junnila, M., Kettula, S. MuseumFinland—Finnish museums on the Semantic Web. Web Semantics: Science, Services and Agents on the World Wide Web 2005, 3(2-3): 224-241.

10. Bojārs, U., Breslin, J. G., Finn, A., Decker, S. Using the Semantic Web for linking and reusing data across Web 2.0 communities. Web Semantics: Science, Services and Agents on the World Wide Web 2008, 6(1): 21-28.

11. Celma, Ò., Raimond, Y. ZemPod: A Semantic Web approach to podcasting. Web Semantics: Science, Services and Agents on the World Wide Web 2008, 6(2): 162-169.

12. Saleem, M., Kamdar, M. R., Iqbal, A., Sampath, S., Deus, H. F., Ngomo, A.-C. Big linked cancer data: Integrating linked TCGA and PubMed. Web Semantics: Science, Services and Agents on the World Wide Web 2014, `http://dx.doi.org/10.1016/j.websem.2014.07.004`.

13. Oinonen, K. (2005) On the road to business application of Semantic Web technology. Semantic Web in Business—How to proceed. In: *Industrial Applications of Semantic Web: Proceedings of the 1st IFIP WG12.5 Working Conference on Industrial Applications of Semantic Web*. International Federation for Information Processing. Springer Science+Business Media, Inc., New York.

14. Murphy, T. (2010) Lin Clark On Why Drupal Matters. Socialmedia. `http://socialmedia.net/2010/09/07/lin-clark-on-why-drupal-matters`. Accessed 9 September 2010.

15. Arenas, M., Bertails, A., Prud'hommeaux, E., Sequeda, J. (eds.) (2012) A Direct Mapping of Relational Data to RDF. `www.w3.org/TR/rdb-direct-mapping/`. Accessed 18 January 2015.

16. Clark, K. (2010) The RDF Database Market. Clark & Parsia, LLC. `http://weblog.clarkparsia.com/2010/09/23/the-rdf-database-market/`. Accessed 18 January 2015.

17. Dertouzos, L. M., Berners-Lee, T., Fischetti, M. (1999) *Weaving the Web: The Original Design and Ultimate Destiny of the World Wide Web by Its Inventor.* Harper San Francisco, San Francisco.

18. Mockapetris, P. (1987) Domain names—Implementation and specification. RFC 1035. The Internet Engineering Task Force. `http://tools.ietf.org/html/rfc1035`. Accessed 18 January 2015.

19. Braden, R. (ed.) (1989) Requirements for Internet Hosts—Application and Support. RFC 1123. The Internet Engineering Task Force. `http://tools.ietf.org/html/rfc1123`. Accessed 18 January 2015.

20. Elz, R., Bush, R. (1997) Clarifications to the DNS Specification. RFC 2181. The Internet Engineering Task Force. `http://tools.ietf.org/html/rfc2181`. Accessed 18 January 2015.

21. Berners-Lee, T., Fielding, R., Masinter, L. (1998) Uniform Resource Identifiers (URI): Generic Syntax. RFC 2396. The Internet Society. `http://tools.ietf.org/html/rfc2396`. Accessed 18 January 2015.

22. Berners-Lee, T., Masinter, L., McCahill, M. (eds.) (1994) Uniform Resource Locators (URL). RFC 1738. The Internet Engineering Task Force. `http://tools.ietf.org/html/rfc1738`. Accessed 18 January 2015.

23. Mealling, M., Denenberg, R. (eds.) (2002) Uniform Resource Identifiers (URIs), URLs, and Uniform Resource Names (URNs): Clarifications and Recommendations. RFC 3305. The Internet Society. `http://tools.ietf.org/html/rfc3305`. Accessed 18 January 2015.

CHAPTER 2

■ ■ ■

Knowledge Representation

To improve the automated processability of web sites, formal *knowledge representation* standards are required that can be used not only to annotate markup elements for simple machine-readable data but also to express complex statements and relationships in a machine-processable manner. After understanding the structure of these statements and their serialization in the Resource Description Framework (RDF), the structured data can be efficiently modeled as well as annotated in the markup, or written in separate, machine-readable metadata files. The formal definitions used for modeling and representing data make efficient data analysis and reuse possible. The three most common machine-readable annotations that are recognized and processed by search engines are RDFa (RDF in attributes), HTML5 Microdata, and JSON-LD, of which HTML5 Microdata is the recommended format. The machine-readable annotations extend the core (X)HTML markup with additional elements and attributes through external vocabularies that contain the terminology and properties of a knowledge representation domain, as well as the relationship between the properties in a machine-readable form. Ontologies can be used for searching, querying, indexing, and managing agent or service metadata and improving application and database interoperability. Ontologies are especially useful for knowledge-intensive applications, in which text extraction, decision support, or resource planning are common tasks, as well as in knowledge repositories used for knowledge acquisition. The schemas defining the most common concepts of a field of interest, the relationships between them, and related individuals are collected by semantic knowledge bases. These schemas are the de facto standards used by machine-readable annotations serialized in RDFa, HTML5 Microdata, or JSON-LD, as well as in RDF files of Linked Open Data datasets.

Vocabularies and Ontologies

Controlled vocabularies of the Semantic Web collect concepts and terms used to describe a field of interest or area of concern. *Ontologies* are more complex, very formal definitions of terms, individuals and their properties, object groups (classes), and relationships between individuals suitable to describe virtually any statement related to the field of interest in a machine-readable form.

For example, to declare a person in a machine-readable format, we need a vocabulary that has the formal definition of "Person." A straightforward choice is the Friend of a Friend (FOAF) vocabulary, which has a Person class that defines typical properties of a person, including, but not limited to, name and homepage. If we write this code in XML serialization, we would get the code in Listing 2-1.

Listing 2-1. Pseudocode for Defining the Class and a Property of a Resource

```
<Person>
  <name>Leslie Sikos</name>
</Person>
```

This code provides hierarchy, inferring that Person is a class and name is a property; however, it is out of context. We have to declare which external vocabulary defines this class and property, using the *namespace mechanism*. In RDF/XML serialization, this can be done using the xmlns attribute in the form xmlns:vocabulary_prefix="vocabulary_namespace:web_address", in our case, xmlns:foaf="http://xmlns.com/foaf/0.1/", which points to the FOAF namespace at http://xmlns.com/foaf/0.1/. The namespace mechanism makes it possible to abbreviate http://xmlns.com/foaf/0.1/ as foaf (also known as prefix), so foaf:Person refers to http://xmlns.com/foaf/0.1/Person, foaf:homepage to http://xmlns.com/foaf/0.1/homepage and so forth (see Listing 2-2).

■ **Note**   These links are often symbolic links that do not always point to a dedicated web page for each individual property and are sometimes forwarded to the domain of the namespace. Some vocabularies have a namespace address mechanism whereby all links point directly to the corresponding section of the machine-readable vocabulary file. The human-readable explanation of the properties of external vocabularies is not always provided. In case of FOAF, the web address of the individual property addresses point to the web site of the specification (http://xmlns.com/foaf/spec/), while the individual properties have their own fragment identifier, such as the Person property's address, http://xmlns.com/foaf/spec/#term_Person.

Listing 2-2. Describing the Name of a Person Using a Class and a Property from a Vocabulary

```
… xmlns:foaf="http://xmlns.com/foaf/0.1/"
…
<foaf:Person>
  <foaf:name>Leslie Sikos</foaf:name>
</foaf:Person>
```

The format and serialization of the structured data are independent of the vocabulary definitions, so, for example, the same schema.org reference can be used in RDF, RDFa, HTML5 Microdata, and JSON-LD. The vocabulary or ontology required depends on the area of interest you want to represent; however, some knowledge domains such as persons and books can be described with classes and properties from more than one vocabulary.

The schema.org Vocabulary Collection

Covering approximately 300 concept definitions, https://schema.org is one of the most frequently used collections of structured data markup schemas. Schema.org was launched by Google, Yahoo!, and Bing in 2011. Schema.org contains the machine-readable definitions of the most commonly used concepts, making it possible to annotate actions, creative works, events, services, medical concepts, organizations, persons, places, and products.

Analogously to the previous example, if we want to describe a book, we need a vocabulary with the definition of "Book" and typical book properties. If we want to add the book title with a more descriptive property than the name property of schema.org, we can use the title property from the *Dublin Core* (*DC*) vocabulary, resulting in two namespace declarations (see Listing 2-3).

Listing 2-3. Describing a Book

```
…
xmlns:schema="http://schema.org/"
xmlns:dc="http://purl.org/dc/terms/"
…
<schema:Book>
  <dc:title>Web Standards: Mastering HTML5, CSS3, and XML</dc:title>
</schema:Book>
```

Here, `schema:Book` abbreviates `http://schema.org/Book`, which is the machine-readable definition of the Book class, while `dc:title` abbreviates `http://purl.org/dc/terms/title`, which is the machine-readable definition of the `title` property.

The most common schema.org types (classes) and properties are collected at `http://schema.org/docs/gs.html#schemaorg_types`, while the full list of properties is available at `http://schema.org/docs/full.html`.

General, Access, and Structural Metadata

General metadata, such as abstract, creator, date, publisher, title, language of web resources (web sites, images, videos), physical resources (books, CDs), and objects such as artworks, can be described using Dublin Core. The Dublin Core elements are widely deployed in machine-readable annotations, used on DMOZ [1], one of the biggest multilingual open-content directories of web links, as well as in XMP metadata of JPEG photos. The namespace of Dublin Core Elements (dc) is `http://purl.org/dc/elements/1.1/`, and the namespace of Dublin Core terms (dcterms) is `http://purl.org/dc/terms/`.

Structured datasets can be described using terms from the *Vocabulary of Interlinked Datasets* (*VoID*). VoID covers general, access, and structural metadata definitions, as well as the description of links between structured datasets. The prefix of VoID is `void`, and the namespace is `http://rdfs.org/ns/void#`.

Person Vocabularies

The features of a person and relationships between people can be described by a variety of controlled vocabularies, as summarized in Table 2-1.

Table 2-1. Person Vocabularies

Vocabulary	Abbreviation	Namespace	Typical Use
Person class from schema.org	`schema:Person`	`http://schema.org/Person`	Given name, family name, gender, affiliation, award, nationality, honorific prefix or suffix, job title, etc.
Friend of a Friend	`foaf`	`http://xmlns.com/foaf/0.1/`	Person, name, gender, home page
Contact: Utility concepts for everyday life	`contact`	`http://www.w3.org/2000/10/ swap/pim/contact`	Contact location, personal title, mother tongue, nearest airport to your residence
vcard	`vcard`	`http://www.w3.org/2001/ vcard-rdf/3.0#`	Electronic business card
Bio	`bio`	`http://vocab.org/bio/0.1/`	Biographical information
Relationship vocabulary	`relationship`	`http://vocab.org/ relationship/`	Relationships between people (`friendOf`, `parentOf`, `spouseOf`, etc.)

Book Vocabularies

Books can be precisely described using properties from `http://schema.org/Book`, defining book formats, the number of pages, the copyright holder, the genre, and other features of books. Dublin Core is often used to declare general metadata of books. The International Standard Book Number (ISBN) of books can be declared not only with the `isbn` property of the Book class of schema.org (defined at `http://schema.org/isbn`), but also using the `isbn` property from the URN vocabulary. Books you intend to read, books you've already read, or your favorite books can be described using the reading list schema through the `http://www.ldodds.com/schemas/book/` namespace.

PRISM: A Publishing Vocabulary

The Publishing Requirements for Industry Standard Metadata (PRISM) describes many components of print, online, mobile, and multimedia content, including the following:

- Creator, contributor, copyright owner
- Locations, organizations, topics, people, and events, conditions of reproduction
- Publication date, including cover date, post date, volume, number
- Restrictions for republishing and reuse

PRISM is commonly used for describing partner syndication, content aggregation, content repurposing, resource discovery, multiple channel distribution, content archiving, capture rights usage information, RSS, XMP, and machine-readable annotations of web sites. The PRISM namespaces are `http://prismstandard.org/namespaces/basic/2.1/` for PRISM 2.1 Basic (typical prefix: `prism`) and `http://prismstandard.org/namespaces/prism-ad/3.0/` for PRISM 3.0 (usual prefix: `prism-ad`).

GoodRelations: An E-commerce Ontology

The de facto ontology for e-commerce is GoodRelations (`gr`), which is suitable for describing businesses, offerings, prices, features, payment options, opening hours, and so on. The namespace of GoodRelations is `http://purl.org/goodrelations/v1#`. GoodRelations is widely deployed and also used by Yahoo! and BestBuy.

Publication Ontologies

While the generic metadata of publications can be expressed in Dublin Core, there are ontologies specially written for describing publications and citations. Table 2-2 summarizes the four most deployed publishing ontologies (FaBiO, PRO, PSO, and PWO) and the four referencing ontologies (CiTO, BiRO, C4O, and DoCO) that are known as the *Semantic Publishing and Referencing Ontologies* (*SPAR*), as well as the Bibliographic Ontology (bibo).

Table 2-2. *Publication and Referencing Ontologies*

Ontology	Abbreviation	Namespace	Typical Use
Bibliographic Ontology	bibo	http://purl.org/ontology/bibo/	Citation, document classification, describe documents, distributors, editors, interviewers, performers, ISBN, etc.
Bibliographic Reference Ontology	biro	http://purl.org/spar/biro/	Bibliographic records, references, collections, and lists
Citation Counting and Context Characterization Ontology	c4o	http://purl.org/spar/c4o/	Number of citations, citation context
Citation Typing Ontology	cito	http://purl.org/spar/cito/	Factual and rhetorical type and nature of citations (e.g., shared authors, one publication confirms the conclusion of another one)
Document Components Ontology	doco	http://purl.org/spar/doco/	Chapter, section, paragraph, table, preface, glossary, etc.
FRBR-aligned Bibliographic Ontology	fabio	http://purl.org/spar/fabio/	Abstracts, articles, artistic works, theses, blog posts, conference proceedings
Publishing Roles Ontology	pro	http://purl.org/spar/pro	Roles of agents (e.g., author, editor, reviewer, publisher)
Publishing Status Ontology	pso	http://purl.org/spar/pso	Status of publication (e.g., submitted manuscript, accepted manuscript, proof)
Publishing Workflow Ontology	pwo	http://purl.org/spar/pwo	Stages of publication workflow (e.g., under review)

DOAP: A Project Management Vocabulary

Description of a project (DOAP) is a vocabulary to describe software projects, especially open source projects and their associated resources, including participants and web resources. The namespace of DOAP is http://usefulinc.com/doap/.

Licensing Vocabularies

ALicensing, such as copyright information, permissions and prohibition regarding the reproduction, distribution, and sharing of creative works, as well as creating derivative works, is best described using Creative Commons (cc) licenses. The namespace of Creative Commons is http://creativecommons.org/ns#.

Media Ontologies

There are ontologies dedicated to media resources, such as music and video files, as summarized in Table 2-3.

Table 2-3. *Media Ontologies*

Ontology	Abbreviation	Namespace	Typical Use
The Music Ontology	mo	http://purl.org/ontology/mo/	Artist, composer, conductor, discography, imdb, record, remixer, singer, tempo, etc.
VidOnt: The Video Ontology	vidont	http://vidont.org/	Movie properties (remake, sequel, narrator, etc.), video file properties (aspect ratio, audio codec, letterboxed, video bitrate, MAR, etc.)

Vocabularies for Online Communities

Posts, user roles, threads, user accounts, and user groups of online communities can be described using *Semantically-Interlinked Online Communities* (*SIOC*). The namespace of SIOC Core is http://rdfs.org/sioc/ns#.

Facebook uses the vocabulary of Facebook OpenGraph (og) to allow web pages the same functionality as any other object on Facebook. The namespace of OpenGraph is http://ogp.me/ns#.

Knowledge Management Standards

The most frequently used knowledge management standards are the Resource Description Framework (RDF), the Web Ontology Language (OWL), and the Simple Knowledge Organization System (SKOS).

Resource Description Framework (RDF)

On the Semantic Web, structured datasets are usually expressed in, or based on, the *Resource Description Framework* (*RDF*) [2]. RDF can be used to create a machine-interpretable description about any kind of web resource, because RDF files can be extended with an arbitrary number of external vocabularies. In fact, RDF and other core Semantic Web standards such as RDFS and OWL have their own vocabularies, which are usually combined with one another and extended using other vocabularies, in order to describe objects and their properties. Keep in mind, however, that RDF is far more than just a vocabulary, as it is a fully featured semantic data-modeling language. The namespace of RDF is http://www.w3.org/1999/02/22-rdf-syntax-ns#.

The RDF vocabulary defines classes for XML literal values (rdf:XMLLiteral), properties (rdf:Property), RDF statements (rdf:Statement), RDF lists (rdf:List), as well as containers of alternatives (rdf:Alt), unordered containers (rdf:Bag), and ordered containers (rdf:Seq). An instance of rdf:List is rdf:nil, which represents the empty list. The RDF vocabulary also defines properties such as rdf:type (an instance of rdf:Property used to express that a resource is an instance of a class), rdf:first (the first item in the subject RDF list), rdf:rest (the rest of the subject RDF list after rdf:first), rdf:value (structured value), rdf:subject (the subject of the RDF statement), rdf:predicate (the predicate of the RDF statement), and rdf:object (the object of the RDF statement).

The RDF data model is based on statements to describe and feature resources, especially web resources, in the form of subject-predicate-object (resource-property-value) expressions called *RDF triples* or *RDF statements*. The predicate (property) describes the relationship between the subject and the object. For example, the natural language sentence "Leslie's homepage is `http://www.lesliesikos.com`" can be expressed as shown in Table 2-4. All elements of the triple are resources defined by a unique URI (see Listing 2-4).

Table 2-4. *An RDF Triple*

	RDF Data Model	**RDF Triple**
Subject	Leslie	`http://www.lesliesikos.com/metadata/sikos.rdf#lesliesikos`
Predicate	The machine-readable definition of "homepage" from the Friend of a Friend (FOAF) external vocabulary	`http://xmlns.com/foaf/0.1/homepage`
Object	`http://www.lesliesikos.com`	`http://www.lesliesikos.com`

Listing 2-4. Describing a Person in RDF/XML

```
<?xml version="1.0" encoding="UTF-8"?>
<rdf:RDF xmlns:rdf="http://www.w3.org/1999/02/22-rdf-syntax-ns#" ↵
 xmlns:foaf="http://xmlns.com/foaf/0.1/">
  <foaf:Person rdf:about="http://www.lesliesikos.com/metadata/sikos.rdf#lesliesikos">
    <foaf:homepage rdf:resource="http://www.lesliesikos.com" />
    <foaf:family_name>Sikos</foaf:family_name>
    <foaf:givenname>Leslie</foaf:givenname>
  </foaf:Person>
</rdf:RDF>
```

The about attribute of RDF declares the subject of the RDF statement, which is, in this case, `http://www.lesliesikos.com/metadata/sikos.rdf#lesliesikos`. The fragment identifier #lesliesikos is used to identify an actual person rather than a document (`sikos.rdf`). Those objects whose value is a web address, such as the home page of a person, are declared using the `resource` attribute of RDF, in contrast to those that are string literals (character sequences), such as Sikos (the value of the `family_name` property from the FOAF vocabulary). The syntax of this example is known as the *RDF/XML serialization* (*RDF/XML*), which is the normative syntax of RDF [3], using the `application/rdf+xml` Internet media type and the `.rdf` or `.xml` file extension. Structured datasets can be written in RDF using a variety of other syntax notations and data serialization formats, for example, RDFa, JSON-LD, Notation3 (N3), Turtle, N-Triples [4], TRiG [5], and TRiX [6], so the syntax of RDF triples varies from format to format. The N3 syntax is, for example, less verbose than the RDF/XML serialization, where the namespace prefix is declared by the `@prefix` directive, the URIs are delimited by the less than (`<`) and greater than (`>`) signs, and the triples are separated by semicolons (`;`) (see Listing 2-5).

Listing 2-5. Describing a Person in N3

```
@prefix :      <http://www.lesliesikos.com/metadata/sikos.rdf#> .
@prefix foaf: <http://xmlns.com/foaf/0.1/> .
@prefix rdf:  <http://www.w3.org/1999/02/22-rdf-syntax-ns#> .

:lesliesikos a foaf:Person ;
  foaf:givenname "Leslie" ;
  foaf:family_name "Sikos" ;
  foaf:homepage <http://www.lesliesikos.com> .
```

Shorthand notation can be used for the most common predicates (see Table 2-5).

Table 2-5. *Shorthand Notation for Common Predicates*

Predicate	Shorthand Notation
`<http://www.w3.org/1999/02/22-rdf-syntax-ns#type>`	a
`<http://www.w3.org/2002/07/owl#sameAs>`	=
`<http://www.w3.org/2000/10/swap/log#implies>`	=> or <=

This is the reason why the RDF type of the person is declared using a. If the Notation 3 code is in an external file, the typical file extension is .n3. The MIME type and character encoding of N3 should be declared as text/n3; charset=utf-8. Tokenizing and whitespace handling are not specified in the N3 grammar. Base URIs to be used for the parsing of relative URIs can be set with the @base directive in the form @base <http://example.com/overview/>. Several N3 rules for string escaping are derived from Python, namely, stringliteral, stringprefix, shortstring, shortstringitem, longstring, longstringitem, shortstringchar, and longstringchar. Additionally, the \U extension, also used in another RDF serialization (N-Triples), can be applied. Legal escape sequences are \newline, \\ (backslash, \), \' (single quote, '), \" (double quote, "), \n (ASCII Linefeed, LF), \r (ASCII Carriage Return, CR), \t (ASCII Horizontal Tab, TAB), \uhhhh (Unicode character in BMP), and \U00hhhhhh (Unicode character in plane 1–16 notation). The escapes \a, \b, \f, and \v cannot be used, because the corresponding characters are not allowed in RDF.

A subset of N3 is the *Terse RDF Triple Language*, often referred to as *Turtle*. Turtle provides a syntax to describe RDF graphs in a compact textual form, which is easy to develop. It is a subset of Notation 3 (N3) and a superset of N-Triples. Turtle is popular among Semantic Web developers and considered an easy-to-read alternative to RDF/XML. The typical file extension of Turtle files is .ttl. The character encoding of Turtle files should be UTF-8. The MIME type of Turtle is text/turtle. Turtle is supported by many software frameworks that can be used for querying and analyzing RDF data, such as Jena, Redland, and Sesame. Turtle files consist of a sequence of directives, statements representing triples, and blank lines. Triples can be written in Turtle as a sequence of subject-predicate-object terms, separated by whitespace, and terminated by a period (.). URIs are written in angle brackets (<>), and string literals are delimited by double quotes ("") such as <http://www.lesliesikos.com/metadata/sikos.rdf#> <http://xmlns.com/foaf/0.1/homepage> <http://www.lesliesikos.com>. Using the URI prefix declaration @PREFIX foaf: <http://xmlns.com/foaf/0.1/> ., this can be abbreviated as <http://www.lesliesikos.com/metadata/sikos.rdf#> foaf:homepage <http://www.lesliesikos.com> ., where foaf:homepage declares the concatenation of http://xmlns.com/foaf/0.1/ with homepage, revealing the original URI http://xmlns.com/foaf/0.1/ homepage.

Figure 2-1 represents the triples of Listing 2-5 as an *RDF graph*, which is a directed, labeled graph in which the *nodes* are the resources and values [7]. The nodes and predicate arcs of the RDF graph correspond to *node elements* and *property elements*. The default node element is rdf:Description, which is very frequently used as the generic container of RDF statements in RDF/XML. To add context to RDF statements and make them globally interpretable, RDF triples are sometimes stored with the name of the graph, called *quads* (subject-predicate-object-graph name), which will be demonstrated in later chapters.

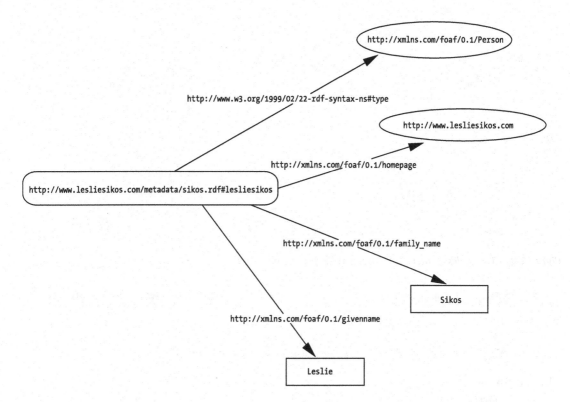

Figure 2-1. *A simple RDF graph*

The example can be extended with properties from other external vocabularies, but the concept remains the same. Once you've created your RDF file, you have a machine-readable metadata file you can upload to your web site. Semantic software agents can find and retrieve the information in such files (see Figure 2-2), display the human-readable part in a visually appealing manner (see Figure 2-3) and generate a scalable graph based on the RDF triples (see Figure 2-4), and infer new information.

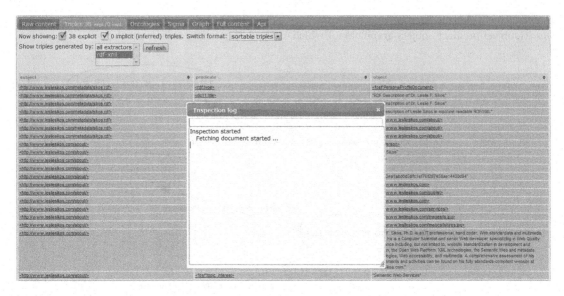

Figure 2-2. *RDF triples extracted by Sindice Web Data Inspector [8]*

Figure 2-3. *A personal description extracted from RDF and displayed on a web page*

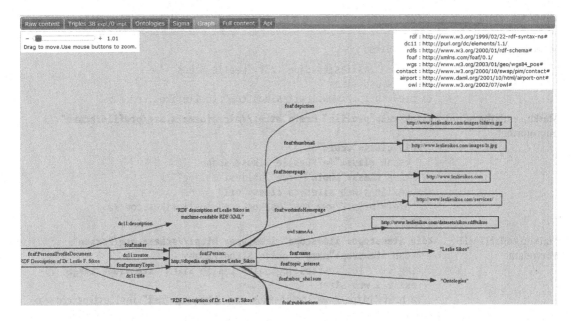

Figure 2-4. *A graph generated from an RDF file*

While such machine-readable RDF files are useful, their primary application is data modeling, so the RDF files are separate from the markup of your web site. You can add structured data directly to the markup, such as (X)HTML5, by using *machine-readable annotations*, which can be processed by semantic data extractors and, if needed, converted into RDF.

Machine-Readable Annotations

There are four machine-readable annotation formats for web sites (by order of introduction):

- *Microformats*, which publish structured data about basic concepts,[1] such as people, places, events, recipes, and audio, through core (X)HTML attributes

- *RDFa*, which expresses RDF in markup attributes that are not part of the core (X) HTML vocabularies

- *HTML5 Microdata*, which extends the HTML5 markup with structured metadata (a HTML5 Application Programming Interface)

- *JSON-LD*, which adds structured data to the markup as JavaScript code

RDFa and JSON-LD can be used in most markup language versions and variants, while HTML5 Microdata can be used in (X)HTML5 only. All these annotation formats have their own syntax. For example, the vocabulary is declared with the vocab attribute in RDFa, the itemtype attribute in Microdata, and context in JSON-LD (see Table 2-6).

---

[1]The other three formats are more advanced, as they can use concepts from any external vocabulary.

23

Table 2-6. *Data Represented as Structured Data in a Microformat, Microdata, RDFa, and JSON-LD*

Markup without Semantic Annotation	```Leslie Sikos```
	
	 ```<img src="lesliesikos.jpg" alt="Leslie Sikos" />```
	 ```Leslie's web site:```
	 ```<a href="http://www.lesliesikos.com">lesliesikos.com</a>```

Markup with the hCard microformat	```<link rel="profile" href="http://microformats.org/profile/hcard" />```
	 ```...```
	 ``` <div class="vcard">```
	 ``` <span class="fn">Leslie Sikos</span>```
	 ``` <img class="photo" src="lesliesikos.jpg" />```
	 ``` Leslie's web site: <a class="url"```
	 ``` href="http://www.lesliesikos.com">lesliesikos.com</a>```
	 ``` </div>```

Markup with HTML5 Microdata	```<div itemscope="itemscope" itemtype="http://schema.org/Person">```
	 ``` <span itemprop="name">Leslie Sikos</span>```
	 ``` <img src="lesliesikos.jpg" alt="Leslie Sikos" itemprop="image" />```
	 ``` Leslie's web site:```
	 ``` <a href="http://www.lesliesikos.com" itemprop="url">lesliesikos.com</a>```
	 ```</div>```

Markup with RDFa	```<div vocab="http://schema.org/" typeof="Person">```
	 ``` <span property="name">Leslie Sikos</span>```
	 ``` <img src="lesliesikos.jpg" alt="Leslie Sikos" property="image" />```
	 ``` Leslie's web site:```
	 ``` <a href="http://www.lesliesikos.com" property="url">lesliesikos.com</a>```
	 ```</div>```

Markup with JSON-LD	```<script type="application/ld+json">```
	 ```{```
	 ``` "@context": "http://schema.org",```
	 ``` "@type": "Person",```
	 ``` "image": "lesliesikos.jpg",```
	 ``` "name": "Leslie Sikos",```
	 ``` "url": "http://www.lesliesikos.com"```
	 ```}```
	 ```</script>```

These syntaxes will be described in the next sections.

Microformats

The results of the very first approach to add machine-readable annotations to the (X)HTML markup are called *microformats* (μF). Some microformats apply and reuse features of existing technologies, such as the rel attribute of (X)HTML, while others, such as hCard, extend the core markup vocabulary the simplest way possible: based on *Plain Old Semantic HTML* (*POSH*). Microformats can be implemented not only in (X)HTML markup but also in XML, RSS, Atom, and so on. Microformats can express site structure, link weight, content type, and human relationships with the class, rel, and rev attribute values. They are very easy to write, and a great deal of software supports them (the Operator and Tails Export add-ons for Firefox, the Michromeformats Google Chrome extension, the microformats transformer Optimus, or the Microformats Bookmarklet for Safari, Firefox, and IE).

However, due to limitations and open issues, other machine-readable annotation formats gradually overtook microformats. Applying various microformats as multiple values on the same a element, such as `rel="nofollow"` and `rel="friend"`, cannot be used. The `rev` attribute used by the Vote Links microformat is not supported by HTML5. Profile URIs provided by the `profile` attribute cannot be used on the head element in HTML5, wherein the `profile` attribute values can be declared for the `rel` attribute on anchors (a) or link elements (`link`). As an example, a profile URI is presented for the hCalender microformat with all the three options. The hCalendar microformat is based on the iCalendar standard (RFC 2445). All contents that use hCalendar notation should refer to the hCalendar XMDP profile, in other words, `http://microformats.org/profile/hcalendar`, as shown in Listing 2-6 or Listing 2-7 for the document head or Listing 2-8 as part of the document body. These methods can also be combined.

Listing 2-6. Providing the hCalendar Head Profile in the Document Head (Cannot Be Used in HTML5)

```
<head profile="http://microformats.org/profile/hcalendar">
```

Listing 2-7. Linking to the hCalendar Profile in the Document Head

```
<link rel="profile" href="http://microformats.org/profile/hcalendar" />
```

Listing 2-8. Using the hCalendar Profile in the Document Body

```
<a rel="profile" href="http://microformats.org/profile/hcalendar">hCalendar</a>
```

■ **Note** New structural elements introduced by HTML5, such as `article` or `section`, are not recognized by all microformat parsers, so the preceding attributes on these elements might not be processed.

In the next sections, I will give you an overview of some of the most popular microformats, namely, hCalendar, hCard, `rel="license"`, `rel="nofollow"`, `rel="tag"`, Vote Links, and XFN.

hCalendar and h-event

You can use the hCalendar microformat to create calendar entries for sport events, anniversaries, reminders, meetings, workshops, conferences, and other events.

The root class name for hCalendar is `vcalendar`. The root class name for events is `vevent`, which is required for all event listings. The properties are represented by the elements of hCalendar. The required classes are `dtstart`, which should be provided in the ISO date format,[2] and `summary`. Listing 2-9 shows an hCalendar example.

Listing 2-9. A Three-Day Conference Represented in hCalendar

```
<link rel="profile" href="http://microformats.org/profile/hcalendar" />
...
<div class="vevent">
  <h1 class="summary">Semantic Web Conference 2015</h1>
  <div class="description">Semantic Web Conference 2015 was announced yesterday.</div>
  <div>Posted on: <abbr class="dtstamp" title="20150825T080000Z">Aug 25, 2015</abbr></div>
```

---

[2]Beyond microformats such as hAtom, hCalendar, hCard, and hReview, several web technologies apply the ISO 8601 date format for date-time representation, such as XML, XML schema datatypes, RDF, and Atom.

```
<div class="uid">uid1@host.com</div>
<div>Organized by: <a class="organizer" href="mailto:js@expl.com">js@expl.com</a></div>
<div>Dates: <abbr class="dtstart" title="20151012T093000Z">October 12 2015, 9.30am ↵
 UTC</abbr> - <abbr class="dtend" title="20151014T200000Z">October 14 2015, 8.00pm ↵
 UTC</abbr></div>
<div>Status: <span class="status">Confirmed</span></div>
<div>Filed under:</div>
<ul>
  <li class="category">Conference</li>
</ul>
</div>
```

Optional properties include, but are not limited to, location, url, dtend (in ISO date format), duration (in ISO date duration format), rdate, rrule, category, description, uid, geo, attendee, contact, organizer, attach, and status. The geo property has the subproperties latitude and longitude, while attendee has the subproperties partstat and role. Those who have to publish new events regularly might find the hCalendar generator *hCalendar-o-matic* useful [9].

The specification has been superseded by the h-event specification, which supports the following properties inside a markup element with class h-event: p-name (event name or title), p-summary (short summary), dt-start (date and time when the event starts), dt-end (date and time when the event ends), dt-duration (duration of the event), p-description (verbose description), u-url (web site), p-category (event category or categories), and p-location (event location, which can include h-card, h-adr, or h-geo). All properties are optional. An example is shown in Listing 2-10.

Listing 2-10. A Three-Day Conference Annotated Using h-event

```
<div class="h-event">
  <h1 class="p-name"> Semantic Web Conference '15</h1>
  <p>From
    <time class="dt-start" datetime="2015-10-12 09:30">12<sup>th</sup> October 2015,
    9:30am</time>
    to <time class="dt-end" datetime="2015-10-14 20:00">14<sup>th</sup> October 2015,
    8:00pm</time>
    at <span class="p-location">Nice Conference Hall</span></p>
  <p class="p-summary">Semantic Web Conference 2015 was announced yesterday.</p>
</div>
```

hCard

The hCard microformat standard can be used to represent contact data of people, companies, and organizations by semantic markup. hCard metadata should be provided on the contact pages of web sites. In summer 2010, hCard crossed the 2 billion mark, according to the now-discontinued Yahoo! SearchMonkey, which made hCard the most popular metadata format for people and organizations up to 2010. Because hCard is based on the vCard standard (RFC 2426), existing vCards can be easily converted to hCard.[3]

---

[3]The vCard notation BEGIN:VCARD is class="vcard" in hCard, N: is class="n", FN: is class="fn", and so on.

■ **Tip** The vCard standard is widely used for storing electronic business cards. For example, Microsoft Outlook uses this format for the business cards available under Contacts. Also, many smartphones use the vCard format to store contacts in the phone memory (when you set up contacts not to be stored on the SIM card).

The hCard class names should be in lowercase.

■ **Caution** The root class name for an hCard is vcard. An element with a class name vcard is itself called an hCard.

The two required attributes in hCard are fn and n. However, the second one is optional if any *implied "N" optimization rules* are in effect.[4] The property n might have the subproperties family-name, given-name, additional-name, honorific-prefix, and honorific-suffix. All other properties are optional, including adr, agent, bday, category, class, email, geo, key, label, logo, mailer, nickname, note, org, photo, rev, role, sort-string, sound, tel, title, tz, uid, and url. Permissible subproperties are post-office-box, extended-address, street-address, locality, region, postal-code, country-name, type, and value for adr; type and value for email; latitude and longitude for geo; organization-name and organization-unit for org; and type and value for tel. A typical hCard code looks like Listing 2-11.

Listing 2-11. A Typical hCard

```
<link rel="profile" href="http://microformats.org/profile/hcard" />
...
<div id="hcard-John-Smith" class="vcard">
  <img src="http://www.example.com/jsmith.jpg" alt="Photo of John Smith" class="photo" />
  <a class="url fn" href="http://www.example.com">John Smith</a>
  <div class="org">Smith and Sons</div>
  <a class="email" href="mailto:smith@example.com">smith@example.com</a>
  <div class="adr">
    <div class="street-address">123 Nice Street</div>
    <span class="locality">Adelaide</span>,
    <span class="region">SA</span>,
    <span class="postal-code">5000</span>
    <span class="country-name">Australia</span>
  </div>
  <div class="tel">+61812345678</div>
</div>
```

The following hCard elements are singular and can be provided just once: fn, n, bday, tz, geo, sort-string, uid, class, and rev. All other properties are allowed to have multiple instances. Generally, the visible property values of markup elements represent the value of the hCard property. However, there are some exceptions. For hyperlinks that are represented by the a element for one or multiple hCard properties, the href attribute provides the property value for all properties with a URL value (for example, photo). In case the img element is used, the src attribute holds the property value for all properties with a URL value. For object elements, the data attribute provides the property value. The content of the element is the property

---

[4]If n is omitted but fn is present, the value of n will be equal to the value of fn.

value for all other properties. If the title attribute is provided for abbr elements with hCard notation, its value is considered as the hCard property instead of the element contents used otherwise.

Although it is easy to create it manually, hCard metadata can be generated by the hCard creator *hCard-o-matic* on the web site of the authors of the specification [10]. You simply fill in a form about the name, organization, country, e-mail, and other contact data, and the software generates the hCard.

To provide additional information, microformats can also be nested. For example, a sport event review might contain not only the review (annotated in hReview) but also personal information (in hCard) at the same time (see Listing 2-12).

Listing 2-12. A Combination of hReview and hCard

```
<link rel="profile" href="http://microformats.org/profile/hreview" />
<link rel="profile" href="http://microformats.org/profile/hcard" />
…
<div class="hreview">
  <h1 class="summary">The Winner Takes It All Review</h1>
  <span class="reviewer vcard">
  by <span class="fn">John Smith</span>, <span class="title">Editor</span> ↵
  at <span class="org">Sport Reviews</span>
  </span>
  Rating: <span class="rating">4.5</span> out of 5.
  <span class="description">A fascinating performance.</span>
</div>
```

The review is described by the hReview microformat (class="hreview"). The name of the reviewer is revealed by span class="reviewer". The hCard microformat is nested inside the hReview microformat in order to provide additional information about him/her (a space-separated list of attribute values in <span class="reviewer vcard">). The hCard properties describe the name (fn), job title (title), and organization (org) of the reviewer.

rel="license"

There are millions of web resources with some or all rights reserved. Many licenses associated with documents and objects are sophisticated, and users cannot be expected to know them. The rel="license" microformat can be added to hyperlinks that point to the description of the license. This is especially useful for images but can be used for any resources. Basic image embeddings apply only the src and alt attributes on the img element, such as in Listing 2-13.

Listing 2-13. A Basic Image Embedding

```
<img src="hotel.jpg" alt="The Palace Hotel" />
```

To declare the image license, the rel and href attributes should also be used. In the case of the *Creative Commons Attribution-ShareAlike license*, for example, it should be in the form shown in Listing 2-14.

Listing 2-14. Declaring an Image License

```
<link rel="profile" href="http://microformats.org/profile/rel-license" />
…
<img src="hotel.jpg" alt="The Palace Hotel" rel="license" ↵
 ref="http://creativecommons.org/licenses/by-sa/4.0/" />
```

The value of the `href` attribute provides the associated URI of the resource in which the license is described. Some of the most commonly used *license deeds* are [11] as follows:

- Creative Commons Attribution (cc by)

  `http://creativecommons.org/licenses/by/4.0/`

- Creative Commons Attribution Share Alike (cc by-sa)

  `http://creativecommons.org/licenses/by-sa/4.0/`

- Creative Commons Attribution No Derivatives (cc by-nd)

  `http://creativecommons.org/licenses/by-nd/4.0/`

- Creative Commons Attribution Non-Commercial (cc by-nc)

  `http://creativecommons.org/licenses/by-nc/4.0/`

- Creative Commons Attribution Non-Commercial Share Alike (cc by-nc-sa)

  `http://creativecommons.org/licenses/by-nc-sa/4.0/`

- Creative Commons Attribution Non-Commercial No Derivatives (cc by-nc-nd)

  `http://creativecommons.org/licenses/by-nc-nd/4.0/`

You should select a license that matches what you let others do with your work (distribute commercially or noncommercially, remix, tweak, share with proper crediting, alter, and so on).

rel="nofollow"

One value of the `rel` attribute deserves extended attention, because it is often used in *search engine optimization* (SEO). When `rel="nofollow"` is added to a hyperlink, the link destination should not be considered for additional ranking by search engines. This attribute value can be applied if document owners require hyperlinks, without affecting the ranking of their web pages or links to external web sites. For example, if a hyperlink is vital on the web page but its destination page has a very low PageRank (PR), the hyperlink should be provided with `rel="nofollow"`, to avoid search engine penalty.

■ **Note** PageRank is a link analysis algorithm used to assign a numerical weighting to each web page, in order to express its relative importance on a 0–10 scale.

For example, if the index page of `lowprsite.com` has a low PR but you have to link to it because of the content presented there, you can use the `rel="nofollow"` microformat, as shown in Listing 2-15.

Listing 2-15. A Link That Will Not Be Considered by Search Engines While Indexing a Page

```
<link rel="profile" href="http://microformats.org/profile/rel-nofollow" />
...
<a href="http://www.lowprsite.com" rel="nofollow">Low PR site</a>
```

Although it is widely used, there are several open issues about this microformat. The rel="nofollow" microformat indicates a behavior rather than a relationship, so the definition is illogical. The name of the microformat does not reflect the real meaning, and it is not a noun. While rel="nofollow" was originally introduced to stop comment spam in blogs, using it alone does not prevent spamming attempts to add marketing to a page (only prevent target pages from benefiting through an increased page rank). Finally, many legitimate non-spam links provided as the attribute value of rel="nofollow" might be ignored or given reduced weight by search engines, which is an undesirable side effect.

rel="tag"

Unlike other microformats and general meta keywords, the rel="tag" microformat can be used for visible links. It can be applied on hyperlink elements to indicate that the destination of the link is a general author-designated tag (keyword) for the current page. An example is shown in Listing 2-16.

Listing 2-16. Using rel="tag"

```
<link rel="profile" href="http://microformats.org/profile/rel-tag" />
...
<a href="http://www.lesliesikos.com/category/textbooks/" rel="tag">Textbooks</a>
```

Vote Links

Vote Links is an elemental microformat with three possible values on the rev attribute of the a element: vote-for, vote-against, and vote-abstain. The values are mutually exclusive. Optionally, visible rollovers can be provided by the title attribute. Listing 2-17 shows an example.

Listing 2-17. A Vote Links Example

```
<link rel="profile" href="http://microformats.org/profile/vote-links" />
...
<a rev="vote-for" href="http://example.com/thumbsup/" ↵
 title="HTML should be the primary markup language">HTML5</a>
<a rev="vote-against" href="http://example.com/thumbsdown/" ↵
 title="XHTML should be the primary markup language">XHTML5</a>
```

XFN

The very first HTML microformat, XHTML Friends Network (XFN), was introduced in December 2003. XFN was designed by Global Multimedia Protocols Group to express human relationships with simple hyperlinks. XFN is especially useful for brochure-style home pages and blog entries. The name of the person should be provided as the text of the hyperlink (between <a> and </a>). The personal web site is the target of the hyperlink, in other words, the value of the href attribute. All relationship data can be provided by the rel attribute on a elements. Multiple values are allowed and should be separated by spaces. The friendship type can be contact, acquaintance, or friend. If the person is known personally, it can be expressed by the met attribute value of the rel attribute. For example, a friend of Leslie Sikos, whom he knows personally, can publish that relationship on his web site by XFN, as shown in Listing 2-18.

Listing 2-18. Link to the Web Site of a Friend

```
<link rel="profile" href="http://gmpg.org/xfn/11" />
...
I am an old friend of <a href="http://lesliesikos.com" rel="friend met">Leslie Sikos</a>.
```

The distance between the residence of the person and that of his friend can be expressed by the co-resident and neighbor values. Relatives can set to child, parent, sibling, spouse, or kin. The professional relationships co-worker and colleague are also supported. Feelings can also be expressed (muse, crush, date, sweetheart).

CSS styles can also be added to XFN metadata. For example, friends can be provided in bold and colleagues in italic, with the CSS rules shown in Listing 2-19.

Listing 2-19. Styling XFN

```
a[rel~="friend"] {
  font-weight: bold;
}

a[rel~="colleague "] {
  font-style: italic;
}
```

Although it is easy to create XFN from scratch, XFN creators such as XFN Creator [12] or Exefen [13] might speed up development.

XMDP

XHTML MetaData Profiles (XMDP) metadata is an XHTML-based format for defining metadata profiles that are both machine- and human-readable. XMDP consists of a property definition list, an optional description, and then, if applicable, one or more definition list items. The profile definition list is identified by the class (see Listing 2-20).

Listing 2-20. XMDP Profile Definition

```
<dl class="profile">
```

The definition term is identified by the id (see Listing 2-21).

Listing 2-21. Definition Term and Data for XMDP

```
<dt id="property1">property1</dt>
<dd>propertydesc</dd>
```

The informatively used meta properties author and keywords, for example, can be defined by XMDP, as shown in Listing 2-22.

Listing 2-22. A Complete XMDP Example

```
<dl class="profile">
  <dt id="author">author</dt>
  <dd>A person who wrote (at least part of) the document.</dd>
  <dt id="keywords">keywords</dt>
  <dd>A comma and/or space separated list of the keywords or keyphrases of the document.</dd>
</dl>
```

Drafts and Future Microformats

You can apply microformats to provide specific metadata on a wide variety of resources. Address information can be described by `adr`. Geographic coordinates (latitude-longitude pairs) can be provided according to the *World Geodetic System* (*WGS*) with the geo microformat. hAtom can be used for web syndication. Information about audio recordings can be embedded by using the hAudio microformat. The hListing microformat can be applied for open, distributed listings. Image, video, and audio media components can be described by hMedia. hNews is a microformat to provide news content on web sites. Product descriptions can be expressed in hProduct. Cooking and baking recipes can be described on the Web with hRecipe. Résumés and CVs can be published with hResume. Document reviews can be written in hReview. The `rel="directory"` microdata can indicate that a link destination is a directory listing that refers to the current page. File attachments provided for downloading can be indicated by the `rel="enclosure"` microformat. `rel="home"` provides a hyperlink to the home page of the web site. The `rel="payment"` microformat is an online payment mechanism. The reworking of the `robots meta` tag is the Robot Exclusion Profile. The xFolk microformat (stands for *xFolksomony*) was designed for publishing collections of bookmarks. The list goes on, and the Microformats Community welcomes metadata enthusiasts to create new microformats; however, other formats, such as RDFa and HTML5 Microdata, seem to replace microformats.

RDFa

RDFa (RDF in attributes) makes it possible to write RDF triples in the (X)HTML markup, XML, or SVG as attribute values. The full RDFa syntax (RDFa Core) [14] provides basic and advanced features for experts to express complex structured data in the markup, such as human relationships, places, and events. Those who want to express fairly simple structured data in their web documents can use the less expressive *RDFa Lite* [15], a minimal subset of RDFa that is easier to learn and suitable for most general scenarios. RDFa Lite supports the following attributes: `vocab`, `typeof`, `property`, `resource`, and `prefix`. In host languages that authorize the use of the `href` and `src` attributes, they are supported by RDFa Lite too.

A bunch of numbers has a different meaning in a math lesson than in the telephone book, while a word often has a different meaning in a poem than in real life. The meaning of words depends on the context, so in order to make computers understand the field or area (knowledge domain), we have to identify the machine-readable vocabulary that defines the terminology of the domain. In RDFa, the vocabulary can be identified by the `vocab` attribute, the type of the entity to describe is annotated by the `typeof` attribute, and the properties with the `property` attribute (see Listing 2-23).

Listing 2-23. Basic Machine-Readable Annotation of a Person in RDFa

```
<p vocab="http://schema.org/" typeof="Person">
  My name is <span property="name">Leslie Sikos</span> and you can find out more about me ↵
  by visiting <a property="url" href="http://www.lesliesikos.com">my web site</a>.
</p>
```

Once the preceding code is published and indexed, search engines will find the "web site of Leslie Sikos" more efficiently. To uniquely identify this entity on the Web, the `resource` attribute is used (see Listing 2-24). The `resource` attribute is one of the options to set the object of statements, which is particularly useful when referring to resources that are not navigable links, such as the ISBN number of a book.

Listing 2-24. A Unique Identifier of the Entity in RDFa

```
<p vocab="http://schema.org/" typeof="Person" resource="#sikos">
  My name is <span property="name">Leslie Sikos</span> and you can find out more about me ↵
  by visiting <a property="url" href="http://www.lesliesikos.com">my web site</a>.
</p>
```

The vocabulary declaration makes it possible to omit the full URI from each property (name refers to http://schema.org/name, url abbreviates http://schema.org/url). However, if you add RDFa annotation for more than one real-world object or person, you can declare the namespace of the vocabulary on the html element of your (X)HTML document (e.g., <html xmlns:foaf="http://xmlns.com/foaf/0.1/" …>) and associate it with a prefix that can be reused throughout the document. Every time you use a term from the vocabulary declared on the top of your document, you add the prefix followed by a colon, such as foaf:name, schema:url, etc. Using prefixes is not only handy but sometimes the only way to annotate your markup. For example, if you need terms from more than one vocabulary, additional vocabularies can be specified by the prefix attribute (see Listing 2-25). You can refer to any term from your most frequently used vocabulary (defined in the vocab attribute value) without the prefix, and terms from your second vocabulary with the prefix you define as the attribute value of the prefix attribute, or define them on the html element with the xmlns attribute followed by the prefix name and the namespace URI.

Listing 2-25. Using the Term "Textbook" from the FaBiO Ontology

```
<p vocab="http://schema.org/" typeof="Person" prefix="fabio: http://purl.org/spar/fabio/" ↵
resource="#sikos">
  My name is <span property="name">Leslie Sikos</span> and you can find out more about me ↵
  by visiting <a property="url" href="http://www.lesliesikos.com">my web site</a>.
  I am the author of <a property="fabio:Textbook" ↵
  href="http://lesliesikos.com/mastering-structured-data-on-the-semantic-web/">Mastering ↵
  Structured Data on the Semantic Web</a>.
```

To make search engines "understand" that the provided link refers to a textbook of Leslie Sikos, we used the machine-readable definition of "textbook" from the FaBiO ontology. If you need more than one additional vocabulary for your RDFa annotations, you can add them to the attribute value of the prefix attribute as a space-separated list.

The most frequently used vocabulary namespaces are predefined in RDFa parsers, so you can omit them in your markup and still be able to use their terms in RDFa annotations (Table 2-7).

Table 2-7. Widely Used Vocabulary Prefixes Predefined in RDFa [16]

Prefix	URI	Vocabulary
cc	http://creativecommons.org/ns#	Creative Commons Rights Expression Language
ctag	http://commontag.org/ns#	Common Tag
dcterms	http://purl.org/dc/terms/	Dublin Core Metadata Terms
dc	http://purl.org/dc/elements/1.1/	Dublin Core Metadata Element Set, Version 1.1
foaf	http://xmlns.com/foaf/0.1/	Friend of a Friend (FOAF)
gr	http://purl.org/goodrelations/v1#	GoodRelations
ical	http://www.w3.org/2002/12/cal/icaltzd#	iCalendar terms in RDF
og	http://ogp.me/ns#	Facebook OpenGraph
rev	http://purl.org/stuff/rev#	RDF Review
sioc	http://rdfs.org/sioc/ns#	SIOC Core
v	http://rdf.data-vocabulary.org/#	Google Rich Snippets
vcard	http://www.w3.org/2006/vcard/ns#	vCard in RDF
schema	http://schema.org/	schema.org

More sophisticated annotations require additional attributes that are supported by RDFa Core only. Beyond the RDFa Lite attributes, RDFa Core supports the about, content, datatype, inlist, rel, and rev attributes.

The *current subject* is the web address[5] of the document or a value set by the host language, such as the base element in (X)HTML. As a result, any metadata written in a document will concern the document itself by default. The about attribute can be used to change the current subject and state what the data is about, making the properties inside the document body become part of a new object rather than referring to the entire document (as they do in the head of the document).

If some displayed text is different from the represented value, a more precise value can be added using the content attribute, which is a character data (CDATA) string to supply machine-readable content for a literal. A value can also optionally be typed using the datatype attribute (see Listing 2-26). Declaring the type ensures that machines can interpret strings, dates, numbers, etc., rather than considering them as a character sequence.

Listing 2-26. Using the content and datatype Attributes

```
<html xmlns="http://www.w3.org/1999/xhtml" ↵
  prefix="xsd: http://www.w3.org/2001/XMLSchema# dc: http://purl.org/dc/terms/">
  <head>
    <title>Leslie's Blog</title>
  </head>
  <body>
    <h1 property="dc:title">Leslie's Blog</h1>
    <p>
      Last modified: <span property="dc:modified"
      content="2014-11-28T12:43:00-09:30"
      datatype="xsd:dateTime">28 November 2014</span>.
    </p>
  </body>
</html>
```

In RDFa, the relationship between two resources (predicates) can be expressed using the rel attribute (see Listing 2-27).

Listing 2-27. Describing the Relationship Between Two Resources in RDFa

```
This document is licensed under the
<a prefix="cc: http://creativecommons.org/ns#" ↵
  rel="cc:license" ↵
  href="http://creativecommons.org/licenses/by-nc-nd/3.0/">Creative Commons By-NC-ND ↵
  License</a>.
```

When a predicate is expressed using rel, the href or src attribute is used on the element of the RDFa statement, to identify the object (see Listing 2-28).

Listing 2-28. Using href to Identify the Object

```
<link about="mailto:leslie@example.com" ↵
      rel="foaf:knows" href="mailto:christina@example.com" />
```

---

[5]Web address (Uniform Resource Identifier, URI), internationalized web address (Internationalized Resource Identifier, IRI), or compact web address (Compact URI, CURIE)

Reverse relationships between two resources (predicates) can be expressed with the rev attribute. The rel and rev attributes can be used on any element individually or together. Combining rel and rev is particularly useful when there are two different relationships to express, such as when a photo is taken by the person it depicts (see Listing 2-29).

Listing 2-29. Combining the rel and rev Attributes

```
<img about="http://www.lesliesikos.com" src="koalahug.jpg" rev="dc:creator" rel="foaf:img" />
```

■ **Caution**   If a triple predicate is annotated using rel or rev only, but no href, src, or resource is defined on the same element, the represented triple will be incomplete [17].

The inlist attribute indicates that the object generated on the element is part of a list sharing the same predicate and subject (see Listing 2-30). Only the presence of the inlist attribute is relevant; its attribute value is always ignored.

Listing 2-30. Using the inlist Attribute

```
<p prefix="bibo: http://purl.org/ontology/bibo/ dc: http://purl.org/dc/terms/" ↵
   typeof="bibo:Website">
  The web site <span property="dc:title">Andrew Peno Graphic and Fine Artist</span> by ↵
    <a inlist="" property="dc:creator" href="http://www.andrewpeno.com">Andrew Peno</a> and ↵
    <a inlist="" property="dc:creator" href="http://www.lesliesikos.com">Leslie Sikos</a>.
</p>
```

RDFa DOM API

RDFa provides a Document Object Model (DOM) Application Programming Interface (API) to extract and utilize structured data from a web page, for advanced user interfaces and interactive applications [18].

HTML5 Microdata

HTML5 Microdata is an HTML5 module defined in a separate specification, extending the HTML5 core vocabulary with attributes for representing structured data [19].

Global Microdata Attributes

HTML5 Microdata represents structured data as a group of *name-value pairs*. The groups are called *items*, and each name-value pair is a *property*. Items and properties are represented by regular elements. To create an item, the itemscope attribute is used.[6] To add a property to an item, the itemprop attribute is used on a descendant of the item (a child element of the container element), as shown in Listing 2-31.

---

[6]In HTML5, most web designers use attribute minimization and omit the attribute value (even if it is irrelevant), which is not allowed in XHTML5. In other words, in HTML5, you can write itemscope on the container element without a value, while in XHTML5 you write itemscope="itemscope", which is more verbose and more precise and validates as HTML5 and XHTML5. The XHTML5 syntax is used throughout the book.

Listing 2-31. A Person's Description in HTML5 Microdata

```
<div itemscope="itemscope" itemtype="http://schema.org/Person">
  <span itemprop="name">Leslie Sikos</span>
  <img src="lesliesikos.jpg" alt="Leslie Sikos" itemprop="image" />
  Leslie's web site:
  <a href="http://www.lesliesikos.com" itemprop="url">lesliesikos.com</a>
</div>
```

Property values are usually strings (sequences of characters) but can also be web addresses, as the value of the `href` attribute on the a element, the value of the `src` attribute on the `img` element, or other elements that link to or embed external resources. In Listing 2-31, for example, the value of the image item property is the attribute value of the `src` attribute on the `img` element, which is `lesliesikos.jpg`. Similarly, the value of the `url` item property is not the content of the a element, `lesliesikos.com`, but the attribute value of the `href` attribute on the a element, which is `http://www.lesliesikos.com`. By default, however, the value of the item is the content of the element, such as the value of the `name` item property in this example: `Leslie Sikos` (delimited by the `<span>` and `</span>` tag pair).

The type of the items and item properties are expressed using the `itemtype` attribute, by declaring the web address of the external vocabulary that defines the corresponding item and properties. In our example, we used the `Person` vocabulary from `http://schema.org` that defines properties of a person, such as `familyName`, `givenName`, `birthDate`, `birthPlace`, `gender`, `nationality`, and so on. The full list of properties is defined at `http://schema.org/Person`, which is the value of the `itemtype`. In the example, we declared the name with the `name` property, the depiction of the person with the `image` property, and his web site address using the `url` property. The allowed values and expected format of these properties are available at `http://schema.org/name`, `http://schema.org/image`, and `http://schema.org/url`, respectively.

The item type is different for each knowledge domain, and if you want to annotate the description of a book rather than a person, the value of the `itemtype` attribute will be `http://schema.org/Book`, where the properties of books are collected and defined, such as `bookFormat`, `bookEdition`, `numberOfPages`, `author`, `publisher`, etc. If the item has a global identifier (such as the unique ISBN number of a book), it can be annotated using the `idemid` attribute, as shown in Listing 2-32.

Listing 2-32. The Description of a Book in HTML5 Microdata

```
<div itemscope="itemscope" itemtype="http://schema.org/Book" ↵
  itemid="urn:isbn:978-1-484208-84-7">
  <img itemprop="image" src="http://www.masteringhtml5css3.com/img/webstandardsbook.jpg" ↵
  alt="Web Standards" />
  <span itemprop="name">Web Standards: Mastering HTML5, CSS3, and XML</span> ↵
  by <a itemprop="author" href="http://www.lesliesikos.com">Leslie Sikos</a>
</div>
```

Although HTML5 Microdata is primarily used for semantic descriptions of people, organizations, events, products, reviews, and links, you can annotate any other knowledge domains with the endless variety of external vocabularies.

Groups of name-value pairs can be nested in a Microdata property by declaring the `itemscope` attribute on the element that declared the property (see Listing 2-33).

Listing 2-33. Nesting a Group of Name-Value Pairs

```
<div itemscope="itemscope">
  <p>Name: <span itemprop="name">Herbie Hancock</span></p>
  <p>Band: <span itemprop="band" itemscope="itemscope">
          <span itemprop="name">The Headhunters</span>
          (<span itemprop="size">7</span> members)
        </span>
  </p>
</div>
```

In the preceding example, the outer item (top-level Microdata item) annotates a person, and the inner one represents a jazz band.

An optional attribute of elements with an itemscope attribute is itemref,[7] which gives a list of additional elements to crawl to find the name-value pairs of the item. In other words, properties that are not descendants of the element with the itemscope attribute can be associated with the item using the itemref attribute, providing a list of element identifiers with additional properties elsewhere in the document (see Listing 2-34). The itemref attribute is not part of the HTML5 Microdata data model.

Listing 2-34. Using the itemref Attribute

```
<div itemscope="itemscope" id="herbie" itemref="a b"></div>
<p id="a">Name: <span itemprop="name">Herbie Hancock</span></p>
<div id="b" itemprop="band" itemscope="itemscope" itemref="c"></div>
<div id="c">
  <p>Band: <span itemprop="name">The Headhunters</span></p>
  <p>Size: <span itemprop="size">7</span> members</p>
</div>
```

The first item has two properties, declaring the name of jazz keyboardist Herbie Hancock, and annotates his jazz band separately on another item, which has two further properties, representing the name of the band as The Headhunters, and sets the number of members to 7 using the size property.

HTML5 Microdata DOM API

HTML5 Microdata has a DOM API for web developers to directly access structured data [20].

JSON-LD

In contrast to RDFa and HTML5 Microdata, the two other mainstream formats to add structured data to the web site markup, *JavaScript Object Notation for Linked Data* (*JSON-LD*) is described as JavaScript code rather than markup elements and attributes. As a result, JSON-LD is completely separate from the (X)HTML code. One of the advantages of this lightweight Linked Data format is that it is easy for humans to read and write. JSON-LD transports Linked Data using the JavaScript Object Notation (JSON), an open standard format using human-readable text to transmit attribute-value pairs [21]. If the JSON-LD code is written in a separate file rather than the markup, the de facto file extension is .jsonld. The Internet media

---

[7]The itemref attribute is not part of the Microdata data model and is purely a syntactic construct to annotate web page components for which creating a tree structure is not straightforward, as, for example, a table in which the columns represent items, and the cells the properties.

type of JSON-LD is application/ld+json and, if written in the markup, the JSON-LD code is delimited by curly braces between the <script> and </script> tags, as shown in Listing 2-35.

Listing 2-35. Compact JSON-LD Code in the Markup

```
<script type="application/ld+json">
{
  "@context": "http://schema.org",
  "@type": "Person",
  "image": "lesliesikos.jpg",
  "name": "Leslie Sikos",
  "url": "http://www.lesliesikos.com"
}
</script>
```

This example uses the compact syntax of JSON-LD, which can be expanded to the full syntax notation demonstrated in Listing 2-36.

Listing 2-36. Expanded JSON-LD Code

```
[
  {
    "@type": [
      "http://schema.org/Person"
    ],
    "http://schema.org/image": [
      {
        "@id": "http://www.lesliesikos.com/images/lesliesikos.jpg"
      }
    ],
    "http://schema.org/name": [
      {
        "@value": "Leslie Sikos"
      }
    ],
    "http://schema.org/url": [
      {
        "@id": "http://www.lesliesikos.com"
      }
    ]
  }
]
```

JSON-LD DOM API

The API of JSON-LD provides a way to transform JSON-LD documents to be more easily consumed by specific applications [22].

GRDDL: XML Documents to RDF

Since valid XML documents comply to a very strict grammar, RDF triples can often be extracted from XML. *Gleaning Resource Descriptions from Dialects of Languages* (*GRDDL*, pronounced as "griddle") is a markup format for transforming XML documents, including XHTML documents (with or without microformats such as hCard or hCalendar) to RDF. These transformations are usually expressed in XSLT, and happen in the following three steps:

1. Source document declaration

2. Link to one or more extractors

3. GRDDL agent extracts RDF from the document

XHTML 1.x documents use the profile attribute on the head element to declare that the document supports GRDDL transformations, while the available transformations are provided as an `.xsl` file (Listing 2-37).

Listing 2-37. An XHTML 1.x Document That Supports GRDDL Transformations

```
<head profile="http://www.w3.org/2003/g/data-view">
<link rel="transformation" href="grddlxfn.xsl" />
```

■ **Caution** The `profile` attribute is not supported in XHTML5.

In XML documents such as the Atom syndication format (used for news feeds) or KML (used to display geographic data in Google Earth and Google Maps), a transformation can be associated with the XML namespace by simply pointing to the namespace (Listing 2-38).

Listing 2-38. An XML Namespace Declaration Pointing to NamespaceTransformation

```
<foo xmlns="http://example.com/1.0/">
```

When the `http://example.com/1.0/` namespace is accessed, it reveals the `namespaceTransformation`, allowing easy deployment of RDF/XML from XML documents.

For XHTML documents that contain microformats, the profile specific to the applied annotations is used. For example, an XHTML document that supports GRDDL and has hCard information has a profile like that shown in Listing 2-39.

Listing 2-39. An XHTML 1.x Document That Supports GRDDL and Contains hCard Information

```
<head profile="http://www.w3.org/2003/g/data-view http://www.w3.org/2006/03/hcard">
```

GRDDL agents can extract all the hCard data from pages that reference the link of profile transformation (Listing 2-40).

Listing 2-40. Profile Transformation Link

```
The RDF data is extracted by <a rel="profileTransformation" ↵
href="hcard2rdf.xsl">this XSL</a> from <a href="http://example.com/hcard/">this hCard</a>.
```

R2RML: Relational Databases to RDF

The majority of dynamic web site contents are powered by relational databases (RDB) such as Microsoft SQL, MySQL, Oracle, IBM DB2, or PostgreSQL. *RDB2RML (R2RML)* is a standard for direct mapping of relational databases to RDF [23], making data more accessible on the Semantic Web (see Figure 2-5).

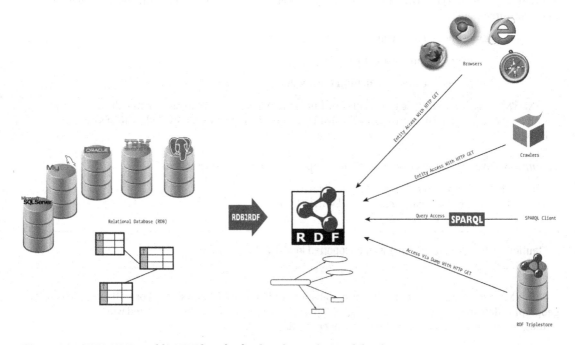

Figure 2-5. *RDB2RML enables RDF benefits for data from relational databases*

The direct mapping represents the RDB data and schema as an RDF graph called a *direct graph* and is described in the Turtle syntax. Assume we have two tables in a relational database, one of which collects people, the other addresses (Listing 2-41).

Listing 2-41. RDB Input

```
CREATE TABLE "Addresses" (
            "ID" INT, PRIMARY KEY("ID"),
                  "city" CHAR(10),
                  "state" CHAR(3)
)

CREATE TABLE "People" (
            "ID" INT, PRIMARY KEY("ID"),
                        "fname" CHAR(10),
                        "addr" INT,
                        FOREIGN KEY("addr") REFERENCES "Addresses"("ID")
)

INSERT INTO "Addresses" ("ID", "city", "state") VALUES (52, 'Adelaide', 'SA')
INSERT INTO "People" ("ID", "fname", "addr") VALUES (5, 'Leslie', 52)
```

Both tables have a unique identifier as the primary key. The address identifier provides the relation between the two tables (Figure 2-6).

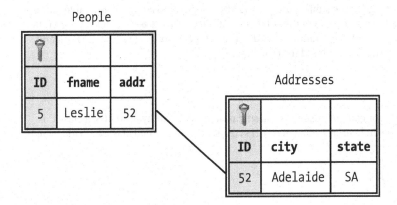

Figure 2-6. RDB input tables

The R2RML direct mapping of this example would create a People class with a Leslie entity with ID 5, an Addresses class with the city and state details of the Leslie entity, and a link between the Leslie entity and the associated address (Listing 2-42).

Listing 2-42. RDF/Turtle Output

```
@base <http://example.com/DB/> .
@prefix xsd: <http://www.w3.org/2001/XMLSchema#> .

<People/ID=5> rdf:type <People> .
<People/ID=5> <People#ID> 5 .
<People/ID=5> <People#fname> "Leslie" .
<People/ID=5> <People#addr> 52 .
<People/ID=5> <People#addr> <Addresses/ID=52>
<Addresses/ID=52> rdf:type <Addresses> .
<Addresses/ID=52> <Addresses#ID> 52 .
<Addresses/ID=52> <Addresses#city> "Adelaide" .
<Addresses/ID=52> <Addresses#state> "SA" .
```

RDFS

While RDF is the cornerstone of the Semantic Web, by itself it is not suitable for describing ontologies. RDFS (RDF Vocabulary Description Language, originally the RDF Schema Language) is a simple, RDF-based language for creating RDF ontologies by defining terms of a knowledge domain and the relationships between them [24]. RDFS is an extension of the RDF vocabulary with basic ontology elements and also reuses RDF properties. RDFS ontologies can be represented as RDF graphs. RDFS is suitable for describing various resource types, using specific properties. The RDFS classes and properties form the RDFS vocabulary, including a specialized set of predefined RDF resources with their meaning and using URI references with the prefix http://www.w3.org/2000/01/rdfschema# and the associated QName prefix rdfs:. The classes of the RDFS vocabulary are used to define a class resource (rdfs:Resource), the class of literal values such as strings and integers (rdfs:Literal), the class of classes (rdfs:Class), the class of RDF datatypes (rdfs:Datatype), the class of RDF containers (rdfs:Container), and the class of container membership properties (rdfs:ContainerMembershipProperty). The properties of RDFS can express that the subject is a subclass of a class (rdfs:subClassOf), the subject is a subproperty of a property (rdfs:subPropertyOf), define a domain (rdfs:domain) or range of the subject property (rdfs:range), add a human-readable name for the subject (rdfs:label), declare a description of the subject resource (rdfs:comment), identify a member of the subject resource (rdfs:member), add information related to the subject resource (rdfs:seeAlso), and provide the definition of the subject resource (rdfs:isDefinedBy).

Defining RDFS Classes

An RDFS class corresponds to a type or category used for classification and hierarchy. In RDFS, a class C is defined by a triple of the form shown in Listing 2-43, where rdfs:Class is a predefined class and rdf:type is a predefined property.

Listing 2-43. Class Definition in RDFS

```
C rdf:type rdfs:Class .
```

For example, the example.com video rental company wants to use RDFS to provide information about movies, including westerns and comedies. The classes to represent these categories can be written as the statements (triples) shown in Listing 2-44.

Listing 2-44. Statements in RDFS

```
ex:Movie rdf:type rdfs:Class .
ex:Western rdf:type rdfs:Class .
ex:Comedy rdf:type rdfs:Class .
```

Defining RDFS Subclasses

Suppose example.com wants to define that westerns and comedies are movies. This can be done with RDFS subclasses shown in Listing 2-45.

Listing 2-45. Subclass Definition in RDFS

```
ex:Western rdfs:subClassOf ex:Movie .
ex:Comedy rdfs:subClassOf ex:Movie .
```

The rdfs:subClassOf property is reflexive, in other words, once an RDFS class is created, it is a subclass of itself, such as the definition of ex:Movie infers that ex:Movie rdfs:subClassOf ex:Movie . The rdfs:subClassOf property is also transitive. The predefined rdfs:subclassOf property is used as a predicate in a statement to declare that a class is a specialization of another more general class. The meaning of the rdfs:subClassOf predefined property in a statement of the form C1 rdfs:subClassOf C2 is that any instance of class C1 is also an instance of class C2. For example, if we have the statements ex:Comedy rdfs:subClassOf ex:Movie . (comedies are movies) and ex:ActionComedy rdf:type ex:Comedy . (action comedies are comedies), the statement ex:ActionComedy rdf:type ex:Movie . (action comedies are movies) can be inferred (knowledge explicitly not stated can be deducted).

Defining RDFS Instances

To define an instance for example.org, such as an individual movie, we can make an RDF statement that the film *Bad Boys* is an action comedy, as shown in Listing 2-46.

Listing 2-46. Instance Definition in RDFS

```
@prefix films:   <http://example.com/films> .
@prefix moviedb: <http://examplefilmdb.com> .

moviedb:BadBoys rdf:type films:ActionComedy .
```

The `rdf:type` predefined property is used as a predicate in a statement I `rdf:type` C . to declare that individual I is an instance of class C. In statements of the form C `rdf:type` `rdfs:Class` ., `rdf:type` is used to declare that class C (viewed as an individual object) is an instance of the `rdfs:Class` predefined class. Defining a class explicitly is optional. If we write a triple such as I `rdf:type` C ., C is inferred to be a class (namely, an instance of `rdfs:Class`). A class is not limited to one hierarchical level and can be a subclass or superclass of other classes that is usually represented as a directed graph (see Figure 2-7).

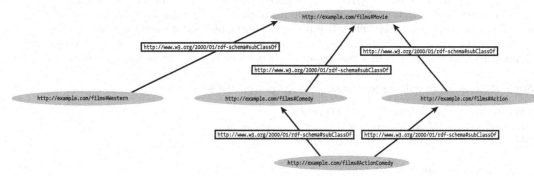

Figure 2-7. *Hierarchy of RDFS classes on a graph*

In our example, the graph represents the machine-readable statements that can be expressed by the ontology (Listing 2-47).

Listing 2-47. RDFS Classes Correspond to Relationships Represented on the Graph

```
@prefix films:   <http://example.com/films> .
@prefix rdf:     <http://www.w3.org/1999/02/22-rdf-syntax-ns#> .
@prefix rdfs:    <http://www.w3.org/2000/01/rdf-schema#> .

films:Movie rdf:type rdfs:Class .
films:Action rdf:type rdfs:Class .
films:Comedy rdf:type rdfs:Class .
films:Western rdf:type rdfs:Class .
films:ActionComedy rdf:type rdfs:Class .
films:Action rdfs:subClassOf films:Movie .
films:Comedy rdfs:subClassOf films:Movie .
films:Western rdfs:subClassOf films:Movie .
films:ActionComedy rdfs:subClassOf films:Comedy .
films:ActionComedy rdfs:subClassOf films:Action .
```

Defining RDFS Properties

Specific properties can be defined without references to classes or to characterize classes. To create a property for a class, one makes the statement that the property to be defined is an instance of the predefined `rdf:Property` class. For example, we write `ex:author rdf:type rdf:Property .`, so that the `ex:author` property can be used as a predicate in an RDF triple, such as `ex:LeslieSikos ex:author ex:WebStandards .` Because RDFS properties are resources too, properties can be either subjects or objects of triples. For example, `ex:author prov:definedBy ke:LeslieSikos` and `ke:LeslieSikos prov:defined ex:author`.

The `rdfs:label` property is an instance of `rdf:Property` that can be used to provide a human-readable version of the name of a resource. The `rdfs:comment` property is an instance of `rdf:Property` suitable for providing a human-readable description of a resource. A very frequently used RDFS property on the Semantic Web is `rdfs:seeAlso`, which is an instance of `rdf:Property` and used to indicate a resource that provides additional information about the subject resource. Assume we have an RDF description for the textbook *Web Standards: Mastering HTML5, CSS3, and XML*. We declare the title of the book with the title property from the Dublin Core vocabulary, so its namespace at `http://purl.org/dc/terms/` has to be included in the namespace declaration. To link the web site of the book to a web page that describes additional books by the author, the `rdfs:seeAlso` property can be used (see Listing 2-48). Because we use RDF and RDFS properties as well, their namespaces have to be added to the namespace declaration.

Listing 2-48. Tagging, Describing, and Linking Resources with RDFS Properties

```
@prefix dcterms: <http://purl.org/dc/terms/> .
@prefix rdf: <http://www.w3.org/1999/02/22-rdf-syntax-ns#> .
@prefix rdfs: <http://www.w3.org/2000/01/rdf-schema#> .

<http://www.masteringhtml5css3.com>
    rdfs:label "RDF Description of the web design book Web Standards" ;
    dcterms:title "Web Standards: Mastering HTML5, CSS3, and XML" ;
    rdfs:comment "Web Standards: Mastering HTML5, CSS3, and XML presents step-by-step ↵
    guides based on solid design principles and best practices, and shows the most common ↵
    web development tools and web design frameworks. You will master HTML5 and its XML ↵
    serialization, XHTML5, the new structuring and multimedia elements, the most important ↵
    HTML5 APIs, and understand the standardization process of HTML 5.1, HTML 5.2, and ↵
    future HTML5 versions." ;
    rdfs:seeAlso <http://www.lesliesikos.com/web-design-books/> .
```

The `rdfs:isDefinedBy` property is an instance of `rdf:Property` that is used to indicate a resource that defines the subject resource, such as a controlled vocabulary in which the resource is described.

Defining RDFS Domains and Ranges

Properties can be declared to apply only to certain instances of classes, by defining their domain and range, which indicate the relationships between RDFS classes and properties and RDF data. The `rdfs:domain` predicate indicates that a particular property applies to instances of a designated class (the domain of the property), in other words, declares the class of those resources that may appear as subjects in a triple with the predicate. The `rdfs:range` predicate indicates that the values of a particular property are instances of a designated class (the class of those resources that may appear as the object in a triple with the predicate, also known as the range of the property), as shown in Listing 2-49.

Listing 2-49. Using RDFS Domain and Range

```
ex:Book rdf:type rdfs:Class .
ex:Person rdf:type rdfs:Class .
ex:author rdf:type rdf:Property .
ex:author rdfs:domain ex:Book .
ex:author rdfs:range ex:Person .
Book1 ex:hasAuthor Author .
```

■ **Note**   Not all properties have a domain or range.

The `rdfs:range` property can also indicate that a property value is declared with a typed literal[8] (Listing 2-50).

Listing 2-50. Using a Typed Literal

```
ex:age rdf:type rdf:Property .
ex:age rdfs:range xsd:integer .
```

Web Ontology Language (OWL)

While simple machine-readable ontologies can be created using RDFS, complex knowledge domains require more capabilities, such as

- Relations between classes (union, intersection, disjointness, equivalence)
- Property cardinality constraints (minimum, maximum, exact number, e.g., a Person has exactly one father)
- Rich typing of properties (object vs. datatype, specific datatypes)
- Characteristics of properties and special properties (transitive, symmetric, functional, inverse functional, e.g., A `ex:hasAncestor` B and B `ex:hasAncestor` C implies that A `ex:hasAncestor` C)
- Specifying that a given property is a unique key for instances of a particular class
- Domain and range restrictions for properties when they are used with a certain class
- Equality of classes, specifying that two classes with different URI references actually represent the same class
- Equality of individuals, specifying that two instances with different URI references actually represent the same individual
- Enumerated classes

---

[8]The datatype can also be expressed by `rdfs:Datatype` such as `xsd:integer rdf:type rdfs:Datatype .` or using `rdf:datatype` as for example `rdf:datatype="http://www.w3.org/2001/XMLSchema#string"`.

Web Ontology Language (*OWL*) is a knowledge representation language especially designed for creating web ontologies with a rich set of modeling constructors, addressing the limitations of RDFS. The development of the first version of OWL was started in 2002, and the second version, OWL2, in 2008. OWL became a W3C Recommendation in 2004 [25], and OWL2 was standardized in 2009 [26, 27]. OWL is based on RDF, semantically extending RDF and RDFS, as well as its predecessor language, *DAML+OIL*.

■ **Note**   The abbreviation of *Web Ontology Language* is intentionally not WOL but OWL [28].

Description Logic

Ontologies on the Semantic Web often implement *mathematical logic*, a subfield of mathematics dealing with formal expressions, deductive reasoning, and formal proof. *Description Logic* (*DL*) is a family of formal knowledge representation languages in Artificial Intelligence used for logical formalism for ontologies, including formal reasoning of the concepts of a knowledge domain. Description Logic languages are more expressive than *propositional logic* (which deals with declarative propositions and does not use quantifiers) and more efficient in decision problems than *first-order predicate logic* (which uses predicates and quantified variables over non-logical objects). A Description Logic can model concepts, roles and individuals, and their relationships. A core modeling concept of a Description Logic is the *axiom*, which is a logical statement about the relation between roles and/or concepts. Most web ontologies written in OWL are implementations of a Description Logic.

Each Description Logic *Knowledge Base* (*KB*) consists of a *terminological part* (*TBox*) and an *assertional part* (*ABox*), both of which contain a set of axioms. A basic Description Logic is $\mathcal{AL}$, the *Attributive Language*, which supports atomic negation,[9] concept intersection, universal restrictions, and limited existential quantification.

■ **Note**   The naming convention of Description Logics is to indicate additional constructors by appending a corresponding letter (see Table 2-8).

Table 2-8. Common Letters Used in Description Logic Names

Symbol	Includes	Example
$\mathcal{C}$	Complex concept constructor negation	The negation of arbitrary concepts
$\mathcal{S}$	An abbreviation of $\mathcal{ALC}$ with transitive roles	Apple's mobile operating system is iOS, and iOS is developed for iPhone smartphones, so iPhone smartphones are made by Apple.
$\mathcal{R}$	Limited complex role inclusion axioms, reflexivity and irreflexivity, role disjointness	"part of" and "has part"
$\mathcal{O}$	Enumerated classes of object value restrictions (nominals)	Africa, Antarctica, Asia, Australia, Europe, North America, South America

(continued)

---

[9]Negation of concept names that do not appear on the left-hand side of axioms.

Table 2-8. (*continued*)

Symbol	Includes	Example
$\mathcal{I}$	Inverse properties	Employ and employed by
$\mathcal{N}$	Cardinality restrictions	Each person has two parents.
$\mathcal{F}$	Functional properties, a special case of uniqueness quantification	"there is one and only one"
$\mathcal{Q}$	Qualified cardinality restrictions	Cardinality restrictions that have fillers other than ⊤
$(\mathcal{D})$	Data type properties, data values, or data types	The number annotated as integer in the statement "Christina is 30 years old"

An extension of $\mathcal{AL}$ is the *Attributive Concept Language with Complements*, the Description Logic abbreviated as $\mathcal{ALC}$. $\mathcal{ALC}$ supports ABox expressions such as individual assignments (e.g., Ford is a car), property assignments (e.g., Leslie has a wife, Christina), TBox expressions such as subclass relationships (⊑) and equivalence (≡), as well as conjunction (⊓), disjunction (⊔), negation (¬), property restrictions (∀,∃), tautology (⊤, a logical formula which is always true), and contradiction (⊥). By combining such mathematical operators, you can construct complex class expressions, which are denoted by the *C* in the name of this Description Logic. $\mathcal{ALC}$ can describe sets of individuals, sets of atomic classes, and sets of roles.

$\mathcal{SR}$ extends the capabilities of $\mathcal{ALC}$ with property chains, property characteristics, and role hierarchies. The property characteristics include transitivity (e.g., Ben has the ancestor Violet), symmetry (e.g., Christina is the spouse of Leslie, and Leslie is the spouse of Christina), asymmetry (e.g., Leslie has the son Ben), reflexivity (e.g., Christina has the relative Linda), irreflexive (e.g., Christina is the parent of Ben), functional (e.g., Christina has a husband) and inverse functional properties (e.g., Leslie is the husband of Christina). $\mathcal{SRO}$ extends $\mathcal{SR}$ with nominals, i.e., enumerated classes of object value restrictions. $\mathcal{SROI}$ adds inverse properties to $\mathcal{SRO}$. $\mathcal{SROIQ}$ extends $\mathcal{SRO}$ with qualified cardinality constraints. $\mathcal{SROIQ}^{(D)}$ extends $\mathcal{SRO}$ $\mathcal{IQ}$ with datatypes, including facets. In addition, $\mathcal{SROIQ}^{(D)}$ supports disjoint properties and adds tautology (⊤) and contradiction (⊥) support for objects and datatypes (see Figure 2-8).

Beyond Abox and TBox, $\mathcal{SROIQ}^{(D)}$ also supports so-called *Role Boxes* (*RBox*) to collect all statements related to roles and the interdependencies between roles. Each RBox consists of a role hierarchy (including generalized role inclusion axioms) and a set of role assertions.

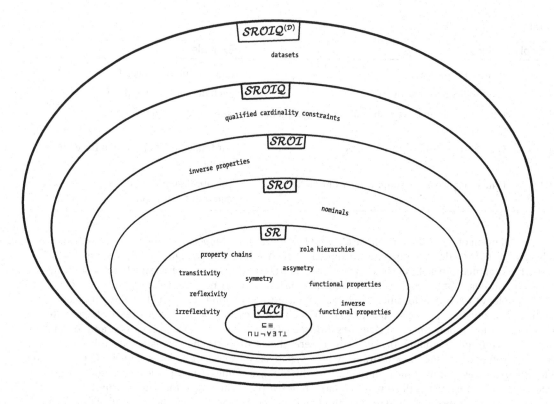

Figure 2-8. *Relationship between the description logic constructors of $\mathcal{ALC}$ and $\mathcal{SROIQ}^{(D)}$*

OWL Variants

There are three flavors of OWL, each constituting different compromises between expressive power and computational complexity (reasoning practicability):

- *OWL-Full*: No restrictions on the use of language constructs: no global restrictions or restrictions for RDF usage. Maximum expressiveness, syntactic freedom, and no computational guarantees. The semantics of OWL-Full is a mixture of RDFS and OWL-DL (*RDF-Based Semantics*).

- *OWL-DL*: A restricted version of OWL-Full that corresponds to a Description Logic. OWL-DL provides maximum expressiveness, computational completeness (all conclusions are guaranteed to be computable), and decidability (all computations can be finished in finite time). It inherits global restrictions from $\mathcal{SROIQ}^{(D)}$. In OWL-DL, RDF can be used only for expressing OWL axioms. OWL-DL implements the model-theoretic semantics of $\mathcal{SROIQ}^{(D)}$ called *OWL2 Direct Semantics*.

- *OWL-Lite*: A subset of OWL-DL designed for easy implementation. OWL-Lite has limited applicability, because it is suitable only for classification hierarchy and simple constraints.

OWL2 provides the expressiveness of the $\mathcal{SROIQ}^{(D)}$ Description Logic; OWL-DL is based on the $\mathcal{SHOIN}^{(D)}$ Description Logic; while OWL-Lite is based on the $\mathcal{SHIF}^{(D)}$ Description Logic.

OWL ontologies are RDF graphs, in other words, sets of RDF triples. Similar to RDF graphs, OWL ontology graphs can be expressed in various syntactic notations. OWL is a higher-level language than RDF; in fact, it is a vocabulary extension of RDF. Consequently, RDF graphs are OWL-Full ontologies. The default OWL namespace is `http://www.w3.org/2002/07/owl#`, which defines the OWL vocabulary. There is no MIME type defined specifically for OWL, but the `application/rdf+xml` or the `application/xml` MIME type is recommended for OWL documents with the `.rdf` or `.owl` file extension.

OWL has three components: classes, properties, and individuals. Classes and individuals are differentiated in OWL using `Class` and `Thing`. While in RDFS only subclasses of existing classes can be created, in OWL, classes can be constructed based on existing classes in any of the following ways:

- Enumerating the content

- Through intersection, union, or complement

- Through property restrictions

Syntaxes

At the high level, the OWL abstract syntax [29] and the OWL2 functional syntax [30] can be used. OWL also supports several exchange syntaxes, including the RDF syntaxes, such as RDF/XML and RDF/Turtle, the OWL2 XML syntax [31], and the Manchester syntax [32], but RDF/XML is the normative syntax.

■ **Note**   In the examples, I use declarations for a hypothetical smartphone ontology.

The OWL2 functional syntax is compatible with the *Unified Modeling Language* (*UML*), one of the most widely deployed general-purpose standardized modeling languages (see Listing 2-51). It is clean, adjustable, modifiable, and easy to parse. The functional syntax is primarily used for defining the formal OWL2 grammar in the W3C specifications.

Listing 2-51. OWL2 Functional Syntax Example

```
Prefix(owl:=<http://www.w3.org/2002/07/owl#>)

Ontology(<http://example.com/smartphone.owl>
  Declaration( Class( :Smartphone ) )
)
```

The notational variant of the OWL2 functional syntax is the OWL/XML syntax, which uses an XML tree structure instead of RDF triples, as shown in Listing 2-52.

Listing 2-52. OWL2 XML Syntax Example

```
<Ontology ontologyIRI="http://example.com/smartphone.owl">
  <Prefix name="owl" IRI="http://www.w3.org/2002/07/owl#"/>
  <Declaration>
    <Class IRI="Smartphone"/>
  </Declaration>
</Ontology>
```

The only normative syntax of OWL 2 is the RDF/XML syntax (see Listing 2-53). Every OWL2-compliant tool supports this syntax.

Listing 2-53. RDF/XML Syntax Example

```
<rdf:RDF ↵
 xmlns:owl="http://www.w3.org/2002/07/owl#" ↵
 xmlns:rdf="http://www.w3.org/1999/02/22-rdf-syntax-ns#">
  <owl:Ontology rdf:about="Phone Ontology"/>
  <owl:Class rdf:about="#Smartphone"/>
</rdf:RDF>
```

A straightforward syntax for representing RDF triples for OWL ontologies is the RDF/Turtle syntax shown in Listing 2-54.

Listing 2-54. RDF/Turtle Example

```
@prefix rdf: <http://www.w3.org/1999/02/22-rdf-syntax-ns#> .
@prefix owl: <http://www.w3.org/2002/07/owl#> .

<http://example.com/smartphone.owl>
  rdf:type owl:Ontology .
  :Smartphone rdf:type owl:Class .
```

The less frequently used Manchester syntax is a compact, user-friendly syntax for OWL-DL that collects information about a particular class, property, or individual into a single construct called a *frame*. The Manchester syntax is easy to read and write, especially for those who are not experts in mathematical logic. Complex descriptions consist of short, meaningful English words, while eliminating the logical symbols and precedence rules represented in other syntaxes, as shown in Listing 2-55.

Listing 2-55. Manchester Syntax Example

```
Prefix: owl: <http://www.w3.org/2002/07/owl#>

Ontology: <http://example.com/smartphone.owl>
Class: Smartphone
```

Properties

In OWL, the following types of properties exist:

- *Object properties* that link individuals to other individuals

- *Datatype properties* that link individuals to data values (subclasses of object properties)

- *Annotation property* (owl:AnnotationProperty)

- *Ontology property* (owl:OntologyProperty)

Property features are defined by the property axioms. The basic form expresses the existence only. For example, in a smartphone ontology, the property hasTouchscreen can be declared to express a major feature of mobile phones (see Listing 2-56).

Listing 2-56. A Property Declaration in OWL

```
<owl:ObjectProperty rdf:ID="hasTouchscreen" />
```

OWL property axioms can also define additional characteristics. OWL reuses RDF Schema constructs such as `rdfs:subPropertyOf`, `rdfs:domain`, and `rdfs:range`. Relations to other properties can be expressed by `owl:equivalentProperty` and `owl:inverseOf` (Listing 2-57).

Listing 2-57. Two Equivalent Smartphone Properties (Accelerometer and G-sensor)

```
<owl:ObjectProperty rdf:ID="hasAccelerometer">
  <owl:equivalentProperty>
    <owl:ObjectProperty rdf:ID="hasGsensor" />
  </owl:equivalentProperty>
</owl:ObjectProperty>
```

Global cardinality constraints are defined by `owl:FunctionalProperty` and `owl:InverseFunctionalProperty` (see Listing 2-58). Symmetry and transitivity features are defined by `owl:SymmetricProperty` and `owl:TransitiveProperty` [33].

Listing 2-58. A `FunctionalProperty` in OWL

```
<owl:ObjectProperty rdf:about="&myMobile;manufactured_by">
  <rdf:type rdf:resource="&owl;FunctionalProperty" />
  <rdfs:domain rdf:resource="&myMobile;Mobile" />
</owl:ObjectProperty>
```

OWL provides precise declarations for expressing relationships, even if they are evident. For example, the *property hierarchy* of two smartphone features can be expressed using `rdfs:subPropertyOf`, as presented in Listing 2-59.

Listing 2-59. Property Hierarchy in OWL

```
<owl:ObjectProperty rdf:ID="hasGeotagging" />
  <owl:ObjectProperty rdf:ID="hasCamera">
  <rdfs:subPropertyOf rdf:resource="hasGeotagging" />
</owl:ObjectProperty>
```

Classes

Similar to RDF, OWL provides classes to group resources. There are six different *class descriptions* in OWL:

1. Class identifier (URI reference). A named instance of `owl:Class`, a subclass of `rdfs:Class`.[10] Listing 2-60 shows an example.

    Listing 2-60. A Class Identifier in OWL

    ```
    <owl:Class rdf:ID="Handheld"/>
    ```

---

[10]In OWL Lite and OWL DL. In OWL-Full they are equivalent.

2. Set of individuals (instances of a class) defined by the `owl:oneOf` property. For example, the class of smartphones can be declared in the RDF/XML syntax, with the RDF construct `rdf:parseType="Collection"`, as shown in Listing 2-61.

Listing 2-61. Declaring Class Instances in OWL

```
<owl:Class>
  <owl:oneOf rdf:parseType="Collection">
    <owl:Thing rdf:about="#Touch" />
    <owl:Thing rdf:about="#Type" />
    <owl:Thing rdf:about="#TouchType" />
  </owl:oneOf>
</owl:Class>
```

3. Property restriction: a value constraint or a cardinality constraint (for example, see Listing 2-62).

Listing 2-62. Property Restrictions in OWL

```
<owl:Restriction>
  <owl:onProperty rdf:resource="hasGPS" />
  <owl:allValuesFrom rdf:resource="#Smartphone" />
</owl:Restriction>
```

4. Intersection of two or more class descriptions. For example, the intersection of the `Smartphone` and the `MadeByApple` classes can be described by `owl:intersectionOf`, stating that iPhones are smartphones made by Apple (see Listing 2-63).

Listing 2-63. Intersection in OWL

```
<owl:Class rdf:ID="IPhone">
  <owl:intersectionOf rdf:parseType="Collection">
    <owl:Class rdf:about="#Smartphone" />
    <owl:Class rdf:about="#MadeByApple" />
  </owl:intersectionOf>
</owl:Class>
```

5. Union of two or more class descriptions.

6. Complement of a class description. The class extension contains exactly those individuals that do not belong to the class extension of the class description that forms the object of the statement. The complement can be described by the `owl:complementOf` property.

Class descriptions can be combined into *class axioms*. Class hierarchy can be expressed by a *subclass axiom* (Listing 2-64).

Listing 2-64. Class Hierarchy in OWL

```
<owl:Class rdf:ID="Slide">
  <rdfs:subClassOf rdf:resource="#smartphone" />
</owl:Class>
```

The equivalence of two classes express that the individuals contained by them are identical. Listing 2-65 shows an example.

Listing 2-65. Equivalent Classes in OWL

```
<owl:Class rdf:about="VirtualKeyboard">
  <owl:equivalentClass rdf:resource="#Softquerty">
</owl>
```

Although individuals can be members of several classes in general, in many cases, memberships are exclusive. For example, smartphones either have a physical keyboard or a virtual keyboard (on the touchscreen). This *class disjointness* can be expressed as shown in Listing 2-66.

Listing 2-66. Class Disjointness in OWL

```
<owl:Class rdf:about="VirtualKeyboard">
  <owl:equivalentClass rdf:resource="#Softquerty" />
  <owl:disjointWith rdf:resource="Keyboard" />
</owl>
```

Simple Knowledge Organization System (SKOS)

Simple Knowledge Organization System (*SKOS*) is a W3C recommendation for representing taxonomies, thesauri, classification schemes, subject-heading systems, and structured controlled vocabularies. Being one of the most frequently implemented Semantic Web standards in industrial applications, SKOS is built upon RDF and RDFS to enable easy publication of controlled vocabularies as linked data. RDF provides interoperability, consistency, and integrity and allows knowledge organization systems to be used in distributed, decentralized metadata applications where metadata are retrieved from multiple resources.

The SKOS standard defines the SKOS data model as an OWL-Full ontology [34]. The elements of the SKOS data model are OWL classes and properties with individual URIs that form the SKOS vocabulary. The classes and properties of SKOS are suitable for representing the common features of thesauri (lists words in groups of synonyms and related concepts). The abstract concepts of SKOS are represented by terms and can be organized in hierarchies using relationships such as broader and narrower or linked by nonhierarchical (associative) relationships, such as related. Further SKOS classes and predicates can be used for basic descriptions (Concept, ConceptScheme), labeling (prefLabel, altLabel, prefSymbol, altSymbol), documentation (definition, scopeNote, changeNote), subject indexing (subject, isSubjectOf), grouping (Collection, OrderedCollection), and subject indication (subjectIndicator). SKOS also provides some inference rules similar to the RDFS inference rules.

Rule Interchange Format (RIF)

The additional information used to automatically make new discoveries on the Semantic Web are based either on ontologies or on *rule sets*. While ontologies focus on the classification methods by defining classes, subclasses, and relations, rule sets focus on general mechanisms for discovering and generating new relations, based on existing relations. Rule sets are collections of IF-THEN constructs called *rules*. If the condition in the IF part of the code holds, the conclusion of the THEN part of the code is processed. Rules are simplifications of a first-order predicate logic, are relatively easy to implement, and beyond syntax and semantics, and they can express existential quantification, disjunction, logical conjunction, negation, functions, non-monotonicity, and other features.

There are many different rule languages, for example, the *Rule Markup Language* (*RuleML*), an XML approach to represent both forward (bottom-up) and backward (top-down) rules, or the *Semantic Web Rule Language* (*SWRL*), which was introduced as an extension to OWL. Due to the different paradigms, semantics, features, syntaxes, and commercial interests of rule languages, there is a need for *rule exchange*.

The *Rule Interchange Format* (*RIF*) was designed for rule sharing and exchange between existing rule systems, in other words, allowing rules written for one application to be shared and reused in other applications and rule engines while preserving semantics. RIF is a collection of rigorously defined rule languages called *dialects*. The Core Dialect of RIF is a common subset of most rule engines. The Basic Logic Dialect (BLD) adds logic functions, equality and named arguments, and supports the Horn logic (a disjunction of literals with at most one positive literal). The Production Rules Dialect (PRD) provides action with side effects in rule conclusion. RIF has a mapping to RDF.

Reasoning

Description logic-based ontologies are crucial in describing the meaning of web resources and can leverage powerful description logic *reasoning tools* to facilitate machine-processability of semantic web sites. *Reasoning* derives facts that are not expressed explicitly in machine-readable ontologies or knowledge bases. Description logic reasoners implement the *analytic tableau method* (truth tree) for semantic reasoning, which is the most popular proof procedure for formulas of first-order predicate logic. Among other benefits, this makes it possible to determine the satisfiability of formula sets. Reasoners can determine whether a description of the concept is not contradictory, or whether a description is more general than another description. They can check consistency and whether an individual is an instance of a concept or not. Reasoners can retrieve all instances of a particular concept and find the most specific concept individuals belong to. Due to decidability, computational complexity, and the level of formality, automatic processing is not always feasible.

Parsers

Semantic parsing is the process of mapping a natural language sentence into a formal representation of its meaning. A basic form of semantic parsing is the case-role analysis (semantic role labeling), which identifies roles such as source or destination. An advanced semantic parsing represents a sentence in predicate logic or other formal language for automated reasoning.

Summary

In this chapter, you became familiar with the most common controlled vocabularies and ontologies, so that you can identify the suitable vocabularies and ontologies for your projects, in addition to the right classes and properties. You know how to model statements in RDF, represent them as directed graphs, and write them in RDF/XML or Turtle, as well as annotate them in RDFa, Microdata, or JSON-LD.

The next chapter will show you how to create datasets from structured data and link them to other datasets, making your dataset part of the Linked Open Data Cloud.

References

1. DMOZ—the Open Directory Project. www.dmoz.org. Accessed 20 March 2015.

2. Cyganiak, R., Wood, D., Lanthaler, M. (eds.) (2014) RDF 1.1 Concepts and Abstract Syntax. World Wide Web Consortium. www.w3.org/TR/rdf11-concepts/. Accessed 18 January 2015.

3. Gandon, F., Schreiber, G. (eds.) (2014) RDF 1.1 XML Syntax. World Wide Web Consortium. www.w3.org/TR/rdf-syntax-grammar/. Accessed 18 January 2015.

4. Carothers, G., Seaborne, A. (2014) RDF 1.1 N-Triples. A line-based syntax for an RDF graph. World Wide Web Consortium. www.w3.org/TR/n-triples/. Accessed 18 January 2015.

5. Bizer, C., Cyganiak, R. (2014) RDF 1.1 TriG. RDF Dataset Language. World Wide Web Consortium. www.w3.org/TR/trig/. Accessed 18 January 2015.

6. Carroll, J. J., Stickler, P. (2004) RDF Triples in XML. HP Laboratories. www.hpl.hp.com/techreports/2003/HPL-2003-268.pdf. Accessed 18 January 2015.

7. Klyne, G., Carroll, J. J., McBride, B. (eds.) (2014) RDF 1.1 Concepts and Abstract Syntax. World Wide Web Consortium. www.w3.org/TR/rdf11-concepts/. Accessed 18 January 2015.

8. Sindice (2014) Sindice Web Data Inspector. Sindice Ltd. http://inspector.sindice.com. Accessed 18 January 2015.

9. King, R., Çelik, T. (2012) hCalendar Creator. http://microformats.org/code/hcalendar/creator.html. Accessed 20 March 2015.

10. Çelik, T. (2005) hCard Creator. The Microformats Community. http://microformats.org/code/hcard/creator. Accessed 18 January 2015.

11. Casserly, C. et al (eds.) (2015) Licenses. Creative Commons. http://creativecommons.org/about/licenses/. Accessed 14 April 2015

12. Mullenweg, M., Çelik, T. (2004) XFN 1.1 Creator. Global Multimedia Protocols Group. http://gmpg.org/xfn/creator. Accessed 18 January 2015.

13. Mullenweg, M. (2014) Exefen. http://ma.tt/tools/exefen.php/. Accessed 18 January 2015.

14. Adida, B., Birbeck, M., McCarron, S., Herman, I. (eds.) (2013) RDFa Core 1.1—Second Edition. Syntax and processing rules for embedding RDF through attributes. World Wide Web Consortium. www.w3.org/TR/rdfa-core/. Accessed 18 January 2015.

15. Sporny, M. (ed.) (2012) RDFa Lite 1.1. World Wide Web Consortium. www.w3.org/TR/rdfa-lite/. Accessed 18 January 2015.

16. Herman, I. (2014) RDFa Core Initial Context. World Wide Web Consortium. www.w3.org/2011/rdfa-context/rdfa-1.1. Accessed 18 January 2015.

17. Adida, B., Birbeck, M., McCarron, S., Herman, I. (eds.) (2012) Completing incomplete triples. In RDFa Core 1.1. www.w3.org/TR/2012/REC-rdfa-core-20120607/#s_Completing_Incomplete_Triples. Accessed 18 January 2015.

18.   Rixham, N., Birbeck, M., Herman, I. (2012) RDFa API. World Wide Web
      Consortium. www.w3.org/TR/rdfa-api/. Accessed 18 January 2015.

19.   Hickson, I. (2013) HTML Microdata. World Wide Web Consortium.
      www.w3.org/TR/microdata/. Accessed 18 January 2015.

20.   Hickson, I. (ed.) (2013) HTML Microdata. World Wide Web Consortium.
      www.w3.org/TR/microdata/#using-the-microdata-dom-api. Accessed
      18 January 2015.

21.   Sporny, M., Longley, D., Kellogg, G., Lanthaler, M., Lindström, N. (2014)
      JSON-LD 1.0. World Wide Web Consortium. www.w3.org/TR/json-ld/. Accessed
      18 January 2015.

22.   Longley, D., Kellogg, G., Lanthaler, M., Sporny, M. (2014) JSON-LD 1.0 Processing
      Algorithms and API. World Wide Web Consortium. www.w3.org/TR/json-ld-api/.
      Accessed 18 January 2015.

23.   Das, S., Sundara, S., Cyganiak, R. (eds.) (2012) R2RML: RDB to RDF Mapping
      Language. World Wide Web Consortium. www.w3.org/TR/r2rml/. Accessed 18
      January 2015.

24.   Brickley, D., Guha, R. V. RDF Schema 1.1. World Wide Web Consortium.
      www.w3.org/TR/rdf-schema/. Accessed 18 December 2014.

25.   Dean, M., Schreiber, G. (eds.), Bechhofer S, van Harmelen F, Hendler J, Horrocks
      I, McGuinness DL, Patel-Schneider PF, Stein LA (2004) OWL Web Ontology
      Language Reference. World Wide Web Consortium. www.w3.org/TR/owl-ref/.
      Accessed 18 January 2015.

26.   Hitzler, P., Krötzsch, M., Parsia, B., Patel-Schneider, P. F., Rudolph, S. (eds.) (2012)
      OWL 2 Web Ontology Language—Primer 2nd ed. World Wide Web Consortium.
      www.w3.org/TR/owl-primer/. Accessed 18 January 2015.

27.   Motik, B., Grau, B. C., Horrocks, I., Wu, Z., Fokoue, A., Lutz, C. (eds.), Calvanese,
      D., Carroll, J., De Giacomo, G., Hendler, J., Herman I., Parsia, B., Patel-Schneider,
      P. F., Ruttenberg, A., Sattler, U., Schneider, M. (2012) OWL 2 Web Ontology
      Language—Profiles. World Wide Web Consortium. www.w3.org/TR/owl2-
      profiles/. Accessed 18 January 2015.

28.   Herman, I. (2010) "Why OWL and not WOL?" Tutorial on Semantic Web
      Technologies. World Wide Web Consortium. www.w3.org/People/Ivan/
      CorePresentations/RDFTutorial/Slides.html#%28114%29. Accessed
      18 January 2015.

29.   Patel-Schneider, P. F., Horrocks, I. (eds.) (2004) Abstract Syntax. In: OWL
      Web Ontology Language. Semantics and Abstract Syntax. World Wide Web
      Consortium. www.w3.org/TR/2004/REC-owl-semantics-20040210/syntax.html.
      Accessed 18 January 2015.

30.   Motik, B., Patel-Schneider, P. F., Parsia, B. (eds.), Bock, C., Fokoue, A., Haase,
      P., Hoekstra, R., Horrocks, I., Ruttenberg, A., Sattler, U., Smith, M. (2012) OWL 2
      Web Ontology Language. Structural Specification and Functional-Style Syntax 2nd Ed.
      World Wide Web Consortium. www.w3.org/TR/owl-syntax/. Accessed
      18 January 2015.

31. Motik, B., Parsia, B., Patel-Schneider, P. F. (eds.), Bechhofer, S., Grau,
     B. C., Fokoue, A., Hoekstra, R. (2012) OWL 2 Web Ontology Language. XML
     Serialization 2nd Ed. World Wide Web Consortium. `www.w3.org/TR/owl-xml-serialization/`. Accessed 18 January 2015.

32. Horridge, M., Patel-Schneider, P. F. (2012) OWL 2 Web Ontology Language.
     Manchester Syntax. World Wide Web Consortium. `www.w3.org/TR/owl2-manchester-syntax/`. Accessed 18 January 2015.

33. Dean, M., Schreiber, G. (eds.), Bechhofer S, van Harmelen F, Hendler J, Horrocks
     I, McGuinness DL, Patel-Schneider PF, Stein LA (2004) Properties. In: OWL Web
     Ontology Language Reference. World Wide Web Consortium. `www.w3.org/TR/owl-ref/#Property`. Accessed 18 January 2015.

34. Miles, A., Bechhofer, S. (2009) SKOS Simple Knowledge Organization System
     Reference. World Wide Web Recommendation. `www.w3.org/TR/skos-reference/`. Accessed 18 January 2015.

CHAPTER 3

■ ■ ■

Linked Open Data

In contracts to the isolated data silos of the conventional Web, the Semantic Web interconnects open data, so that all datasets contribute to a global data integration, connecting data from diverse domains, such as people, companies, books, scientific publications, films, music, reviews, television and radio programs, medicine, statistics, online communities, and scientific data. The union of the structured datasets forms the Linked Open Data Cloud, the decentralized core of the Semantic Web, where software agents can automatically find relationships between entities and make new discoveries. Linked Data browsers allow users to browse a data source, and by using special (typed) links, navigate along links into other related data sources. Linked Data search engines crawl the Web of Data by following links between data sources and provide expressive query capabilities over aggregated data. To support data processing for new types of applications, Linked Open Data (LOD) is used by search engines, governments, social media, publishing agencies, media portals, researchers, and individuals.

Linked Data Principles

Conventional web pages are hypertext documents connected with hyperlinks (or simply links). These hyperlinks point to other documents or a part of another document; however, they do not hold information about the type of relationship between the source and the destination resources. While the link relation can be annotated using the `rel` attribute on the `link`, `a`, and `area` markup elements, they are suitable for annotating external CSS files, script files, or the favicon. As mentioned before, some microformats such as `rel="tag"` and XFN also declare link relations. Other specific relation types can be defined in the Atom syndication format and XLink. On the Semantic Web, links can be typed using `rdf:type` or its equivalent in other serializations, such as the `datatype` attribute in RDFa, to provide a machine-interpretable definition for an arbitrary relationship between the source and destination resources. Those structured datasets derived from different resources that are published with such *typed links* between them are called *Linked Data* (also known as *Linking Data*) [1].

Berners-Lee outlined four *Linked Data principles* for publishing and interlinking data on the Web in a human- and machine-readable way, using Semantic Web technologies, so that all published data becomes part of a single global data space [2].

1. Use URIs as names for the "things" of the Web of Data (real-world objects and people). In other words, a *dereferenceable* Uniform Resource Identifier (URI), such as a web address, is assigned to each resource rather than an application-specific identifier, such as a database key or incremental numbers, making every data entity individually identifiable.

■ **Note**   The dereferenceable URIs must be *HTTPRange-14*-compliant. For years, HTTPRange-14 was a design issue of the Semantic Web, because when HTTP was extended from referring only to documents to referring to "things" (real-world objects and persons), the domain of HTTP GET became undefined, leading to ambiguous interpretations of Semantic Web resources. The resolution is to check the web server's answer to the GET request, and if an HTTP resource responds with a 2xx response, the resource identified by that URI is an information resource; if it is a 303 (See Other) response, the resource identified by that URI could be any resource. A 4xx (error) response means that the nature of the resource is unknown [3].

---

2. Use HTTP URIs, so that people can look up the resource names. In other words, provide the URIs over the HTTP protocol into RDF representations for dereferencing.

3. When someone looks up a URI, provide useful information using Semantic Web standards, such as RDF. By providing metadata about the published data, clients can assess the quality of published data and choose between different means of access.

4. Include links to other URIs, so that users can discover related information. When RDF links are set to other data resources, users can navigate the Web of Data as a whole by following RDF links.

The benefits of Linked Data are recognized by more and more organizations, businesses, and individuals. Some industrial giants that already have LOD implementations are Amazon.com, BBC, Facebook, Flickr, Google, Thomson Reuters, The New York Times Company, and Yahoo!, just to name a few.

The Five-Star Deployment Scheme for Linked Data

Publishing Linked Data (following the Linked Data principles) does not guarantee data quality. For example, the documents the URIs in LOD datasets point to might be documents that are difficult to reuse. Pointing to a fully machine-interpretable RDF file is not the same as pointing to a PDF file containing a table as a scanned image. A five-star rating system is used for expressing the quality of Linked Data which are not open, and Linked Open Data (open data and Linked Data at the same time) [4]. The five-star rating system is cumulative, meaning that on each level, the data has to meet additional criteria beyond the criteria of the underlying level(s) [5]:

★   Data is available on the Web in any format, which is human-readable but not machine-interpretable, due to a vendor-specific file format or lack of structure. All following stars are intended to make the data easier to discover, use, and understand. For example, a scanned image of tabular data in a PDF file is one-star data. Data reusability is limited.

★★   Data is available as machine-readable structured data. For example, tabular data saved in an Excel file is two-star data.

★★★   Data is available in a nonproprietary (vendor-independent) format. For example, tabular data saved as a CSV file is three-star data.

(continued)

★★★★	Published using open standards from the W3C (RDF and SPARQL). For example, tabular data in HTML with RDFa annotation using URIs is four-star data.
★★★★★	All of the above plus links to other, related data to provide context. For example, tabular data in HTML with RDFa annotation using URIs and semantic properties is five-star data. Maximum reusability and machine-interpretability.

The expression of rights provided by licensing makes free data reuse possible. Linked Data without an explicit open license[1] (e.g., public domain license) cannot be reused freely, but the quality of Linked Data is independent from licensing. When the specified criteria are met, all five ratings can be used both for Linked Data (for Linked Data without explicit open license) and Linked Open Data (Linked Data with an explicit open license). As a consequence, the five-star rating system can be depicted in a way that the criteria can be read with or without the open license. For example, the Linked Open Data mug can be read with both green labels for five-star Linked Open Data, or neither label for five-star Linked Data, as shown in Figure 3-1. For example, Linked Data available as machine-readable structured data is two-star Linked Data, while the same with an open license is two-star Linked Open Data.

Figure 3-1. *The requirements of 5 ★ Linked Data and 5 ★ Linked Open Data*

Because converting a CSV file to a set of RDF triples and linking them to another set of triples does not necessarily make the data more (re)usable to humans or machines, even four-star and five-star Linked Open Data have many challenges. One of the challenges is the lack of provenance information, which can now be provided about Linked (Open) Data using standards such as the PROV-O ontology [6]. Another challenge

---

[1]This licensing concept is used on the conventional Web too, in which the term *Open Data* refers to the free license.

is querying Linked Data that do not use machine-readable definitions from a vocabulary, which is difficult and almost impossible to interpret with software agents. Furthermore, the quality of the definitions retrieved from vocabularies and ontologies varies greatly, and the used vocabularies might not restrict the potential interpretations of the used classes and roles towards their intended meaning.

LOD Datasets

A meaningful collection of RDF triples covering a field of interest according to the Linked Open Data principles is called an *LOD dataset*. LOD datasets collect descriptions of entities within the field of interest, and these descriptions often share a common URI prefix (as, for example, http://dbpedia.org/resource/). The authors of the largest datasets provide advanced features that enable easy access to their structured data, such as downloadable compressed files of the datasets or an infrastructure for efficient querying.

RDF Crawling

Similar to the web crawlers that systematically browse conventional web sites for indexing, Semantic Web crawlers browse semantic contents to extract structured data and automatically find relationships between seemingly unrelated entities. LOD datasets should be published in a way so that they are available through *RDF crawling*.

RDF Dumps

The most popular LOD datasets are regularly published as a downloadable compressed file (usually Gzip or bzip2), called an *RDF dump*, which is the latest version of the dataset. RDF dumps should be valid RDF files. The reason why the RDF dump files are compressed is that the datasets containing millions of RDF triples are quite large. The size of Gzip-compressed RDF dumps is approximately 100MB per every 10 million triples, but it also depends on the RDF serialization of the dataset. Table 3-1 summarizes the most popular RDF dumps.

Table 3-1. *Popular RDF Dumps*

Dataset	RDF Dump
DBpedia	http://wiki.dbpedia.org/Downloads2014
WikiData	http://dumps.wikimedia.org/wikidatawiki/
GeoNames	http://download.geonames.org/all-geonames-rdf.zip
LinkedGeoData	http://downloads.linkedgeodata.org/releases/
Open Directory	http://rdf.dmoz.org/
MusicBrainz	ftp://ftp.musicbrainz.org/pub/musicbrainz/data/

SPARQL Endpoints

Similar to relational database queries in MySQL, the data of semantic datasets can also be retrieved through powerful queries. The query language designed specifically for RDF datasets is called *SPARQL* (pronounced "sparkle," it stands for *SPARQL Protocol and RDF Query Language*), which will be discussed in detail in Chapter 7. Some datasets provide a *SPARQL endpoint*, which is an address from which you can directly run SPARQL queries (powered by a back-end database engine and an HTTP/SPARQL server).

Frequently Used Linked Datasets

LOD datasets are published in a variety of fields. Interdisciplinary datasets such as DBpedia (http://dbpedia.org) and WikiData (http://www.wikidata.org) are general-purpose datasets and are, hence, among the most frequently used ones. Geographical applications can benefit from datasets such as GeoNames (http://www.geonames.org) and LinkedGeoData (http://linkedgeodata.org). More and more universities provide information about staff members, departments, facilities, courses, grants, and publications as Linked Data and RDF dump, such as the University of Florida (http://vivo.ufl.edu) and the Ghent University (http://data.mmlab.be/mmlab). Libraries such as the Princeton University Library (http://findingaids.princeton.edu) publish bibliographic information as Linked Data. Part of the National Digital Data Archive of Hungary is available as Linked Data at http://lod.sztaki.hu. Even Project Gutenberg is available as Linked Data (http://wifo5-03.informatik.uni-mannheim.de/gutendata/). Museums such as the British Museum publish some of their records as Linked Data (http://collection.britishmuseum.org). News and media giants publish subject headings as Linked Data, as for example the New York Times at http://data.nytimes.com. MusicBrainz (http://dbtune.org/musicbrainz/) provides data about music artists and their albums, served as Linked Data and via available through a SPARQL endpoint. Data about musicians, music album releases, and reviews are published as Linked Data by BBC Music at www.bbc.co.uk/music, which is largely based upon MusicBrainz and the Music Ontology. The Linked Movie DataBase (LinkedMDB) at http://www.linkedmdb.org is an LOD dataset dedicated to movies, with high quality and quantity of interlinks to other LOD data sources and movie-related web sites. More and more government portals publish publicly available government data as Linked Data, as, for example, the US government's http://data.gov or the UK government's http://data.gov.uk. Some of the most popular LOD datasets will be discussed in the following sections.

DBpedia

The hundreds of concept definitions on schema.org are suitable to annotate common knowledge domains, such as persons, events, books, and movies, but complex machine-readable statements require far more.

DBpedia, hosted at http://dbpedia.org, extracts structured factual data from Wikipedia articles, such as titles, infoboxes, categories, and links. Because Wikipedia contains nearly 5 million articles in English, DBpedia is suitable to describe virtually anything in a machine-readable manner. DBpedia contains approximately 3.4 million concepts described by 1 billion triples.

■ **Note**   Wikipedia infoboxes are the most straightforward for DBpedia extraction, because they contain attribute-value pairs of the corresponding Wikipedia page to be displayed on the right-hand side of the article as a summary of the most important facts in a tabular form. However, structured data extraction is challenging, because the template system changed over time on Wikipedia, resulting in the lack of uniformity, whereby the same attributes have different names, such as placeofbirth and birthplace.

The unique resource identifiers of DBpedia are written as URI references of the form http://dbpedia.org/resource/*Name*, where *Name* is derived from the URL of the Wikipedia article of the form http://en.wikipedia.org/wiki/*Name*. As a result, each resource is a direct mapping of a Wikipedia article. The DBpedia URI references of the form http://dbpedia.org/resource/*Resource:Name* are set up (through content negotiation, where the same content is served in a different format, depending on the query of the client) to return the machine-readable description in RDF when accessed by Semantic Web agents, and the same information in XHTML, when accessed by traditional web browsers (see Figure 3-2).

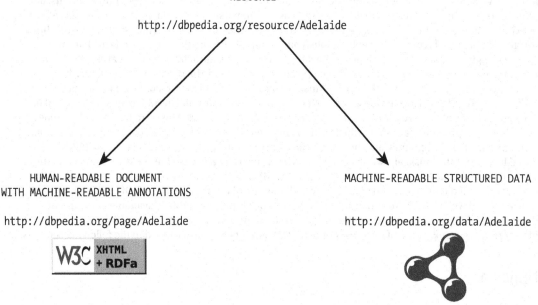

Figure 3-2. DBpedia resources return XHTML or RDF through content negotiation

Assume we want to describe a Semantic Web researcher in RDF who lives in Adelaide, is interested in Web standards, and is a member of the W3C. To do this, we need the corresponding DBpedia URIs that identify the non-information resources (in the form http://dbpedia.org/resource/*Resource:name*) declared as the attribute value of rdf:resource (see Listing 3-1).

Listing 3-1. Linking to DBpedia Resources

```
<?xml version="1.0" encoding="UTF-8"?>
<rdf:RDF ↵
xmlns:foaf="http://xmlns.com/foaf/0.1/" ↵
 xmlns:contact="http://www.w3.org/2000/10/swap/pim/contact#" ↵
 xmlns:rdf="http://www.w3.org/1999/02/22-rdf-syntax-ns#">
  <foaf:person rdf:about="http://www.lesliesikos.com/datasets/sikos.rdf#sikos">
    <foaf:name>Leslie Sikos</foaf:name>
    <foaf:based_near rdf:resource="http://dbpedia.org/resource/Adelaide" />
    <foaf:topic_interest rdf:resource="http://dbpedia.org/resource/Web_standards" />
    <contact:nearestAirport rdf:resource="http://dbpedia.org/resource/Adelaide_Airport" />
  </foaf:person>
  <rdf:Description rdf:about="http://dbpedia.org/resource/W3C">
    <foaf:member rdf:resource="http://www.lesliesikos.com/datasets/sikos.rdf#sikos" />
  </rdf:Description>
</rdf:RDF>
```

The SPARQL endpoint of DBpedia is http://dbpedia.org/sparql, where you can run queries on DBpedia resources, say, the list of people born in Budapest before the 20th century (see Listing 3-2). Querying with SPARQL will be described later, in Chapter 7.

Listing 3-2. A SPARQL Query on DBpedia

```
PREFIX dbo: <http://dbpedia.org/ontology/>

SELECT ?name ?birth ?death ?person WHERE {
    ?person dbo:birthPlace :Budapest .
    ?person dbo:birthDate ?birth .
    ?person foaf:name ?name .
    ?person dbo:deathDate ?death .
    FILTER (?birth < "1901-01-01"^^xsd:date) .
}
ORDER BY ?name
```

Wikidata

Wikidata is one of the largest LOD databases that features both human-readable and machine-readable contents, at http://www.wikidata.org. Wikidata contains structured data from Wikimedia projects, such as Wikimedia Commons, Wikipedia, Wikivoyage, and Wikisource, as well as from the once popular directly editable Freebase dataset, resulting in approximately 13 million data items.

In contrast to many other LOD datasets, Wikidata is collaborative—anyone can create new items and modify existing ones. Like Wikipedia, Wikidata is multilingual. The Wikidata repository is a central storage of structured data, whereby data can be accessed not only directly but also through client Wikis. Data is added to items that feature a label, which is a descriptive alias, connected by site links. Each item is characterized by statements that consist of a property and property value. Wikidata supports the Lua Scribunto parser extension to allow embedding scripting languages in MediaWiki and access the structured data stored in Wikidata through client Wikis. Data can also be retrieved using the Wikidata API.

GeoNames

GeoNames is a geographical database at http://www.geonames.org that provides RDF descriptions for more than 7,500,000 geographical features worldwide, corresponding to more than 10 million geographical names. All features are categorized as one of the nine feature classes, and subcategorized into one of the 645 feature codes. Place-names are stored in the database in multiple languages. GeoNames also contains data such as latitude and longitude, elevation, population, administrative subdivision, and postal codes of cities. The coordinates are expressed in the World Geodetic System 1984 (WGS84) standard used in cartography, geodesy, and navigation.

The GeoNames resources use 303 (See Other) redirection to distinguish a concept (thing as is) from the document describing the resource. For example, the city of Adelaide has two addresses on GeoNames: http://sws.geonames.org/2078025/ and http://sws.geonames.org/2078025/about.rdf. The first represents the city (in a form used in Linked Data references); the second is a document with information about Adelaide.

LinkedGeoData

The *LinkedGeoData* dataset at `http://linkedgeodata.org` uses the information collected by OpenStreetMap data (a free editable world map), makes it available as an LOD dataset, and interlinks this data with other LOD datasets. The authors of the dataset provide their own semantic browser, called *LGD Browser and Editor*, at `http://browser.linkedgeodata.org` (see Figure 3-3).

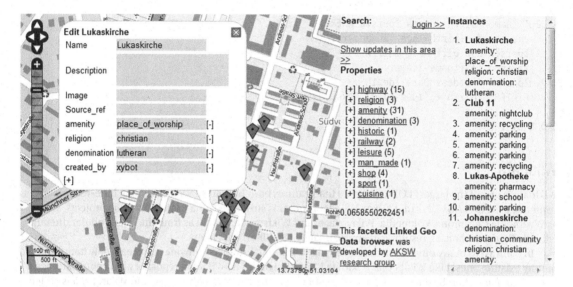

Figure 3-3. *LinkedGeoData in the LGD Browser and Editor*

A good example for the unambiguity on the Semantic Web is searching for "Adelaide" in the LGD Browser. Because there is a city with this name in South Australia, another one in South Africa, and three in the United States (one in Colorado, one in Idaho, and one in Washington), the software will ask for clarification and provide the city map and details according to your choice (see Figure 3-4).

Figure 3-4. *Linked Data is unambiguous*

YAGO

YAGO (Yet Another Great Ontology) is a dataset containing more than 10 million entities and 120 million facts about them, which are automatically extracted from Wikipedia categories, redirects, and infoboxes; synsets and hyponymy from the lexical database WordNet; and GeoNames.

In contrast to other datasets automatically extracting data from LOD datasets, YAGO is more accurate, as a large share of facts is manually evaluated. YAGO entities and facts are often linked to the DBpedia ontology. The SPARQL endpoint of YAGO is `http://lod2.openlinksw.com/sparql`, but queries can also be executed through a web interface at `https://gate.d5.mpi-inf.mpg.de/webyagospotlx/WebInterface`.

LOD Dataset Collections

LOD datasets can be registered and managed using *Datahub* at `http://datahub.io`, an open data registry. Datahub is used by governments, research institutions, and other organizations. Powered by structured data, datahub.io provides efficient search and faceting, browsing user data, previewing data using maps, graphs, and tables. As you will see, a datahub.io registry is a prerequisite for merging new datasets of the LOD Cloud Diagram with existing ones.

Ontobee, available at `http://www.ontobee.org`, is a SPARQL-based linked ontology data server and browser that has been utilized for more than 100 ontologies containing over 2 million ontology terms.

The LOD Cloud Diagram

The *LOD Cloud Diagram* represents datasets with at least 1,000 RDF triples and the links between them (Figure 3-5) [7]. The size of the bubbles corresponds to the data amount stored in each dataset. In the middle of the cloud, you can see the largest datasets, DBpedia and GeoNames, followed by FOAF-Profiles, Freebase, and the W3C.

If you have a big enough dataset that contains at least 1,000 triples and fulfills the requirements of Linked Open Data, you can make a request to add it to the LOD Cloud Diagram. The resources of the dataset must have resolvable `http://` or `https://` URIs that resolve, with or without content negotiation, to RDF data as RDFa, RDF/XML, Turtle, or N-Triples. The dataset must be connected through at least 50 RDF links to arbitrary datasets of the diagram. The dataset must be accessible via *RDF crawling*, via an *RDF dump*, or via a *SPARQL endpoint*. The dataset must be registered on Datahub, and you have to e-mail the authors of the LOD Cloud Diagram (`richard@cyganiak.de` and `mail@anjajentzsch.de`).

An alternate visualization of the LOD Cloud Diagram is created by Stanford University's Protovis, using the CKAN API, and published at `http://inkdroid.org/lod-graph/` (see Figure 3-6).

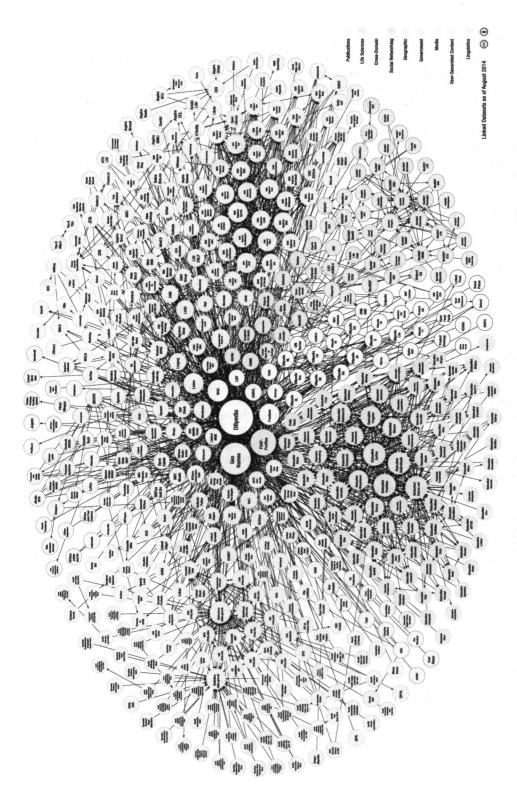

Figure 3-5. The LOD Cloud Diagram (courtesy of Max Schmachtenberg, Christian Bizer, Anja Jentzsch and Richard Cyganiak)

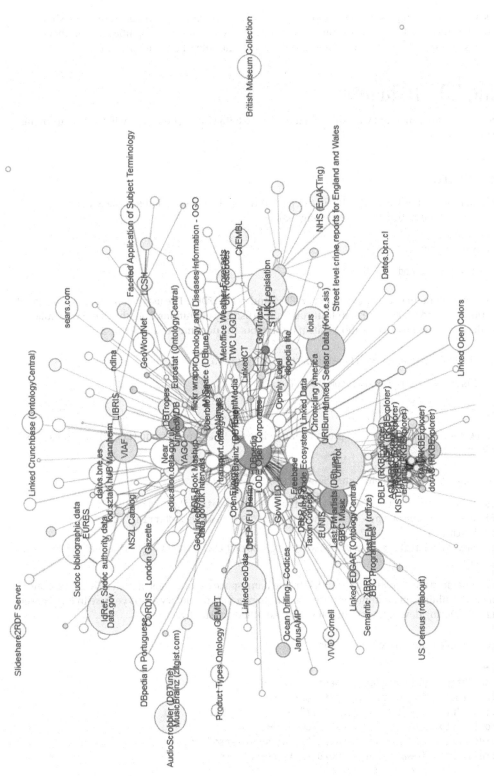

Figure 3-6. *The LOD Graph generated by Protovis*

The CKAN ratings are represented by colors, by which datasets with high average ratings are shown in green, and the ones with low average ratings in red. The intensity of the color signifies the number of received ratings, where white means no rating, and the darker the color the higher the rating.

Creating LOD Datasets

While large datasets are generated with software tools, in the following sections, you will see how to create LOD datasets manually.

RDF Structure

Let's create a dataset file in RDF/XML! The first step is to create a UTF-8 encoded text file with an `.rdf` extension and to add the XML prolog (see Listing 3-3).

Listing 3-3. XML Prolog

```
<?xml version="1.0" encoding="UTF-8"?>
```

The document content will be between `<rdf:RDF>` and `</rdf:RDF>`. The list of namespaces is declared as `xmlns` attributes on `rdf:RDF`. For example, if you want to use any definitions from the FOAF vocabulary, you have to declare its namespace to abbreviate it throughout the document (see Listing 3-4).

Listing 3-4. The Main Container with One Namespace Declaration

```
<rdf:RDF xmlns:foaf="http://xmlns.com/foaf/0.1/">

</rdf:RDF>
```

From now on, you can use the `foaf` prefix to abbreviate the Friend of a Friend (FOAF) namespace, as shown in Listing 3-5.

Listing 3-5. Using the `foaf` Prefix to Abbreviate the FOAF Namespace

```
<foaf:Person rdf:about="http://www.lesliesikos.com/metadata/sikos.rdf#sikos">
  <foaf:firstname rdf:datatype="http://www.w3.org/2001/XMLSchema#string">Leslie ↵
  </foaf:firstname>
  <foaf:surname rdf:datatype="http://www.w3.org/2001/XMLSchema#string">Sikos</foaf:surname>
</foaf:Person>
```

The list of namespaces is typically extended by the namespace declarations of RDF, RDFS, OWL, and so on, along with Dublin Core, schema.org, etc., depending on the vocabulary terms you use in the dataset (see Listing 3-6). During development, the list will be extended constantly.

Listing 3-6. Multiple Namespace Declarations

```
<rdf:RDF ↵
    xmlns:dc="http://purl.org/dc/elements/1.1/" ↵
    xmlns:dcterms="http://purl.org/dc/terms/" ↵
    xmlns:foaf="http://xmlns.com/foaf/0.1/" ↵
    xmlns:owl="http://www.w3.org/2002/07/owl#" ↵
    xmlns:rdf="http://www.w3.org/1999/02/22-rdf-syntax-ns#" ↵
    xmlns:rdfs="http://www.w3.org/2000/01/rdf-schema#" ↵
    xmlns:schema="http://schema.org/">
```

After the namespace list, one can provide dataset information, including licensing, followed by the actual data (RDF statements) of the dataset that will be linked to classes and entities of other LOD datasets with typed links.

Licensing

Linked Open Data without an explicit license is just Linked Data. To make our LOD datasets truly "open," we have to declare the license explicitly, which prevents potential legal liability issues and makes it clear to users what usage conditions apply.

The licensing information of a dataset can be provided in the dataset file or in an external metadata file, such as a VoID (Vocabulary of Interlinked Datasets) file. The license under which the dataset has been published can be declared using the dcterms:license property. The most frequently used license URIs for Linked Open Data are the following:

- http://opendatacommons.org/licenses/pddl/
  Public Domain Dedication and License (PDDL)—"Public Domain for data/databases"

- http://opendatacommons.org/licenses/by/
  Open Data Commons Attribution (ODC-By)—"Attribution for data/databases"

- http://opendatacommons.org/licenses/odbl/
  Open Database License (ODC-ODbL)—"Attribution Share-Alike for data/databases"

- https://creativecommons.org/publicdomain/zero/1.0/
  CC0 1.0 Universal—"Creative Commons public domain waiver"

- https://creativecommons.org/licenses/by-sa/4.0/
  Creative Commons Attribution-ShareAlike (CC-BY-SA)

- http://gnu.org/copyleft/fdl.html
  GNU Free Documentation License (GFDL)

The first four licenses are specifically designed for data, so their use for LOD dataset licensing is highly recommended. Licensing of datasets is a complex issue, because datasets are collections of facts rather than creative works, so different laws apply. Creative Commons and GPL are quite common on the Web; however, they are based on copyright and are designed for creative works, not datasets, so they might not have the desired legal result when applied to datasets.

Community norms (nonbinding conditions of use) can be expressed using the waiver:norms property (http://vocab.org/waiver/terms/norms). A common community norm is ODC Attribution ShareAlike (www.opendatacommons.org/norms/odc-by-sa/), which permits data use from the dataset, but the changes and updates are supposed to be public too, along with the credit given, the source of the data linked, open formats used, and no DRM applied. For example, if we have an ExampleLOD dataset published under the terms of the Open Data Commons Public Domain Dedication and License, and users are encouraged, but not legally bound, to follow the community norms mentioned above, the licensing of the dataset would be as shown in Listing 3-7.

Listing 3-7. LOD Dataset Licensing Example

```
<?xml version="1.0" encoding="UTF-8"?>
<rdf:RDF ↵
    xmlns:dcterms="http://purl.org/dc/terms/" ↵
    xmlns:rdf="http://www.w3.org/1999/02/22-rdf-syntax-ns#" ↵
    xmlns:wv="http://vocab.org/waive/terms/">
```

```
<rdf:Description rdf:about="http://www.examplelod.com/loddataset.rdf#examplelod">
  <dcterms:license rdf:resource="http://www.opendatacommons.org/odc-public-domain-↵
  dedication-and-licence" />
  <wv:norms rdf:resource="http://www.opendatacommons.org/norms/odc-by-sa/" />
  <wv:waiver rdf:datatype="http://www.w3.org/2001/XMLSchema#string">To the extent ↵
  possible under law, Example Ltd. has waived all copyright and related or neighboring ↵
  rights to this dataset.</wv:waiver>
</rdf:Description>
```

■ **Note** The Datahub registration requires an open license to be selected from a drop-down list as a field value, and the license URI as a separate field set as the dataset properties, not just the licensing information provided in the dataset or VoID file.

RDF Statements

The most generic objects of datasets are collected in `rdf:description` containers. Those objects that are representations of real-world objects already defined in a machine-readable vocabulary are usually collected under the corresponding object class (persons in `schema:person`, books in `schema:book`, and so on). Because a basic requirement of Linked Open Data is to identify everything with a dereferenceable web address, make sure that the addresses and fragment identifiers are correct. Whenever possible, use typing to differentiate string literals, numbers, dates, and so on.

Making a statement about another statement is called *reification*. It allows triples to be used in multiple contexts but can affect the formal semantics of your dataset.

Interlinking

Government agencies, large enterprises,[2] media institutes, social media portals, and researchers work with large amounts of data that can be represented as structured data and published as Linked Data. Describing your government data, university research department, colleagues, books, or any other knowledge domain in RDF results in an isolated dataset file, which is not part of the Semantic Web until it is linked to other datasets.

Creating links between the structured datasets of the Semantic Web is called *interlinking*, which makes isolated datasets part of the LOD Cloud, in which all resources are linked to one another. These links enable semantic agents to navigate between data sources and discover additional resources. Interlinking typically happens with `owl:sameAs`, `rdfs:seeAlso`, `foaf:holdsOnlineAccount`, `sioc:user`, and similar predicates. In contrast to conventional hyperlinks of (X)HTML documents, LOD links are *typed links* between two resources. The URIs of the subject and the object of the link identify the interlinked resources. The URI of the predicate defines the type of the link. For example, an RDF link can state that a person is employed by a company, while another RDF link can state that the person knows other people. *Dereferencing* the URI of the link destination yields a description of the linked resource, usually containing additional RDF links that point to other, related URIs, which, in turn, can also be dereferenced, and so on.

Consider the machine-readable description of the book *Web Standards: Mastering HTML5, CSS3, and XML*, at http://www.masteringhtml5css3.com/metadata/webstandardsbook.rdf#book, which declares the title of the book using the `title` property from the Dublin Core vocabulary, and, among many other properties, declares a machine-readable resource describing the author, using `schema:author` (Figure 3-7). Further resources related to the book could be declared using `rdfs:seeAlso`.

---

[2]If the Linked Data is behind a corporate firewall, it is called Linking Enterprise Data.

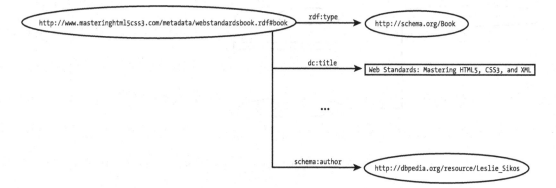

Figure 3-7. *Linking a dataset to a related entity of another dataset*

The DBpedia resource of the author reveals properties of the author, such as his home page address, defined using `foaf:homepage`, and, among many other classifications, links the author to Australian writers, with YAGO (Figure 3-8).

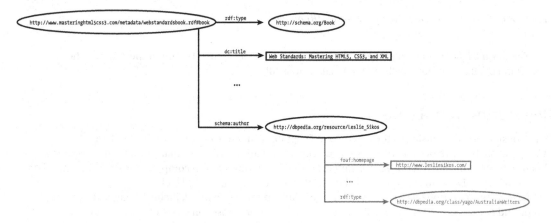

Figure 3-8. *The DBpedia resource links the dataset to another dataset*

Based on `yago:AustralianWriters`, semantic agents will find other authors in the same category (Figure 3-9). By linking to datasets already on the LOD Cloud Diagram (such as pointing to a definition on DBpedia), your dataset will become part of the LOD Cloud.

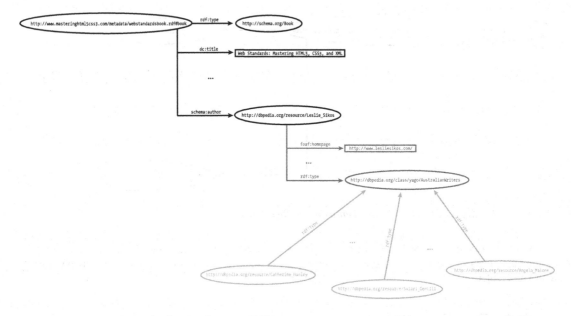

Figure 3-9. *Two RDF graphs sharing the same URI merge*

The *Giant Global Graph*, the other name for the Web of Data coined by Tim Berners-Lee, is the supergraph of all the automatically merged LOD graphs [8].

Registering Your Dataset

To be considered for inclusion in the LOD Cloud Diagram, your dataset must be registered on `http://datahub.io`. To be able to register, you need an affiliation with a company or research institute already on Datahub, or if it is not yet registered, you have to request a new company registration. Candidate datasets of the LOD Cloud Diagram are validated through four compliance levels.

Level 1 (basic compliance) requires basic metadata about your dataset, including name, title, URL, author, and contact e-mail, as well as the `lod` tag added to your dataset on Datahub. Level 2 (minimal compliance) requires a topic tag for your dataset, which can be one of the following: `media`, `geographic`, `lifesciences`, `publications`, `government`, `ecommerce`, `socialweb`, `usergeneratedcontent`, `schemata`, or `crossdomain`. You have to provide an example link URI in the `Data` and `Resources` section with the `example/serialization_format` (`example/rdf+xml`, `example/turtle`, `example/ntriples`, `example/x-quads`, `example/rdfa`, or `example/x-trig`), to help people get a feel for your data before they decide to use it. You also have to provide links to the dump file or the SPARQL endpoint of the dataset. Level 3 (complete compliance) requires additional information, such as the last modification date or version of the dataset (as the value of the field `version`), a dataset description (`notes`), the open license of your dataset (selected from the drop-down menu), a short name for LOD bubble (`shortname`), a link to the license of the dataset (`license_link`), and the instance namespaces (`namespace`). Beyond these custom fields, Level 3 compliance also requires metadata such as VoID file (`meta/void` format), XML sitemap (`meta/sitemap` format), RDF Schema (`meta/rdf-schema` format), and vocabulary mappings (`mapping/` format). Depending on whether you use proprietary vocabularies defined within your top-level domain or not, you have to add the `no-proprietary-vocab` tag (you don't use proprietary vocabularies), or either the `deref-vocab` tag (use dereferenceable propriatory vocabularies) or the `no-deref-vocab` tag (use proprietary vocabularies that are not dereferenceable). Once you are ready with the dataset registration, you can validate it using `http://validator.lod-cloud.net/`.

■ **Note** Since the introduction of the LOD Cloud Diagram, some of the CKAN/Datahub fields used by the Datahub LOD Validator have been changed or discontinued. As a consequence, the Validator might give errors, even on correctly registered datasets. If this happens to your dataset, you have to contact the authors of the LOD Cloud Diagram, via e-mail, for manual approval.

The last step is to e-mail the authors (richard@cyganiak.de and mail@anjajentzsch.de). Further tags are used by the authors of the LOD Cloud Diagram to annotate whether your dataset has any issues or when it is ready to be added to the next update of the LOD Cloud Diagram. Level 4 compliance means that your dataset has been reviewed and added to lodcloud group by the authors who use this group to generate the LOD Cloud Diagram.

Linked Data Visualization

Linked Data visualization tools make the analysis and manipulation of Linked Data easier. The list of Linked Data visualization techniques includes, but is not limited to, comparison of values, analysis of relationships and hierarchies, analysis of temporal or geographical events, text-based visualizations as tag cloud or network of phrases, and representing multidimensional data.

LOD Visualization (http://lodvisualization.appspot.com) can produce visual hierarchies using treemaps and trees from live access to SPARQL endpoints. *LodLive* (http://en.lodlive.it) provides a graph visualization of Linked Data resources. Clicking the nodes can expand the graph structure. LodLive can be used for live access to SPARQL endpoints (see Figure 3-10).

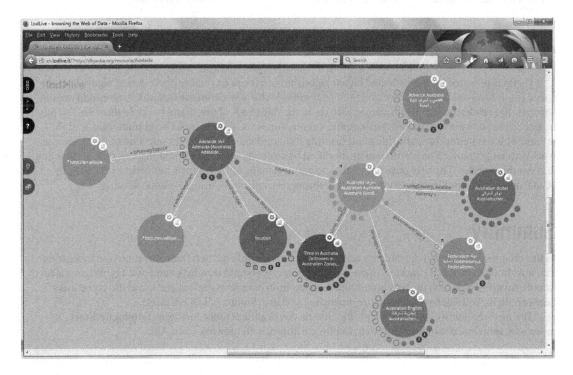

Figure 3-10. *Browsing the Web of Data with LodLive*

The open source graph visualization and manipulation software package Gephi, downloadable from `https://gephi.github.io/`, is ideal for Linked Data visualization. The program helps explore and understand graphs, modify the representation, and manipulate the structures, shapes, and colors to reveal hidden properties (see Figure 3-11).

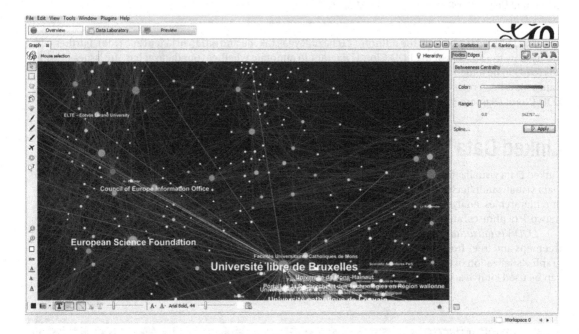

Figure 3-11. *Advanced graph visualization with Gephi*

Gephi is powered by sophisticated layout algorithms, to focus on quality (force-based algorithms) or speed (multilevel refinements through *graph coarsening*). The asynchronous OpenGL exploration engine supports flat rendering and 3D rendering with customizable levels of detail and multiple threads. The other engine of the software tool, called the mapping engine, supports refinements, vector rendering, and SVG output, which is perfect for publishing and drawing infographics. The highlight selection makes it easy to work with large graphs. The graphs can be modified by selecting, moving, annotating, resizing, connecting, and grouping nodes. The very powerful real-time graph visualization supports networks with a maximum of 50,000 nodes and 1 million edges and iteration, through visualization using dynamic filtering.

Summary

In this chapter, you learned the concept and requirements of Linked Open Data and about the industries that link thousands of LOD datasets to one another. You understand now how semantic agents can make new discoveries, based on the machine-readable definition of objects and subjects, and the typed links between them. You learned the structure, licensing, and interlinking of LOD datasets.

The next chapter will introduce you to semantic development tools, including ontology editors, reasoners, semantic annotators, extractors, software libraries, frameworks, and APIs.

References

1. Bizer, C., Heath, T., Berners-Lee, T. Linked data—The story so far. Semantic Web and Information Systems 2009, 5(3):1–22.

2. Berners-Lee, T. (2006) Linked Data—Design Issues. www.w3.org/DesignIssues/LinkedData.html. Accessed 25 March 2014.

3. Fielding, R. T. (2005) httpRange-14 Resolved. http://lists.w3.org/Archives/Public/www-tag/2005Jun/0039.html. Accessed 28 March 2015.

4. The Open Definition—Defining Open in Open Data, Open Content and Open Knowledge. http://opendefinition.org. Accessed 18 January 2015.

5. Hausenblas, M. (2012) 5 ★ Open Data. http://5stardata.info. Accessed 18 January 2015.

6. Lebo, T., Sahoo, S., McGuinness, D. (eds.) (2013) PROV-O: The PROV Ontology. www.w3.org/TR/prov-o/. Accessed 27 March 2015.

7. Schmachtenberg, M., Bizer, C., Jentzsch, A., Cyganiak, R. (2014) The LOD cloud diagram. http://lod-cloud.net. Accessed 18 January 2015.

8. Berners-Lee, T. (2007) Giant Global Graph | Decentralized Information Group (DIG) Breadcrumbs. http://dig.csail.mit.edu/breadcrumbs/node/215. Accessed 28 March 2015.

CHAPTER 4

∎ ∎ ∎

Semantic Web Development Tools

Extracting and manipulating RDF from semistructured data and writing client applications to handle RDF data are common tasks that can be made easier and more efficient using software tools. Web designers and search engine optimization (SEO) experts often generate machine-readable annotations or convert existing structured data to a different serialization. While web site markup can be edited in any text editor, some advanced features are desired when working with semantic annotations, so an advanced text editor is a fundamental tool. Annotators can be used for semantically annotating your web pages and RDFizers to convert text, HTML, and XML documents to RDF. Application developers writing Semantic Web applications in Java, JRuby, Clojure, Scala, Python, and other programming languages often work with Integrated Development Environments, many of which support the integration of semantic software libraries. Ontology editors are widely deployed and used in ontology engineering, many of which support reasoning as well. Linked Data software tools are useful for extracting Linked Data, visualizing Linked Data interconnections, as well as exporting and publishing Linked Data. Semantic Web browsers can display structured data extracted from web pages, generate a map from geospatial data on your smartphone, and provide advanced navigation and interactivity features unavailable in traditional web browsers.

Advanced Text Editors

In contrast to word processors such as Microsoft Word or OpenOffice.org Writer, *plain-text editors* cannot be used for document formatting, but they are suitable for creating and modifying web pages. However, basic text editors are not convenient for web design, because some vital features are missing from them. For example, many of them do not handle control characters and whitespaces correctly. The most well-known examples are Notepad under Windows and vi under Linux. *Advanced text editors* such as WordPad provide text formatting and other additional features. Some advanced text editors are also source code editors with additional tools specifically designed for web designers and software engineers. While not suitable for structured data conversions or LOD processing, advanced text editors are fundamental programs in the toolbox of every Semantic Web developer, owing to advanced features such as the following:

- Comprehensive character encoding support, including full Unicode support

- Whitespace character support

- Control character support, for example, CR+LF (Windows), LF only (UNIX), and Apple (CR only) break rows

- Multifile editing with tabs

- Customizable color schemas for *syntax highlighting* (HTML, CSS, XML,[1] scripts, and so on)

- Undo/redo

- Forced word wrap

- Line numbering

- Auto-indent

- Guides for tag pairs and element nesting

- OS integration (adds application to right-click menu)

The selected editor should be integrated with at least one of your browsers as the default source code editor, which you can use to open the currently rendered web document with a hot key (usually Ctrl+U). There are additional features of text editors that are not vital but can be useful.

- Customized color and font settings

- Customizable toolbars

- Spell checker

- Templates

- Bookmarks

- Full drag-and-drop support

- Built-in FTP client or integration with an (S)FTP client

- Conversions (uppercase, lowercase, invert case, and initial caps)

- International versions (can be convenient for some developers)

- Support for double-byte character systems (DBCS) used in Far East Asian languages, such as Chinese or Japanese (if required)

- Browser preview (launching the default or selected web browser for debugging and testing)

Some of the most well-known advanced text editors are EditPlus and NotePad++ (free, open source [1]) for Windows, BlueFish [2] and Komodo Edit [3] for Linux, and BBEdit [4] and TextWrangler [5] for Mac OS. A comprehensive cross-platform editor is Arachnophilia, which is available for Windows, Linux, Unix, FreeBSD, and Mac OS [6].

As an example, let's look at the major features of Notepad++ . It is a multifile editor with convenient file manager options. Notepad++ saves multiple files with a single click, opens recently edited files, and provides tabs for each opened file. It has a fully customizable interface with advanced features such as line markers, guides for opening and closing tag pairs, structuring guides to collapse or reveal the currently edited level of the DOM tree, and syntax highlighting (see Figure 4-1).

---

[1]On Windows systems, the file format used for syntax highlighting depends on the file extension, so an entire RDF/XML file with the .rdf extension might be white by default, while the same file in the same editor would be syntax-highlighted when saved as .xml.

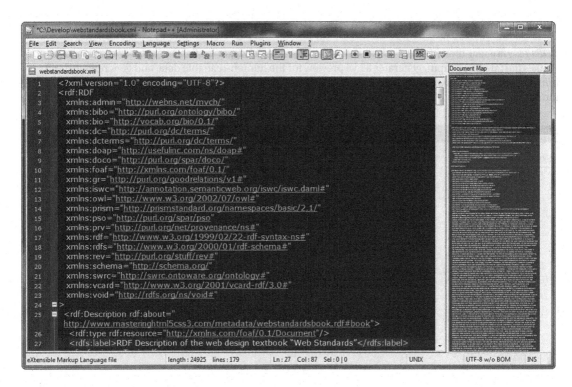

Figure 4-1. *Syntax highlighting and tag pair guides in Notepad++*

There is a variety of programming and web development languages supported in syntax highlighting, from HTML to XML and from PHP to Ruby. There are several predefined color themes you can select from, or you can create new ones to your taste. The different document components (indent guidelines, marks, carets, whitespaces, tag pairs, active and inactive tabs, and so on) can be styled individually. Notepad++ can change text direction of documents. It also supports a variety of character encodings, can add and remove byte-order marks, supports big-endian and little-endian Unicode files, and converts files from one encoding to another.[2] The documents opened in the application can be previewed in any installed browsers.

Notepad++ also provides advanced text transformation functionalities, such as escaping certain characters, transforming lowercase characters to uppercase (or vice versa), searching for matching strings, converting decimal numbers to their hexadecimal equivalents, inserting the current date and time, sorting lists ascending or descending, automatically converting leading spaces to tabs, and so on. Notepad++ also supports macros, which you can run multiple times. The list of features can be extended through additional plug-ins, such as the MIME tools for Base64 encoding and decoding.

Semantic Annotators and Converters

While there are templates available for all machine-readable metadata annotations and one might also write them manually from scratch, you can use software tools that can evaluate your code, provide a preview of the human-readable part of your markup, as well as extract RDF triples, generate the RDF graph of your structured data, and/or convert the annotation to other formats, which can be very handy, owing to the large number of RDF serializations.

---

[2]This feature should be used for those encodings that can be reasonably converted to another, more advanced encoding without sacrificing special characters (for example, ANSI to UTF-8).

RDFa Play

RDFa Play is a real-time RDFa 1.1 editor, data visualizer, and debugger available at `http://rdfa.info/play/`. It takes the raw RDFa input, generates a live preview for the human-readable data, and generates a graph from the triples (see Figure 4-2). If you modify the code, RDFa Play regenerates the browser preview and the graph.

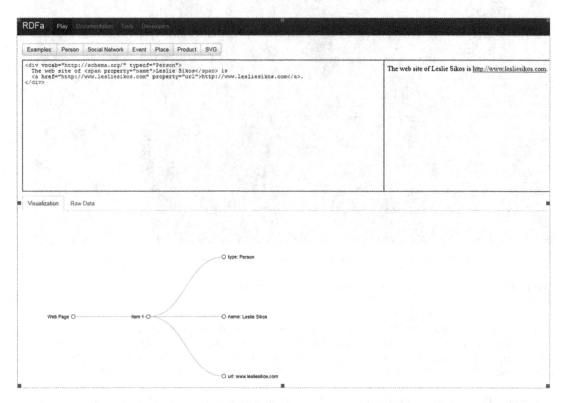

Figure 4-2. *Live browser preview and graph in RDFa Play*

RDFa Play provides RDFa annotation examples for persons, events, and places using schema.org, personal data expressed in FOAF, product description in GoodRelations, and Dublin Core metadata in SVG.

RDFa 1.1 Distiller and Parser

W3C's *RDFa 1.1 Distiller and Parser* at `http://www.w3.org/2012/pyRdfa/` processes your HTML markup containing RDFa and converts the triples to Turtle, RDF/XML, JSON-LD, or N-Triples. The RDFa 1.1 Distiller and Parser is written in Python and powered by RDFLib (`https://rdflib.readthedocs.org`). It accepts online RDFa code fragments, uploaded files, and RDFa annotations copied and pasted. The supported host languages for file upload and direct input are HTML5+RDFa, XHTML+RDFa, SVG+RDFa, Atom+RDFa, and XML+RDFa.

RDF Distiller

The *RDF Distiller* at `http://rdf.greggkellogg.net/distiller` integrates RDF graphs, readers, and writers to Ruby projects. The distiller can be used to transform data between different RDF serializations. The web interface provides a form, which takes the user input through a URI or as direct input in JSON, JSON-LD, HTML5 Microdata, N3, N-Quads, N-Triples, RDFa, RDF/XML, TRiG, TRiX, or Turtle, and converts the code to any of the formats (see Figure 4-3).

```
From URL    From Form Input
┌─Distill RDF Information─────────────────────────────────────────────┐
│  URI  [                                                          ]   │
├─────────────────────────────────────────────────────────────────────┤
│ ┌─Options──────────────────────────────────────────────────────────┐│
│ │                                                                  ││
│ │ Input Format: [ Content Detect ▾ ] Output Format: [ turtle    ▾ ]││
│ │                                                                  ││
│ │ Show Parser debug information: ☐                                 ││
│ │ Validate Input: ☐                                                ││
│ │ Expand graph (RDFa only): ☐                                      ││
│ │ Don't Verify SSL: ☐                                              ││
│ │ Output Graph (RDFa only): [ output              ▾ ]              ││
│ │ Raw Output: ☑                                                    ││
│ └──────────────────────────────────────────────────────────────────┘│
│ ┌─Markup───────────────────────────────────────────────────────────┐│
│ │ <div vocab="http://schema.org/" typeof="Person">                 ││
│ │   <span property="name">Leslie Sikos</span>                      ││
│ │   <img src="lesliesikos.jpg" alt="Leslie Sikos" property="image" />││
│ │   Leslie's web site:                                             ││
│ │   <a href="http://www.lesliesikos.com" property="url">lesliesikos.com</a>││
│ │ </div>                                                           ││
│ └──────────────────────────────────────────────────────────────────┘│
│ [ Submit ]                                                          │
└─────────────────────────────────────────────────────────────────────┘
```

Result

Note, to see result directly, such as formatted HTML for RDFa output, choose the 'Raw Output' option above.

```
@prefix rdf: <http://www.w3.org/1999/02/22-rdf-syntax-ns#> .
@prefix rdfa: <http://www.w3.org/ns/rdfa#> .
@prefix schema: <http://schema.org/> .
@prefix xsd: <http://www.w3.org/2001/XMLSchema#> .

<> rdfa:usesVocabulary schema: .

[
    a schema:Person;
    schema:image <lesliesikos.jpg>;
    schema:name "Leslie Sikos";
    schema:url <http://www.lesliesikos.com>
] .
```

***Figure 4-3.** RDFa to Turtle conversion in RDF Distiller*

The Distiller can automatically detect the input format, which can also be explicitly selected from a drop-down list.

DBpedia Spotlight

DBpedia Spotlight is a tool for annotating DBpedia concepts in plain text [7]. It has three basic functions: annotation, disambiguation, and marking candidates. DBpedia Spotlight's web application visualizes the user's input with DBpedia resource annotations (see Figure 4-4).

Figure 4-4. *Annotation with DBpedia Spotlight*

The RESTful, SOAP-based web API exposes the functionality of annotating and disambiguating entities. The annotation Java/Scala API exposes the underlying logic that performs the annotation or disambiguation. The indexing Java/Scala API executes the data processing necessary to enable the annotation or disambiguation algorithms used.

Google Structured Data Testing Tool

The *Google Structured Data Testing Tool* at `http://www.google.com/webmasters/tools/richsnippets` is suitable for machine-readable metadata testing, including Microformats, RDFa, and HTML5 Microdata annotations online or through direct input. The code length of the direct input is limited to 1,500 characters. The tool provides a preview of Google's representation of your site on Search Engine Result Pages (SERPs), along with the extracted structured data as item, type, and properties (see Figure 4-5).

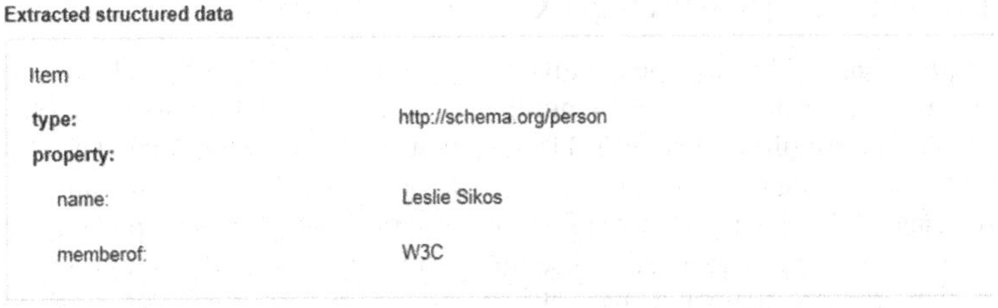

Extracted structured data

Item	
type:	http://schema.org/person
property:	
name:	Leslie Sikos
memberof:	W3C

Figure 4-5. *Triples extracted by the Google Structured Data Testing Tool*

The tool can identify incomplete triples and provides a short explanation if any mandatory property is missing. The Google Structured Data Testing Tool also indicates properties that are not parts of the vocabulary used for the object.

■ **Note** Google does not use machine-readable metadata annotations on Search Engine Result Pages if certain properties are missing for a particular object type. For example, an hCard description will be used by Google only if you provide not only the name but also at least two of the following three properties: organization, location, or role, while code validity can be achieved even if you omit them.

The tool provides machine-readable metadata examples for applications, authors, events, music, people, products, product offers, recipes, and reviews; however, you must log in to your Google account to retrieve the HTML markup of the examples. All other functionalities are available without logging in.

RDFizers

Those software tools that convert application and web site data to RDF are called *RDFizers*. They can be used for a one-time migration effort or implemented as middleware components of Semantic Web software tools such as OpenLink Data Explorer. RDFizers are often available as a software library.

Apache Any23

Apache *Anything To Triples* (Any23) is a Java library, RESTful web service, and command-line tool available at https://any23.apache.org. Any23 extracts structured data from a variety of Web documents, including RDF serializations such as RDF/XML, Turtle, Notation 3, and RDFa; Microformats such as Adr, Geo, hCalendar, hCard, hListing, hRecipe, hReview, License, XFN and Species; HTML5 Microdata; JSON-LD; CSV (Comma Separated Values exported from, for example, Microsoft Excel); as well as vocabularies such as Dublin Core, DOAP, FOAF, GeoNames, Open Graph Protocol, schema.org, and vCard. Any23 can also be used for data conversion such as Turtle to N-Triples.

Apache Any23 can perform validation for code quality assurance. It automatically fixes the DOM structure if it detects incorrect HTML element nesting. Any23 can identify not only structuring markup elements but also meta tags and RDFa annotations. If, for example, a prefix mapping is missing for an RDFa annotation, the RDFa parser will find it out of context and will not be able to handle it. To address this, Apache Any23 provides the Validator classes to implement a Rule precondition, which, when matched, will trigger the Fix method to correct the code.

Owing to its comprehensive features, Any23 is implemented in major Semantic Web applications, such as Sindice.

General Architecture for Text Engineering (GATE)

The *General Architecture for Text Engineering* (*GATE*), an open source text processor tool developed by the University of Sheffield, uses Natural Language Processing (NLP) methods to generate RDF from text files [8]. GATE's Ontology plug-in provides an API for manipulating OWL-Lite ontologies that can be serialized as RDF and RDFS. If you work with OWL-DL ontologies, classes that are subclasses of restrictions supported in OWL-Lite are usually shown, but the classes that are subclasses of other restrictions will not be displayed. Similarly, plain RDF/RDFS files will not be shown correctly, because there is no way for the API to represent many constructs that are allowed in RDF but not allowed in OWL-Lite.

OpenRefine

OpenRefine is a tool for exploring large datasets, cleaning and transforming data from one format to the other, reconciling and matching data, extending data with web services, and linking data to LOD databases [9]. With OpenRefine, you can filter and partition data with regular expressions, use named-entity extraction on full-text fields to automatically identify topics, and perform advanced data operations with the General Refine Expression Language.

Ontology Editors

Ontology editors are software tools specifically designed for ontology engineering. They cover the common tasks of all major stages of ontology development, namely they

- Determine domain and scope. What is the knowledge domain the ontology will cover? What are the potential implementation areas? What types of questions does it intend to answer?

- Consider reuse. Assess other ontologies of similar knowledge domains.

- Enumerate important terms. Create a comprehensive list of terms for the chosen knowledge domain, without focusing on class hierarchy, properties, overlapping terms, or relationships.

- Define classes and class hierarchy.

- Define properties, and characteristics of properties. Define property types, including simple properties and relationships to classes, domains and ranges, as well as universal, existential, and cardinality restrictions.

- Create individuals.

Protégé

Stanford University's *Protégé* is the most widely used open source ontology editor and knowledge management toolset, which can be downloaded from http://protege.stanford.edu. It supports reasoners such as HermiT and FaCT++ to validate ontologies for consistency, as well as a variety of other plug-ins. Originally developed as a Learning Health System for translating raw biomedical data into machine-readable data for decision making, Protégé is now suitable for modeling, ontology-driven application development, and collaborative ontology engineering. The ontologies can be exported in many formats, such as RDFS, and various OWL syntaxes.

While the ontologies can be created in Protégé through a Graphical User Interface (GUI), the software is Java-based, so when it is executed, it opens a command line (see Figure 4-6) behind the GUI in a separate window. The ontologies created in Protégé can be accessed from Java programs through the Protégé-OWL API.

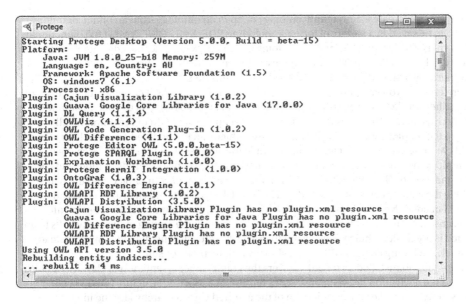

Figure 4-6. Protégé's command line

The GUI of Protégé features a main menu, an address bar, and a tab-based editor (see Figure 4-7).

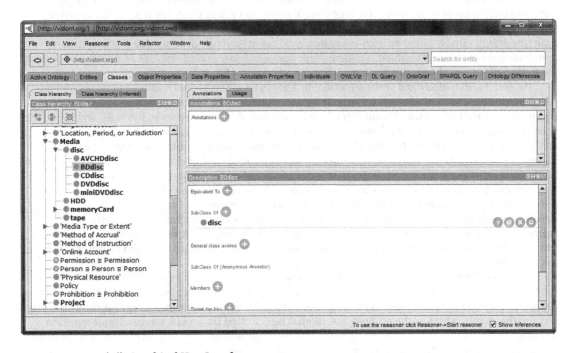

Figure 4-7. Protégé's Graphical User Interface

In the File menu, you can create a new, empty ontology or open an ontology from an offline or online .owl file. Ontologies can be saved in a variety of formats, including RDF/XML, OWL/XML, OWL Functional Syntax, Manchester Syntax, OBO (Open Biomedical Ontologies format), KRSS2 (Knowledge Representation System Specification v2), Latex, or Turtle. The wide range of plug-ins available for Protégé can be downloaded and the already installed plug-ins updated also from this menu.

Under File ➤ Preferences, you can handle hidden annotation URIs. To make it easier to automatically generate unique identifiers to classes, properties, and individuals of an ontology, you can set up or modify the structure of entity URIs for a particular ontology. Once you set up the base URI of the ontology, all fragment identifiers of the ontology will start with this address, which can be modified any time later (New Ontologies tab in File ➤ Preferences). This can be very useful if the address structure has to be changed after creating the ontology, because the developer does not have to change the hundreds or thousands of addresses manually one by one. The default base URI can be a web address of your choice, and the path can optionally include the actual year, month, and day. The base URI typically ends in a #, but this can be changed to / or :, if needed (New Entities tab in File ➤ Preferences). The number sign is the default setting, however, because it creates valid fragment identifiers. You can set the ending of the entity URIs to an arbitrary name, which is the default choice. If you want to use automatically generated identifiers instead, you can set entity labels, including custom URIs and a globally unique prefix or suffix.

OWLViz, a Protégé plug-in installed by default, powers the graphical representation of class hierarchies of OWL ontologies and the navigation between the classes represented as a tree structure (OWLViz tab in File ➤ Preferences). OWLViz makes the comparison of the asserted class hierarchy and the inferred class hierarchy possible. By default, Protégé automatically checks for plug-in updates at program startup, which can also be disabled (Plugins tab in File ➤ Preferences). The default plug-in repository is set to GitHub, which can be changed. The Reasoner tab in File ➤ Preferences can display or hide class, object property, data property, and object inferences or initialize reasoners by setting up precomputation tasks such as classification or realization to be done when the reasoner is launched. The tree hierarchy can be automatically expanded under Tree Preferences in File ➤ Preferences by setting an auto-expansion depth limit (the default value is 3) and an auto-expansion child count limit (the default value is 50). By default, automatic tree expansion is disabled. Accidentally performed changes on any tab can be reverted by clicking the Reset preferences... button on the bottom right-hand corner of File ➤ Preferences.

The core functionalities and views are available through tabs. The Active Ontology tab shows general ontology metadata, such as title, creator, description, in addition to the reused ontologies and statistics about ontology metrics, such as the number of axioms, classes, object properties, individuals, and so on. Protégé also displays all the prefixes used in the opened ontology. Protégé features a dedicated tab for Entities, Classes, Object Properties, Data Properties, Annotation Properties, and Individuals. The class hierarchy is shown as a tree structure, wherein each node can be opened or closed individually. The selected entity, class, or property details are shown in separate panels. Class descriptions provide information about equivalent classes, subclasses, class axioms, members, etc., of the selected class, as well as the option to change the values or add new ones. The classes in Protégé are subclasses of Thing and overlap by default. Class hierarchies can be created from the Tools menu. The object or data type properties can have subproperties or inverse properties. The properties can be functional, transitive, symmetric, asymmetric, reflexive, or irreflexive. Protégé automatically updates inverse properties (such as hasChild and isSonOf in a family relationship ontology).

The Object Properties and Data Properties tabs also have a Characteristics panel. For object properties, the Characteristics panel features checkboxes for Functional, Inverse functional, Transitive, Symmetric, Asymmetric, Reflexive, and Irreflexive properties. The Individuals tab shows not only the class hierarchy but also the members list and the property assertions. The OntoGraf tab provides a visual representation of any part of the ontology (see Figure 4-8). When you hover the mouse over any part of the graph, Protégé shows the fragment identifier, as well as the subclasses/superclasses (if any).

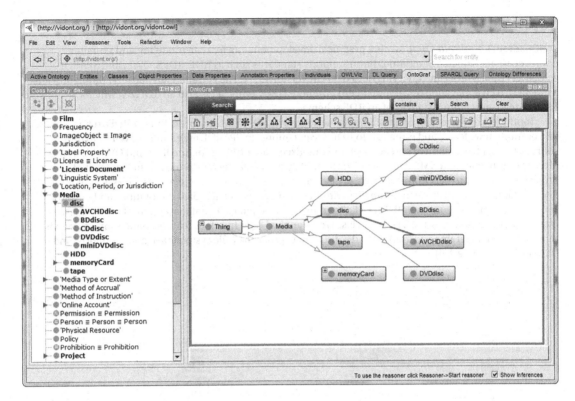

Figure 4-8. *Graph visualization in Protégé*

The SPARQL Query tab provides an interface to execute SPARQL queries. Protégé enumerates the prefixes, provides an editable SELECT query template, which you can modify or delete, and adds arbitrary queries.

Protégé also has an online version at http://webprotege.stanford.edu, which has collaboration support.

SemanticWorks

Altova's *SemanticWorks* is a visual Semantic Web editor that features a graphical RDF and RDFS editor and a graphical OWL editor, supports OWL-Lite, OWL-Full, and OWL-DL dialects [10]. SemanticWorks provides syntax and format checking options and the evaluation of ontology semantics with direct links to errors. Context-sensitive entry helpers display the list of valid input options, depending on the serialization being used. SemanticWorks can generate code in RDF/XML and N-Triples and convert RDF/XML to N-Triples and vice versa. The program features a printing option for RDF and OWL diagrams. New class instances can be defined using intelligent shortcuts. The instances, properties, and classes are organized on tabs, and, similar to software engineering environments, properties and property values can also be manipulated through separate subwindows. The Overview subwindow is very useful when editing large, complex diagrams, when the currently displayed portion of the diagram is indicated as a red rectangle. You can switch between the diagram and the code view at any time.

TopBraid Composer

TopQuadrant's *TopBraid Composer* is a graphical development tool for data modeling and semantic data processing. The free Standard Edition supports standards such as RDF, RDFS, OWL, and SPARQL, as well as visual editing and querying, and data conversions [11]. The commercial Maestro Edition provides a model-driven application development environment [12]. Composer is also an RDFizer, which can convert Excel spreadsheets into instances of an RDF schema.

TopBraid Composer can open ontologies serialized in RDF/XML or Turtle, import RDFa data sources, RSS or Atom news feeds, and e-mails into RDF. It can connect to SPARQL endpoints as well as RDBMS sources, import tab-delimited spreadsheet files and Excel spreadsheets, online RDF and OWL files, UML files, XML Schemas, and XML catalogs. Wizards guide you in creating new projects, such as faceted project resources, projects from CSV files, JavaScript projects, static web projects, as well as XML editing and validation. You can create markup files with RDFa and HTML5 Microdata annotations and develop semantic web applications and RDF/OWL file connections to Jena SDB databases, Jena TDB databases, Oracle databases, and Sesame 2 repositories. The Graphical User Interface features panels for classes, visual representation (diagrams and graphs) and source code, properties, file system navigation, imports, and "baskets" (see Figure 4-9).

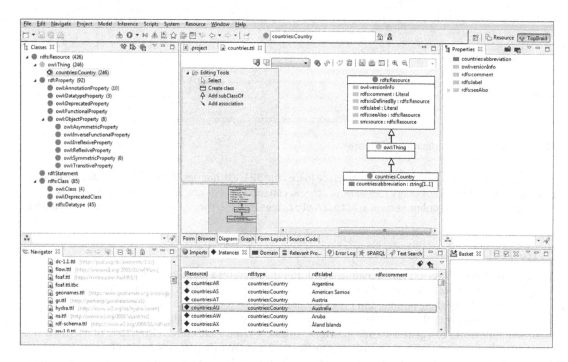

Figure 4-9. *Ontology editing with TopBraid Composer Maestro*

On the Classes panel, you can navigate in your ontologies, represented as a tree structure, create and delete classes, create subclasses and siblings, group components by namespace, and search by name. The Properties panel features, among property manipulation, GoogleMaps integration too. On the Imports panel, the resources can be displayed, along with their rdf:type, rdfs:label, and rdfs:comment values (if provided), as well as rules, instances, errors, SPARQL queries, and text searches. On the Baskets panel, you can load contents from, and save contents to, a text file; add selected resources; add matching properties; add subclasses, subproperties, instances, individuals, and unreferences resources; and perform batch operations.

Apache Stanbol

Apache Stanbol is a semantic data modeler and comprehensive ontology manager [13].

It includes a content-management system that supports Semantic Web services and web application functions such as tag extraction, text completion in search fields, and e-mail routing, based on extracted entities. The functionalities of the Stanbol components are available through a RESTful web service API. The RESTful services return results in RDF, JSON, and JSON-LD. Apache Stanbol can be run as a stand-alone application (packaged as a runnable JAR) or as a web application (packaged as .war) deployable in servlet containers such as Apache Tomcat. It is compatible with Apache frameworks such as Solr (for semantic search), Tika (for metadata extraction), and Jena (for storage).

Stanbol has a built-in RDFizer that processes traditional web contents sent in a POST request with the MIME type specified in the Content-type header and adds semantic information ("RDF enhancement") to it, serialized in the format specified in the Accept header.

Stanbol also provides a reasoner component, which implements a common API and supports different reasoners and configurations through OWLApi and Jena-based abstract services, with implementations for Jena RDFS, OWL, OWLMini, and HermiT. The reasoner module can perform a consistency check, which returns HTTP Status 200 if data is consistent and 204 if not. The reasoner can also be used for classification, in other words, to materialize all inferred rdf:type statements. The semantic enrichment materializes all inferred statements.

The Apache Stanbol Ontology Manager supports multiple ontology networks by interconnecting seemingly unrelated knowledge represented in different ontologies, ontology libraries, a central ontology repository, as well as common ontology engineering tasks, such as reasoning and rule execution. Stanbol can also store and cache semantic information and make it searchable through its persistence services.

Fluent Editor

Fluent Editor is an ontology editor, which can handle RDF, OWL, and SWRL files [14]. Fluent Editor uses a proprietary representation language and query language compatible with Semantic Web standards. The tool has been designed for managing complex ontologies. It features a reasoner window, a SPARQL window for queries, an XML preview window, a taxonomy tree view, and an annotation window. Fluent Editor has two types of plug-ins: a Protégé interoperability plug-in, which supports data export to and import from Protégé, and R language plug-ins that support the development of analytical models with R and rOntorion and plug-in development for Fluent Editor with the R language.

Ontology Analysis Tools

There are software tools for ontology mapping and specific ontology engineering tasks not supported by general-purpose ontology editors such as semantic similarity estimation.

ZOOMA

ZOOMA is an application for discovering optimal ontology mappings and automatic mapping of text values to ontology terms using mapping repositories [15]. ZOOMA can reuse mappings already asserted in the database, explore mapping best suitable for multiple mappings, derive better mappings by recording contextual information, and suggest new terms. The commonly observed values can be processed automatically.

ZOOMA finds all optimal mappings automatically where one text value maps to the same set of terms every time. When using mapping repositories, it can detect errors, in other words, it finds all the text value to ontology term mappings that are potentially incorrect. ZOOMA can also propose new mappings to terms based on the input values; however, selecting the best mapping requires human evaluation and assessment. ZOOMA can easily be used as a software library, as, for example, within an Apache Maven project.

Semantic Measures Library

The *Semantic Measures Library* (*SML*) is a Java library for semantic measure analysis, such as estimating semantic similarity and relatedness by using ontologies to define the distance between terms or concepts [16]. SML functionalities can be accessed also through a set of command-line tools called *SML-Toolkit*. The library supports RDF and RDFS, OWL ontologies, WordNet (a lexical database), Medical Subject Headings (MeSH, a controlled vocabulary for life science publishing), the Gene Ontology, and so on.

Reasoners

Reasoners derive new facts from existing ontologies and check the integrity of ontologies. The various software tools are different in terms of reasoning characteristics, practical usability, and performance, owing to the different algorithms implemented for Description Logic reasoning. Not all reasoners can evaluate all possible inferences, so their soundness and completeness vary. Some ontologies support rules for combining ontologies with rules. A common feature of reasoners is *ABOX reasoning*, the reasoning of individuals that covers instance checking, conjunctive query answering, and consistency checking. Advanced reasoners support the OWL API, a standard interface for application development with OWL reasoning. Another feature of advanced reasoners is the OWLLink support, leveraging an implementation-neutral protocol to interact with OWL 2 reasoners.

HermiT

HermiT is one of the most popular OWL 2 reasoners that can be used to determine ontology consistency, identify relationships between classes, and perform further tasks [17]. HermiT uses its own algorithm, called the *"hypertableau" calculus,* to check the consistency of OWL ontologies and identify subsumption relationships between classes. HermiT can be used as a Protégé plug-in (see Figure 4-10), through the command line, or in Java applications. The latest Protégé versions come with a preinstalled HermiT plug-in. From the command line, you can perform classification, querying, and other common reasoning tasks. As for the Java applications, HermiT supports the OWLReasoner interface from the OWL API, providing access to OWL API objects, such as ontologies and class expressions.

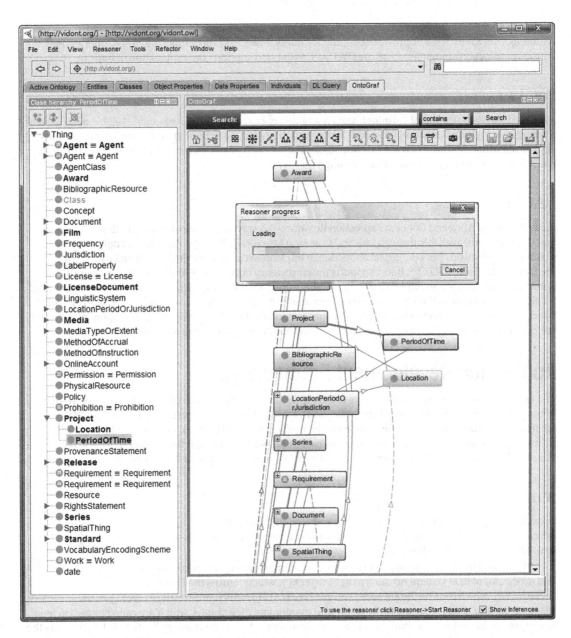

Figure 4-10. *The HermiT reasoner running in Protégé*

Pellet

Clark & Parsia's *Pellet* is an OWL 2 DL reasoner, which can be used in Protégé, Jena, TopBraid Composer, or in Java programs through the OWL API interface [18]. It is based on the *tableau algorithm* to break down complex statements into smaller and simpler pieces to detect contradictions and supports expressive Description Logics. Pellet supports different incremental reasoning, including incremental consistency checking and incremental classification, where updates (additions or removals) can be processed and applied to an ontology without having to perform all the reasoning steps from scratch. Pellet also supports reasoning with SWRL rules. It provides conjunctive query answering and supports SPARQL queries. Pellet reasons ontologies through Jena and the OWL API. Pellet also supports the explanation of bugs.

FaCT++

FaCT++ (Fast Classification of Terminologies) is a tableaux-based OWL 2 DL reasoner[3] [19]. It can be used as a description logic classifier and for modal logic satisfiability testing. It implements a sound and complete tableau algorithm for expressive description logics. FaCT++ is available as a stand-alone tool, as a Protégé plug-in, and can be used in applications through the OWL API.

RACER

Racer (Renamed ABox and Concept Expression Reasoner) is a server-side reasoner for building ontology-based applications, available through Java and Common Lisp APIs [20]. Racer provides not only standard reasoning mechanisms but also logical abduction. It implements a highly optimized tableau calculus for the Description Logic $\mathcal{SRIQ}^{(D)}$. Racer supports the consistency check of RDF data descriptions and OWL 2 ontologies and can open multiple ontologies simultaneously for ontology merging. It can find implicit subclass relationships induced by the axioms of an ontology and find synonyms for properties, classes, or instances. Racer can retrieve information from OWL/RDF documents via SPARQL queries and also support incremental queries. It supports FaCT optimization techniques and optimization for number restrictions and ABoxes.

Application Development Frameworks

The most common programming tasks are collected in software libraries, so that you do not have to write frequently used code. In Semantic Web applications, for example, a common task is to covert an RDF file from one serialization to another, which can be easily performed by tools such as Apache Jena. Such software libraries can be used in a variety of environments, such as through the command line or as a plug-in of an Integrated Development Environment (IDE) such as Eclipse or NetBeans.

Jena

Apache *Jena* is an open source Semantic Web and Linked Data application development framework, which supports the storage, retrieval, and analysis of structured data written in RDF [21].

The core RDF API of Jena has dedicated methods for extracting subjects, objects, and predicates of RDF statements such as getSubject(), which returns the Resource, getObject(), which returns the RDFNode, and getPredicate(), which returns the Property of the statement. Using the Jena RDF API, you can easily create and manipulate RDF graphs, which are called *models* in Jena and represented by the Model interface. For example, to describe a person using the RDF API, first define the URI or the subject and the string of the object (see Listing 4-1), then create an empty, memory-based Model using the createDefaultModel() method (see Listing 4-2).

Listing 4-1. Constant Declaration in Jena

```
static String personWebsite  = "http://www.lesliesikos.com";
static String personName = "Leslie Sikos";
```

---

[3]FaCT++ has a partial support for OWL 2 key constraints and datatypes.

Listing 4-2. Creating a Memory-Based Model

```
Model model = ModelFactory.createDefaultModel();
```

The resource will be created using the Model (see Listing 4-3).

Listing 4-3. Creating a Resource

```
Resource lesliesikos = model.createResource(personWebsite);
```

Finally, add a property to the resource using addProperty (see Listing 4-4).

Listing 4-4. Adding Property to a Resource

```
lesliesikos.addProperty(FOAF.Name, personName);
```

To retrieve statements from an RDF graph (Jena Model), the listStatements() method can be used (see Listing 4-5).

Listing 4-5. Extracting RDF Triples

```
StmtIterator iter = model.listStatements();
```

If you need more details, you can list all the predicated, subjects, and objects from the RDF graph, as shown in Listing 4-6.

Listing 4-6. Listing All Triple Components Individually

```
while (iter.hasNext()) {
  Statement stmt      = iter.nextStatement();
  Resource  subject   = stmt.getSubject();
  Property  predicate = stmt.getPredicate();
  RDFNode   object    = stmt.getObject();

  System.out.print(subject.toString());
  System.out.print(" " + predicate.toString() + " ");
  if (object instanceof Resource) {
    System.out.print(object.toString());
  } else {
    System.out.print(" \"" + object.toString() + "\"");
  }

  System.out.println(" .");
}
```

Jena supports SPARQL queries, including SPARQL, over the JDBC driver framework. In fact, it can serve RDF data over HTTP, using *Fuseki*, a SPARQL server that provides REST-style SPARQL HTTP update, SPARQL querying, and SPARQL update [22]. The Jena rules engine, along with other inference algorithms, can derive consequences from RDF models. The *Inference API* provides reasoning to expand and check triplestore contents. You can not only use built-in OWL and RDFS reasoners but also configure your own inference rules. The Jena *Ontology API* can work with data models, RDFS, and OWL, including partial support for OWL 1.1 features. Jena has its own *high performance triplestore* component called TDB, which stores triples directly to disk and can be directly accessed from a Java Virtual Machine. SQL DB provides a persistent triplestore for Jena, using relational databases, namely, an SQL database for RDF data storage and querying. Jena supports advanced text and spatial search. Jena can be integrated into Eclipse, the popular software development environment for Java developers.

Sesame

Sesame is an open source framework for RDF data analysis and SPARQL querying [23]. The approach implemented to the Sesame framework is different from other semantic frameworks in a way that it features an extensible interface and that the storage engine is segregated from the query interface. *Alibaba*, a Sesame API, is used for mapping Java classes to ontologies and generating Java source files from ontologies, making it possible to directly exploit RSS, FOAF, and Dublin Core from Java. Sesame provides its RDF triplestore as a Java web application (.war), which can be easily deployed to application servers such as Apache Tomcat or Eclipse Jetty. It supports both memory-based (*MemoryStore*) and disk-based (*NativeStore*) storage. The RDF triplestore provides a SPARQL query endpoint. Sesame can be integrated to software development environments such as Eclipse and Apache Maven.

The *Repository API* provides methods for data file uploading, querying, extracting, and manipulation. One of its implementations, *SailRepository*, translates calls to a SAIL implementation of your choice, while another implementation, *HTTPRepository*, offers transparent client-server communication with a Sesame server over HTTP. The HTTP Server, the topmost component of Sesame, has Java servlets for accessing Sesame repositories over HTTP. Using the Repository API of Sesame, you can create a local repository directly from your application, with the capability to store, query, and modify RDF data (see Listing 4-7).

Listing 4-7. Creating a Basic Local Repository in Sesame

```
import org.openrdf.repository.Repository;
import org.openrdf.repository.sail.SailRepository;
import org.openrdf.sail.memory.MemoryStore;
…
Repository repo = new SailRepository(new MemoryStore());
repo.initialize();
```

This repository will use the main memory for data storage, which is by far the fastest RDF repository type. However, the created repository is volatile, meaning that the content is lost when the object is garbage collected or when the program execution is finished. For persistent storage, you need to save the data to a file (see Listing 4-8).

Listing 4-8. Creating a Local Repository with File Storage in Sesame

```
import org.openrdf.repository.Repository;
import org.openrdf.repository.sail.SailRepository;
import org.openrdf.sail.nativerdf.NativeStore;
…
File dataDir = new File("/path/to/datadir/");
Repository repo = new SailRepository(new NativeStore(dataDir));
repo.initialize();
```

To create a repository with RDF Schema inferencing, you have to create a Repository object by passing it a reference to the appropriate Sail object (see Listing 4-9).

Listing 4-9. Creating a Repository with RDF Schema Inferencing

```
import org.openrdf.repository.Repository;
import org.openrdf.repository.sail.SailRepository;
import org.openrdf.sail.memory.MemoryStore;
import org.openrdf.sail.inferencer.fc.ForwardChainingRDFSInferencer;
…
Repository repo = new SailRepository(
  new ForwardChainingRDFSInferencer(
  new MemoryStore()));
repo.initialize();
```

If you use a remote Sesame server rather than a local one, the remote connection has to be set up by initializing the RemoteRepositoryManager (see Listing 4-10).

Listing 4-10. Initializing a RemoteRepositoryManager

```
import org.openrdf.repository.manager.RemoteRepositoryManager;
…
String serverUrl = "http://localhost:8080/openrdf-sesame";
RemoteRepositoryManager manager = new RemoteRepositoryManager(serverUrl);
manager.initialize();
```

The *Storage And Inference Layer API* (*SAIL*) separates storage and inference. The SAIL API is primarily used by triplestore developers. The *RIO API*, which stands for "RDF I/O," contains parsers and writers for RDF serialization. The parsers can transform RDF files to statements, while the writers can transform statements to RDF files. The RIO API can be used independently from all the other Sesame components.

The *RDF Model API* defines the representation of RDF building blocks such as statements, URIs, blank nodes, literals, graphs, and models. The RDF statements are represented by the org.openrdf.model. Statement interface, in which each statement has a subject, predicate, object, and (optionally) a context. Each of these items is an org.openrdf.model.Value, which covers org.openrdf.model.Resource and org.openrdf.model.Literal. Each resource represents an RDF value that is either a blank node (org.openrdf.model.BNode) or a URI (org.openrdf.model.URI). Literals represent RDF literal values such as strings, dates, and integer numbers. New triples and values can be created using org.openrdf. model.ValueFactory (see Listing 4-11).

Listing 4-11. Using a Default ValueFactory Implementation

```
ValueFactory factory = ValueFactoryImpl.getInstance();
```

Once you obtain your ValueFactory, you can create new URIs, literals, and triples (see Listing 4-12).

Listing 4-12. Adding URIs, Literals, and Triples to a ValueFactory Implementation

```
URI webstand = factory.createURI("http://yourbookdataset.com/webstand");
URI title = factory.createURI("http://yourbookdataset.com/title");
Literal webstandsTitle = factory.createLiteral("Web Standards");
Statement titleStatement = factory.createStatement(webstand, title, webstandsTitle);
```

The *Graph API* represents an RDF graph as a Java object. The org.openrdf.model.Graph class handles RDF graphs from the Java code. Graphs can be created in two ways: writing them programmatically by adding statements to them or created using a construct query. Empty graphs can be obtained by creating a GraphImpl object (see Listing 4-13).

Listing 4-13. Creating an Empty Graph

```
Graph myGraph = new org.openrdf.model.impl.GraphImpl();
```

Next, the RDF statement components (subject-predicate-object) have to be created using the ValueFactory object (see Listing 4-14). This prepares the graph to support triples and adds the WebDesignBook subject, the Title predicate, and the Web Standards object to the graph.

Listing 4-14. Adding Triple Support to a Graph

```
ValueFactory myFactory = myGraph.getValueFactory();
String namespace = "http://www.foo.com/bar#";

URI mySubject = myFactory.createURI(namespace, "WebDesignBook");
URI myPredicate = myFactory.createURI(namespace, "Title");
Literal myObject = myFactory.createLiteral("Web Standards");

myGraph.add(mySubject, myPredicate, myObject);
```

Another option is to use the URIs directly to add properties (see Listing 4-15).

Listing 4-15. Using URIs Directly to Add Triples to a Graph

```
URI bookClass = myFactory.createURI(namespace, "Book");
URI rdfType = myFactory.createURI(org.openrdf.vocabulary.RDF.TYPE);
mySubject.addProperty(rdfType, bookClass);
```

Integrated Development Environments

Integrated Development Environments (IDEs) provide an interface for efficient Semantic Web application development, including a source editor with syntax highlighting for a variety of programming languages, such as Java and Python. IDEs have wizards and built-in applications to simplify software development, file handlers, and other tools to support deploying, running, and testing applications. IDEs consist of a runtime system, a workbench, and other features, such as a remote debugger or data modeler.

Eclipse

Eclipse is one of the most popular IDEs for Java developers, providing essential tools, such as a Java IDE, a CVS client, a Git client, an XML Editor, and Apache Maven integration [24].

Eclipse is one of the popular IDEs to use Apache Jena and Sesame. The installation of Eclipse can be done as follows:

1. A prerequisite of Eclipse is the Java Development Kit (JDK). Download it from http://www.oracle.com/technetwork/java/javase/downloads/ and install it (Figure 4-11).

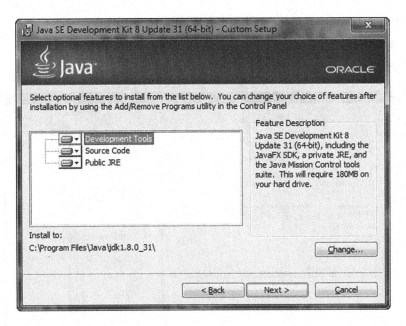

Figure 4-11. Installing the Java Development Kit for Eclipse

■ **Caution**   The Java Development Kit is different from the Java Runtime Environment (JRE), also known as the Java Virtual Machine (JVM), which is a secure computing environment for running Java programs on your computer.

---

2.   Visit http://www.eclipse.org and download the installer. Eclipse is available for Windows, Linux, and Mac OS X. The Windows binary is distributed as a ZIP archive, the Linux and the Apple installers as gzipped TAR archives.

3.   Extract the installation files and execute eclipse.exe.

4.   You have to specify a folder for Eclipse project files. If you want to use the same path every time you launch Eclipse, you can set the folder to the default Eclipse project folder.

Set Up Apache Jena in Eclipse

Once you have Eclipse installed, you can set up Apache Jena.

1.   Go to http://jena.apache.org/download/, select a download mirror, and download the binary distribution suitable for your platform (.zip or .tar.gz).

2.   Extract the Jena files from the archive.

3.   In Eclipse, select File ➤ New ➤ Java Project.

4.   Right-click the name of the newly created project and select Properties (or select File ➤ Properties).

5. Select Java Build Path and click the Libraries tab.

6. Click Add Library... on the right.

7. Select User Library as the library type (see Figure 4-12).

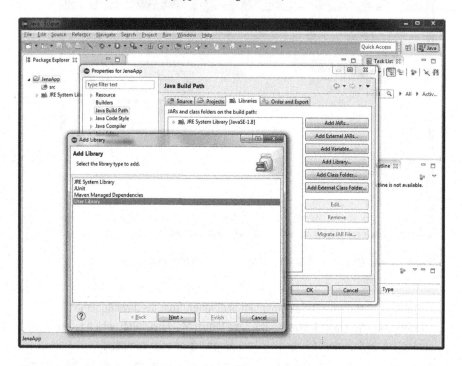

Figure 4-12. *Load the Apache Jena software library to Eclipse*

8. Click the Next ➤ button on the bottom.

9. Click User Libraries... on the right.

10. Click the New... button.

11. Add a name to your library, such as JenaLib.

12. Click the Add external JARs... button on the right.

13. Browse to your Jena directory (`apache-jena-versionNumber`) and go to the `lib` subdirectory.

14. Select all the `.jar` files (for example, with Ctrl+A) and click Open (see Figure 4-13).

15. Click OK.

16. Click Finish.

17. Once you click OK, the Jena software library will be added to your Eclipse project.

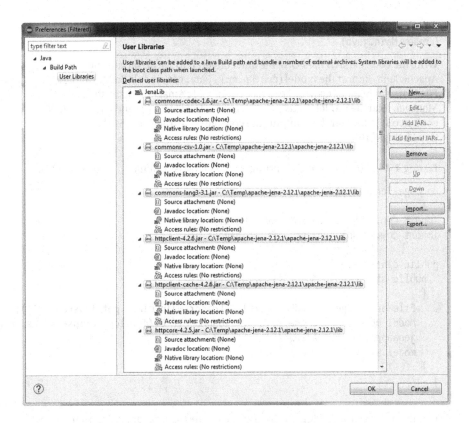

Figure 4-13. *Apache Jena to be added to the Eclipse project*

To see the Jena library in action, let's create a Java program to convert your RDF/XML serialized FOAF file to Turtle!

1. In the Package Explorer, right-click src and select New ➤ Package and create a package.

2. Click the package name and select New ➤ File.

3. Specify a file name and click Finish.

4. Add the file content (type in directly or copy-paste it). If you don't have a FOAF file yet, create one manually in RDF/XML serialization or generate one using FOAF-a-matic at http://www.ldodds.com/foaf/foaf-a-matic.html. The asterisk (*) in front of the file name on the file's tab indicates that the file has been changed. When you save the file with File ➤ Save or Ctrl+S, the character disappears. Save the file as, for example, foaf.rdf.

___

■ **Note**   If you have characters not supported by Windows-1252, Eclipse offers you the option to save the file with UTF-8 encoding to avoid character loss.

___

5. Right-click the package and select New ➤ Class and add a name such as Main (creates Main.java).

6. Write the code to open the FOAF file and convert it to Turtle serialization using Apache Jena. Import the model (com.hp.hpl.jena.rdf.model.Model) and the File Manager of Jena (com.hp.hpl.jena.util.FileManager). Using the File Manager, load the model (FileManager.get().loadModel()) and write the RDF content out to the standard output (the console) in Turtle using System.out (see Listing 4-16).

Listing 4-16. Loading and Converting an RDF File Using Jena

```
package JenaPackage;

import com.hp.hpl.jena.rdf.model.Model;
import com.hp.hpl.jena.util.FileManager;

public class Main {
  public static void main(String args[])
  {
    FileManager.get().addLocatorClassLoader(Main.class.getClassLoader());
    Model model = FileManager.get().loadModel("C:/develop/eclipse/workspace/ ↵
    jenaapp/src/jenapackage/foaf.rdf");
    model.write(System.out,"TURTLE");
  }
}
```

7. Run the program by clicking the Run button on the top toolbar (white triangle in green circle) or Run under the Run menu. The Console shows the output in Turtle (see Figure 4-14).

Figure 4-14. Using Apache Jena to convert RDF/XML to Turtle

Set Up Sesame in Eclipse

Once you have Eclipse installed, you can add Sesame to your environment, similar to Jena.

1. Go to `http://sourceforge.net/projects/sesame/` and download the binary distribution.

2. Extract the Sesame files from the archive.

3. In Eclipse, select File ➤ New ➤ Java Project.

4. Right-click the name of the newly created project and select Properties (or select File ➤ Properties).

5. Select Java Build Path and click the Libraries tab.

6. Click Add Library... on the right.

7. Select User Library as the library type.

8. Click the Next > button on the bottom.

9. Click User Libraries... on the right.

10. Click the New... button.

11. Add a name to your library, such as JenaLib.

12. Click the Add external JARs... button on the right.

13. Browse to your Sesame directory (`openrdf-sesame-version`*Number*) and go to the `lib` subdirectory.

14. Select all the `.jar` files (for example, with Ctrl+A) and click Open (see Figure 4-15).

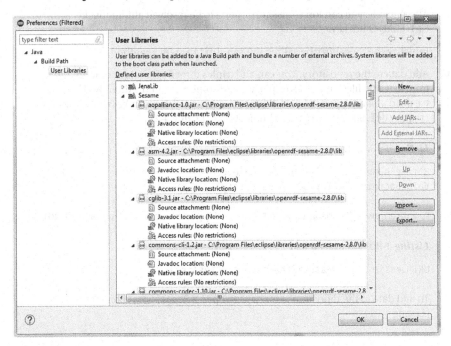

Figure 4-15. *Adding Sesame to Eclipse*

15. Click OK.

16. Click Finish.

17. Once you click OK, the Sesame software library will be added to your Eclipse project.

To see the Sesame library in action, let's create a Java program, to initialize a repository, and add data to and retrieve data from that repository!

1. Create a new Java class. To make it easier to write our code, on the New Java Class window, tick the checkbox public static void main(String[] args) under Which method stubs would you like to create?

2. To store RDF data, we first have to create a repository. While there are many different types of repositories, for our example, we need a simple local repository with fast in-memory store (see Listing 4-17).

   Listing 4-17. Creating a Local Repository in Sesame

   ```
   Repository rep = new SailRepository(new MemoryStore());
   ```

   To use this code, however, we have to write some import statements manually (see Listing 4-18).

   Listing 4-18. Import Packages from the Sesame Library

   ```
   import org.openrdf.repository.Repository;
   import org.openrdf.repository.sail.SailRepository;
   import org.openrdf.sail.memory.MemoryStore;
   ```

   Alternatively, you can force missing imports to be resolved automatically, using the Ctrl+Shift+O hot key.

3. Initialize the repository by calling the rep.initialize() method.

4. Add data to the repository. You can add triples directly from Java or load them from external files. In this example, we add some statements directly. To do so, we need a namespace to be used for creating new URIs and a ValueFactory for creating URI, BNode, and Literal objects (see Listing 4-19).

   Listing 4-19. Adding Data to the Repository

   ```
   String namespace = "http://example.com/";
   ValueFactory f = rep.getValueFactory();
   ```

5. Create a new URI through an identifier for the person Leslie (see Listing 4-20).

   Listing 4-20. Creating a URI

   ```
   URI leslie = f.createURI(namespace, "leslie");
   ```

6. To add data to the repository, you have to open a RepositoryConnection (Listing 4-21).

Listing 4-21. Opening a Connection

```
RepositoryConnection conn = rep.getConnection();
```

7. To ensure that any connection is open only when needed, create a try-finally code block (see Listing 4-22). The try clause holds the tasks to be performed during a connection, while the finally clause is used to close the connection when it is not needed anymore or if something goes wrong.

Listing 4-22. A try-finally Block

```
try {

}
finally {
    conn.close();
}
```

8. In the try clause, add triples to the repository (see Listing 4-23).

Listing 4-23. Adding RDF Statements to a Sesame Repository

```
conn.add(leslie, RDF.TYPE, FOAF.PERSON);
conn.add(leslie, RDFS.LABEL, f.createLiteral("Leslie",
XMLSchema.STRING));
```

The first triple describes Leslie as a Person, the second states Leslie's name as a string.

■ **Note** The frequently used namespaces (RDF, RDFS, FOAF, etc.) are predefined as constants in Sesame.

---

9. Retrieve the data from our repository using the getStatements method (see Listing 4-24), which has four arguments.

Listing 4-24. Data Retrieval from a Repository

```
RepositoryResult<Statement> statements = conn.getStatements(null,
null, null, ↵
true);
```

The first three arguments represent the subject, predicate, and object to be matched. In this case, we want to retrieve all triples. The first three arguments will be null. The last argument is a Boolean value for indicating whether those statements that are inferred by a reasoner should be included. In this example, we do not use any reasoners, so the fourth value won't have any effect on the output. Alternatively, one could use SPARQL queries as well, to extract data from the repository.

10. Convert the result to a Sesame Model (see Listing 4-25), which is a Java Collection.

Listing 4-25. Converting the Result to a Model

```
Model model = Iterations.addAll(statements, new LinkedHashModel());
```

11. To provide a neat output, we need some namespace abbreviations, so that the output won't include full URIs. Again, we can use the predefined constants for the RDF, RDFS, XMLSchema, and FOAF namespaces (see Listing 4-26).

Listing 4-26. Namespace Declaration

```
model.setNamespace("rdf", RDF.NAMESPACE);
model.setNamespace("rdfs", RDFS.NAMESPACE);
model.setNamespace("xsd", XMLSchema.NAMESPACE);
model.setNamespace("foaf", FOAF.NAMESPACE);
model.setNamespace("ex", namespace);
```

12. Display the output in Turtle on the Console, using the Sesame toolkit *Rio* ("RDF I/O") (see Listing 4-27).

Listing 4-27. Sending the Output to the Console

```
Rio.write(model, System.out, RDFFormat.TURTLE);
```

The final code should look like Listing 4-28.

Listing 4-28. A Complete Sesame Code Example

```
package sesamePackage;

import info.aduna.iteration.Iterations;

import org.openrdf.model.Statement;
import org.openrdf.model.URI;
import org.openrdf.model.Model;
import org.openrdf.model.ValueFactory;
import org.openrdf.model.impl.LinkedHashModel;
import org.openrdf.model.vocabulary.FOAF;
import org.openrdf.model.vocabulary.RDF;
import org.openrdf.model.vocabulary.RDFS;
import org.openrdf.model.vocabulary.XMLSchema;
import org.openrdf.repository.Repository;
import org.openrdf.repository.RepositoryConnection;
import org.openrdf.repository.RepositoryException;
import org.openrdf.repository.RepositoryResult;
import org.openrdf.repository.sail.SailRepository;
import org.openrdf.sail.memory.MemoryStore;
import org.openrdf.rio.RDFFormat;
import org.openrdf.rio.RDFHandlerException;
import org.openrdf.rio.Rio;
```

```java
public class SesameApp {

    public static void main(String[] args) throws RepositoryException,
    RDFHandlerException {

        Repository rep = new SailRepository(new MemoryStore());
        rep.initialize();

        String namespace = "http://example.com/";
        ValueFactory f = rep.getValueFactory();

        URI leslie = f.createURI(namespace, "leslie");

        RepositoryConnection conn = rep.getConnection();
        try {
            conn.add(leslie, RDF.TYPE, FOAF.PERSON);
            conn.add(leslie, RDFS.LABEL, f.createLiteral("Leslie", XMLSchema.
            STRING));

            RepositoryResult<Statement> statements = conn.getStatements(null,
            null, null, true);

            Model model = Iterations.addAll(statements, new LinkedHashModel());
            model.setNamespace("rdf", RDF.NAMESPACE);
            model.setNamespace("rdfs", RDFS.NAMESPACE);
            model.setNamespace("xsd", XMLSchema.NAMESPACE);
            model.setNamespace("foaf", FOAF.NAMESPACE);
            model.setNamespace("ex", namespace);

            Rio.write(model,  System.out, RDFFormat.TURTLE);
            }
            finally {
                conn.close();
            }

    }

}
```

Finally, you can run the application. The data stored in and retrieved from the repository is displayed on the Console (see Figure 4-16).

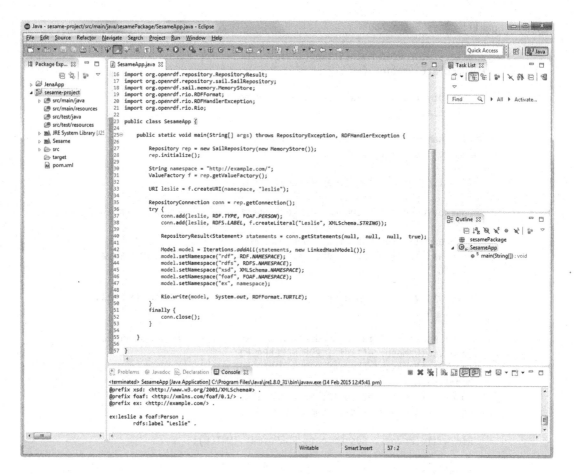

Figure 4-16. *Using Sesame to store and retrieve RDF triples*

NetBeans

NetBeans is another popular Integrated Development Environment for Java [25].
NetBeans is powered by Apache Ant and supports Apache Maven, refactoring, version control, etc. All the functions of the IDE are provided through modules.

Setup Apache Jena in NetBeans

Integrating Apache Jena in NetBeans is similar to the installation we discussed for Eclipse.

1. Go to `http://jena.apache.org/download/`, select a download mirror, and download the binary distribution suitable for your platform (`.zip` or `.tar.gz`).

2. Extract the Jena files from the archive.

3. In NetBeans, select File ➤ New Project ➤ JavaWeb.

4. Give a name to the project and select servers.

5. Select File ➤ Project Properties.

6. Select the Libraries category and select Add JAR/Folder.

7.   Select the required files.

8.   When the files are listed, verify and click OK.

To use Jena in your project, you have to import the required packages, as discussed in the previous sections. If you use Apache Maven integration in NetBeans, you can also start a Jena project as follows:

1.   Select File ➤ New Project ➤ Maven ➤ Java Application.

2.   Add a name to the project and additional information, such as location, then click Finish.

3.   Once NetBeans has created a new Maven project and opened it, right-click Dependencies and choose Add Dependency….

4.   Declare the Group ID, such as `org.apache.jena`, the Artifact ID, such as `jena-core`, and the version of your Jena integration.

5.   Open the `Dependencies` directory and check the dependencies.

■ **Note**   The download of declared dependencies can be forced by right-clicking Dependencies and choosing Download Declared Dependencies.

CubicWeb

CubicWeb is an object-oriented Semantic Web application framework written in Python [26]. It supports RDF and OWL, features semiautomatic XHTML/XML/JSON/text generation, and a proprietary query language similar to SPARQL. CubicWeb supports SQL databases and LDAP directories. The rapid application development is powered by a library of reusable components called "cubes," including a data model and views for common tasks. For example, the `file` cube contains the `file` entity type, gallery view functionality, and a file import utility. If you build a blog application, you create a new cube, such as `mycube`, and reuse the blog cube (see Figure 4-17).

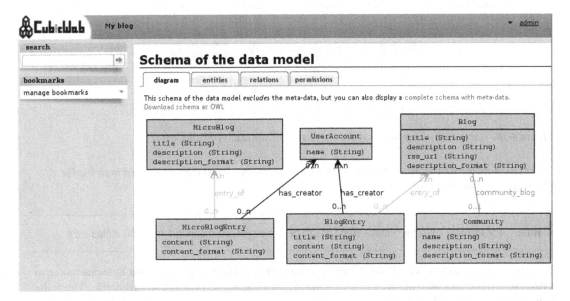

Figure 4-17.   Visualization of the data model in CubicWeb

When you develop a new web application, you create a new cube, select building blocks from existing cubes, create class definitions in your cube's schema, and create instances. The cubes have a standard folder structure to store the Python scripts, style sheets, JavaScript files, and translation files.

Linked Data Software

Sindice

Sindice is one of the most popular Linked Data platforms. Sindice collects, processes and integrates Linked Data from RDF, RDFa, Microformats, and HTML5 Microdata [27]. One of Sindice's components is the *Sindice Web Data Inspector* at `http://inspector.sindice.com`, which is a comprehensive semantic data extractor tool. The tool can be used to extract RDF triples from markup, RDF/XML, Turtle, or N3 documents provided either by URI or by direct input. Sindice Web Data Inspector can be used for retrieving semantic data (Inspect button), combined semantic data extraction and validation (Inspect + Validate button), or ontology analysis and reasoning (see Figure 4-18).

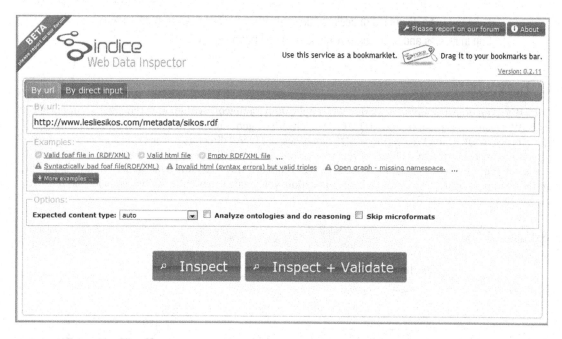

Figure 4-18. *Comprehensive options on the start screen of Sindice Web Data Inspector*

As a result, the tool provides the full list of subject-predicate-object triples retrieved from the file. The output format can also be changed to N-triples or RDF/XML.

■ **Note**   For usability reasons, Sindice Web Data Inspector displays a maximum of 1,000 triples only.

The "Sigma" option is a really good demonstration of machine-readable metadata. Software tools can extract structured data from properly written semantic documents and display them arbitrarily. This is the true essence of the Semantic Web !

A useful feature of Sindice Web Data Inspector is that a scalable graph can be generated from your semantic document. The graph not only presents the triples but also provides a quick summary of the ontologies and vocabularies used in the file.

The Sindice Web Data Inspector also has a validation feature with two different options. The first one, called "RDF syntax validation ," performs an RDF syntax validation according to the W3C specification. The second option is the "Pedantic validator ," which is a validation over the extracted triples. In case of a valid document, both validators give the result "Valid document."

Apache Marmotta

Apache *Marmotta* is a Linked Data server, SPARQL server, and Linked Data development environment [28]. Marmotta provides a Linked Data Platform (LDP) for human-readable and machine-readable read-write data access via HTTP content negotiation.

Marmotta features modules and libraries for LD application development. The modular server architecture makes it possible to implement the required functionalities only. For instance, if you don't need reasoning for your project, you can exclude the reasoner module. Marmotta provides a collection of Linked Data libraries for common LD tasks such as access to LD resources and query Linked Data (through LDPath, a simple LD query language). The triplestore is segregated from the server, so it can be used independently. The Apache Marmotta platform is implemented as a Java web application and deployed as a `.war` file. It is a service-oriented architecture using Contexts and Dependency Injection (CDI), a set of services of Java web application development. The *Marmotta Core*, a fundamental component of Apache Marmotta, provides Linked Data access, RDF import and export functionality, and an admin interface. Marmotta Core unites the service and dependency injection, the triplestore, the system configuration, and logging.

As a SPARQL server, Marmotta provides a public SPARQL 1.1 query and update endpoint and full support for SPARQL 1.1 through HTTP Web services. Marmotta features a fast, native SPARQL implementation in KiWi triplestore, a high-performance, highly scalable transactional triplestore back end for OpenRDF Sesame building on top of a relational database such as MySQL, PostgreSQL, or H2. To make SPARQL queries easier, Apache Marmotta provides Squebi, a lightweight user interface. Beyond KiWi, Marmotta's default triplestore back end, you can also choose Sesame Native (based on Sesame Native RDF back end), BigData (based on the BigData clustered triplestore), or Titan (based on the Titan graph database). *Marmotta Reasoner*, an optional module, is a rule-based reasoner for the KiWi triplestore. It implements datalog-style rules over RDF triples. The *Marmotta Loader* is a command-line tool for loading RDF data in various formats to different triplestores. It supports RDF serializations and can also import directories, split-files, gzip and bzip2 compressed files, as well as Tar and Zip archives.

The Marmotta software libraries can be used not only as components of the Marmotta platform but also as stand-alone lightweight Java libraries. The Apache *Marmotta LDClient* library is a flexible and modular RDFizer suitable for Linked Data projects to retrieve remote Linked Data resources via different protocols and data providers [29]. The modules of Marmotta support RDF/XML, Turtle, N3, JSON-LD, RDFa, XML, HTML, and can process Freebase, Facebook, YouTube, Vimeo, and MediaWiki contents. The software library is extensible through Java's `ServiceLoader` class, enabling custom wrappers for legacy data sources such as RDF, RDFa, Facebook, YouTube, and Wikipedia, as well as base classes for mapping other formats such as XML and JSON. *Marmotta LDCache*, another library, can access remote Linked Data resources as if they were local. It supports wrapping for legacy data sources such as Facebook Graph. LDCache features a local triplecache. Another optional library is *Marmotta LDPath*, a query language less expressive than SPARQL but specifically designed for querying Linked Data in the cloud. LDPath features a path-based navigation, which starts at the resource and follows the links.

■ **Note**   If you use SPARQL queries, LDPath is recommended over LDCache.

LDPath includes a large function library that can be integrated in your own applications. LDPath can be used with LDCache and LDClient and supports back ends such as Jena and Sesame.

sameAs.org

Because interlinking is fundamental in the Linked Open Data cloud, you will often define resources that describe the same object you express in RDF. For example, you refer to the machine-readable definition of your city of residence, pointing to its resource page on DBpedia, GeoNames, and Freebase. Because finding equivalent resource pages can be time-consuming, you might find the tool at `www.sameas.org`, which finds equivalent resource pages across different datasets, useful (see Figure 4-19).

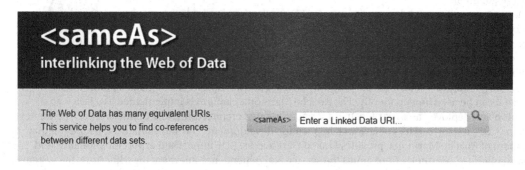

Figure 4-19. sameAs finds equivalent resource definitions from different LOD datasets

Callimachus

Callimachus[4] is an integrated Linked Data application development environment for graph storage, visualization, RDFa templating, data processing with XSLT and XProc, SPARQL querying, and Linked Open Data publishing [30]. It is suitable for standardizing metadata and combining data from different systems and combining enterprise data with open data from the Web.

Callimachus extends the RDFa syntax by allowing variables as well as URIs to be used in attributes. Callimachus further extends the RDFa syntax by introducing expressions that allow values to be substituted within attribute values or within text nodes. Callimachus converts the attributes into graph patterns. Blank nodes and empty property contents are treated as wildcards. Graph patterns with wildcards or variables partners are optionally joined in the result.

Neologism

Neologism is a free and open source vocabulary publishing platform [31]. It is distributed as a Drupal plug-in and supports RDF and RDFS and partially supports OWL. Neologism can import offline and online files written in RDF/XML, RDFa, Turtle, or OWL (see Figure 4-20). The form fields of Neologism feature client-side validation for correct input. Neologism displays relationships between terms in both directions. You can add arbitrary triples in Turtle to any vocabulary's RDF output.

---

[4]Named after Callimachus (310/305?–240 BC), the "Father of Bibliography," who worked at the ancient Great Library of Alexandria.

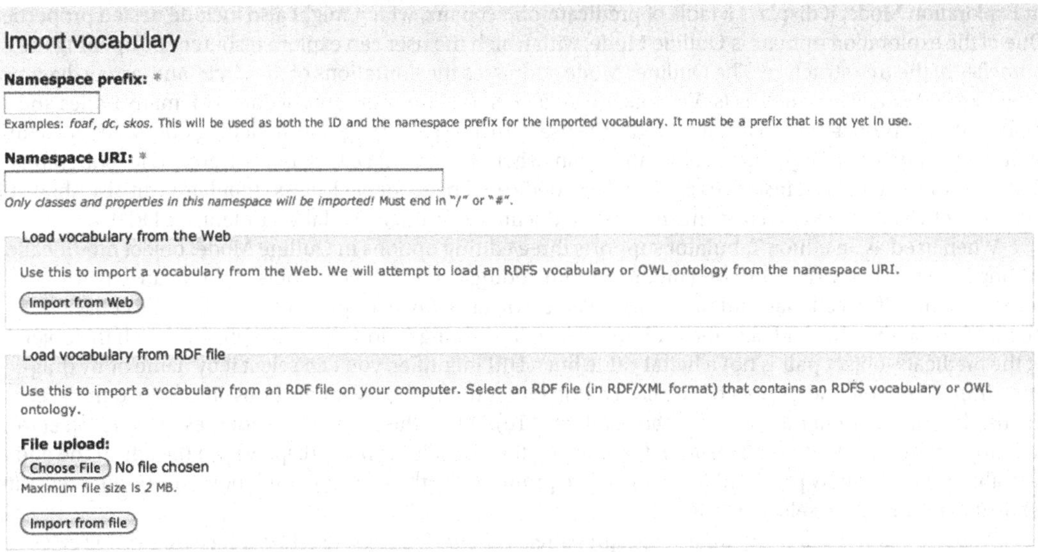

Import vocabulary

Namespace prefix: *

Examples: *foaf, dc, skos*. This will be used as both the ID and the namespace prefix for the imported vocabulary. It must be a prefix that is not yet in use.

Namespace URI: *

Only classes and properties in this namespace will be imported! Must end in "/" or "#".

Load vocabulary from the Web

Use this to import a vocabulary from the Web. We will attempt to load an RDFS vocabulary or OWL ontology from the namespace URI.

(Import from Web)

Load vocabulary from RDF file

Use this to import a vocabulary from an RDF file on your computer. Select an RDF file (in RDF/XML format) that contains an RDFS vocabulary or OWL ontology.

File upload:
(Choose File) No file chosen
Maximum file size is 2 MB.

(Import from file)

Figure 4-20. *Neologism can import vocabulary and ontology files written in any of the mainstream RDF serializations*

LODStats

LODStats is an extensible framework written in Python for high-performance dataset analytics [32]. It gathers statistical dataset characteristics such as class usage count, class hierarchy depth, property hierarchy depth, distinct entities, and so on. LODStates is so powerful that its developers integrated the framework with CKAN, the LOD cloud metadata registry to generate timely and comprehensive statistics about the LOD cloud.

Semantic Web Browsers

Semantic Web browsers are browsing tools for exploring and visualizing RDF datasets enhanced with Linked Data such as machine-readable definitions from DBpedia or geospatial information from GeoData. Semantic Web browsers provide exploration, navigation, and interactivity features different from conventional web browsers. They display not only human-readable but also machine-readable annotations and extracted RDF triples. While conventional browsers use hyperlinks for navigating between documents, Semantic Web browsers provide mechanisms for forward and backward navigation with typed links. Semantic Web browsers support *facet-based* (*faceted*) *browsing* by processing the list of discrete filter attributes called *facets*, gradually refining the search on a collection of information and visualizing the result (such as generating a map from geospatial data). Semantic Web browsers also support *pivoting* (rotation), the dimensional orientation of data. For example, pivoting the initially aggregated Book, Publisher, and Date yields Publisher, Date, and Book. Semantic Web browsers can convert non-linked data to Linked Data and create links to related URIs. They provide text search or SPARQL queries, or both, and support the five-star data deployment scheme discussed in Chapter 3, for data consumption, generation, aggregation, augment, and reinterpretation.

Tabulator

Tabulator is W3C's Semantic Web browser and editor available as a web application and a Firefox plug-in at http://www.w3.org/2005/ajar/tab. It can display Linked Data in various visualization formats. Tabulator contains an RDF store written in JavaScript. The tool has two modes: Exploration Mode and Query Mode.

113

In Exploration Mode, it displays a table of predicate-object pairs, which might also include nested properties. One of the exploration options is Outline Mode, with which the user can explore resources by opening the branches of the tree structure. The Outliner Mode addresses the limitations of the circle-and-arrow diagrams used by RDF visualizers, such as IsaViz, that are inefficient for large amounts of data with many nodes and many different properties. In Outliner Mode, the user can also perform graph-matching queries by selecting a number of fields and pressing the Find All button, when the Linked Data graph is searched for subgraphs matching the given fields. Instances are listed of a dedicated pane for each class. Tabulator can also show the network activity involved in retrieving the opened document, human-readable content, and RDF.

When used as an editor, Tabulator supports three editing options in Outline Mode: object modification, adding a new object with an existing predicate, and adding a new predicate-object pair to an existing subject. To modify a cell that contains a literal value, you click once (or press Enter) when the cell is highlighted, so that the field becomes editable. Once the editing is done, you just press Enter. If the object of the predicate-object pair is not a literal value but a URI identifier, you can select it by name or by drag-and-drop. Tabulator always tries to display a name rather than a URI whenever possible (for example, a textual description rather than rdfs:label or dc:title). When the predicate is not present, a new fact to the property or object table can be added by clicking the blue plus symbol displayed to the left, at the end of the table. When the new pair is added, you will be prompted with an auto-completion box for the predicate, while the object can be selected as usual.

When you perform a query for a subgraph pattern, a table is generated. Inserting a new row creates a new subgraph that matches the query. When a cell value is edited, a statement is removed and another inserted in the same document.

Marbles

Marbles is a server-side application and linked data engine for semantic data retrieval and storage. As a Semantic Web browser, it displays colored "marbles" to indicate the relationship between data origin and data sources. Marbles can also be used as a SPARQL endpoint that supports SELECT, CONSTRUCT, and DESCRIBE queries. Once you download the .war file from http://sourceforge.net/projects/marbles/files/, you can place it into a J2EE web container such as Tomcat to install Marbles automatically. For manual installation, invoke the ant install and remove tasks on the source distribution, then invoke the servlet at the directory root. Among others, Marbles is implemented in DBpedia Mobile.

OpenLink Data Explorer (ODE)

OpenLink Data Explorer (ODE, originally OpenLink RDF Browser) is a browser extension to exploit structured data. ODE adds two options to the standard View menu, both in the main menu and the context menu (see Figure 4-21).

The Data Explorer is available for Internet Explorer, Firefox, Safari, Google Chrome, and Opera (http://ode.openlinksw.com/#Download). Let's install the add-on, say, for Firefox!

1. Go to http://s3.amazonaws.com/opldownload/ajax-tools/ode/1.1/firefox3.0/ode.xpi.

2. Depending on your security settings, Firefox might prevent automatic installation. Click Allow to download the add-on.

3. The Software Installation pop-up asks for permission to proceed ("Install add-ons from authors whom you trust.") Click Install Now.

4. Restart Firefox.

Figure 4-21. *ODE options in the context menu*

Once installed, the plug-in becomes available from the View menu as well as the context menu. The View Entity Description option gives a structured description of the current page. View Data Sources provides raw data display options for the structured data retrieved from the current page (see Figure 4-22).

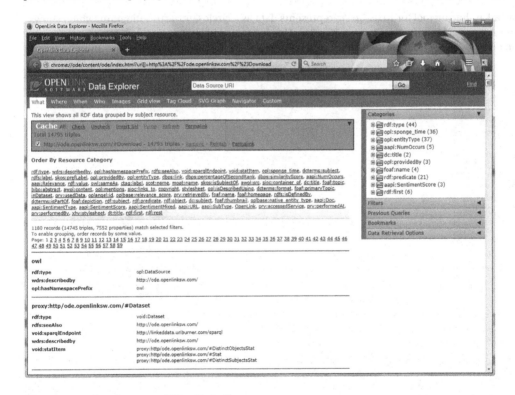

Figure 4-22. *Result screen of View Data Sources*

The settings of the plug-in are available via Tools ➤ OpenLink Data Explorer ➤ Options. First, you can select the viewer. The default one is OpenLink Data Explorer, but you can also choose Zitgist Data Viewer, Marbles, DISCO, Tabulator, or a custom viewer. For Linked Data access, there is an RDFizer service, a SPARQL Endpoint, and you can also define HTTP headers. The default host for RDFizer and the SPARQL endpoint is linkeddata.uriburner.com, which can be modified arbitrarily. The RDFizer is Virtuoso Sponger (http://virtuoso.openlinksw.com/dataspace/doc/dav/wiki/Main/VirtSponger), a component of Virtuoso's SPARQL Processor and Proxy Web Service. Sponger supports RDFa, GRDDL, Amazon Web Services, eBay Web Services, Freebase Web Services, Facebook Web Services, Yahoo! Finance, XBRL Instance documents, Document Object Identifiers (DOI), RSS and Atom feeds, ID3 tags of MP3 music files, vCard, Microformats, Flickr, and Del.icio.us contents.

OpenLink Data Explorer handles RDF, Turtle, and Notation3 MIME data. The default viewer for MIME data is Virtuoso Describe, but you can also choose Virtuoso About or Virtuoso ODE with or without SSL.

DBpedia Mobile

DBpedia Mobile is a location-aware DBpedia client application for mobile devices, providing a map view and a GPS-enabled launcher application [33]. Based on the GPS position of your mobile device, DBpedia Mobile displays a map that contains information about nearby locations extracted from the DBpedia dataset. Approximately 300,000 geographical locations are covered. DBpedia Mobile is powered by the rendering engine and SPARQL capabilities of the Marbles Linked Data Browser. Once the map is rendered, you can browse additional information about the location and go directly to DBpedia, GeoNames, Flickr, and other datasets.

IsaViz

Being a visual authoring tool for RDF, *IsaViz* represents data as a circle-and-arrow diagram, which shows "things" related to each other (see Figure 4-23) [34]. This is useful when analyzing data structures. On an IsaViz diagram you can see clustering when a large number of "things" are related by the same properties.

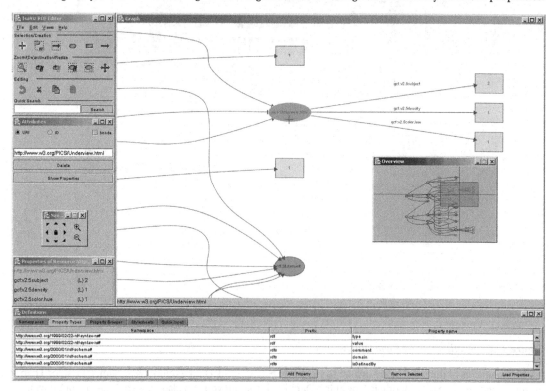

Figure 4-23. *An RDF graph in IsaViz*

RelFinder

RelFinder (Relationship Finder) can be used to visualize, filter, and analyze large amounts of relationships between objects. It is suitable for knowledge representation and knowledge discovery. RelFinder provides standard SPARQL access to datasets. The online version is available at `http://www.visualdataweb.org/relfinder/relfinder.php`, which can generate a directed graph based on the selected objects and their relationships (see Figure 4-24).

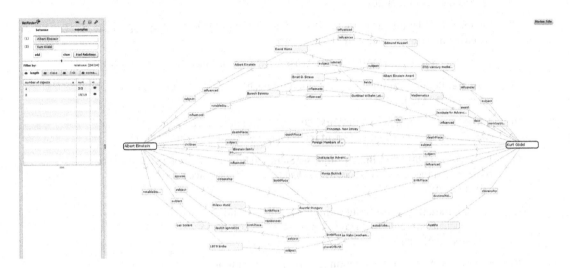

Figure 4-24. *Visualizing connections with RelFinder*

Summary

In this chapter, you became familiar with frequently used software tools that can generate, store, extract, and visualize RDF data. You learned how to generate RDFa annotation for your web site and test RDFa and Microdata annotations with Google Structured Data Testing Tool. You saw how to set up Integrated Development Environments to use software libraries for writing Semantic Web applications and examples for storing RDF data in, and retrieving RDF data from, repositories. You know the most popular Linked Data platforms to import, edit, and serialize datasets.

The next chapter will introduce you to Semantic Web service standards, including protocols, interfaces, and languages used by services such as location-aware applications and semantic e-commerce portals.

References

1. Ho, D. et al. (2014) Notepad++. Don Ho. `http://notepad-plus-plus.org`. Accessed 31 March 2015.

2. Sessink, O. (2014) BlueFish. The Bluefish Project Team. `http://bluefish.openoffice.nl/`. Accessed 4 November 2014.

3. ActiveState Software (2014) Komodo. ActiveState Software. `www.activestate.com/komodo-ide`. Accessed 4 November 2014.

4.   Bare Bones Software (2014) BBEdit. Bare Bones Software, Inc. www.barebones.com/products/bbedit/. Accessed 4 November 2014.

5.   Bare Bones Software (2014) TextWrangler. Bare Bones Software, Inc. www.barebones.com/products/textwrangler/index.html. Accessed 4 November 2014

6.   Lutus, P. (2014) Arachnophilia. www.arachnoid.com/arachnophilia/. Accessed 4 November 2014.

7.   GitHub (2015) DBpedia Spotlight. https://github.com/dbpedia-spotlight/dbpedia-spotlight. Accessed 31 March 2015.

8.   The GATE project team (2015) GATE. https://gate.ac.uk. Accessed 31 March 2015.

9.   The OpenRefine community (2015) OpenRefine. http://openrefine.org. Accessed 31 March 2015.

10.   Altova (2012) Altova SemanticWorks 2012 User and Reference Manual. www.altova.com/documents/SemanticWorks.pdf. Accessed 31 March 2015.

11.   TopQuadrant (2015) TopBraid Composer Standard Edition. www.topquadrant.com/tools/modeling-topbraid-composer-standard-edition/. Accessed 31 March 2015.

12.   TopQuadrant (2015) TopBraid Composer Maestro Edition. www.topquadrant.com/tools/ide-topbraid-composer-maestro-edition/. Accessed 31 March 2015.

13.   The Apache Software Foundation (2015) Apache Stanbol. http://stanbol.apache.org. Accessed 31 March 2015.

14.   Fluent Editor. www.cognitum.eu/semantics/FluentEditor/. Accessed 15 April 2015.

15.   The European Bioinformatics Institute (2015) ZOOMA. www.ebi.ac.uk/fgpt/zooma/. Accessed 31 March 2015.

16.   Harispe, S. (2014) Semantic Measures Library & ToolKit. www.semantic-measures-library.org. Accessed 29 March 2015.

17.   Motik, B., Shearer, R., Glimm, B., Stoilos, G., Horrocks, I. (2013) HermiT OWL Reasoner. http://hermit-reasoner.com. Accessed 31 March 2015.

18.   Clark & Parsia (2015) Pellet: OWL 2 Reasoner for Java. http://clarkparsia.com/pellet/. Accessed 31 March 2015.

19.   Tsarkov, D., Horrocks, I. (2007) FaCT++. http://owl.man.ac.uk/factplusplus/. Accessed 31 March 2015.

20.   University of Luebec (2015) Racer. www.ifis.uni-luebeck.de/index.php?id=385. Accessed 31 March 2015.

21.   The Apache Software Foundation (2015) Apache Jena. http://jena.apache.org. Accessed 31 March 2015.

22.   The Apache Software Foundation (2015) Apache Jena Fuseki. http://jena.apache.org/documentation/fuseki2/. Accessed 31 March 2015.

23. Broekstra, J., Ansell, P., Visser, D., Leigh, J., Kampman, A., Schwarte, A. et al. (2015) Sesame. http://rdf4j.org. Accessed 31 March 2015.

24. The Eclipse Foundation (2015) Eclipse. www.eclipse.org. Accessed 31 March 2015.

25. Oracle Corporation (2015) NetBeans IDE. https://netbeans.org. Accessed 31 March 2015.

26. Logilab (2015) CubicWeb Semantic Web Framework. www.cubicweb.org. Accessed 31 March 2015.

27. Digital Enterprise Research Institute (2015) Sindice—The Semantic Web index. http://sindice.com. Accessed 31 March 2015.

28. The Apache Software Foundation (2015) Apache Marmotta. http://marmotta.apache.org. Accessed 31 March 2015.

29. The Apache Software Foundation (2015) http://marmotta.apache.org/ldclient/. Accessed 31 March 2015.

30. 3 Round Stones (2015) Callimachus—Data-driven applications made easy. http://callimachusproject.org. Accessed 31 March 2015.

31. National University of Ireland (2011) Neologism—Easy Vocabulary Publishing. http://neologism.deri.ie/. Accessed 31 March 2015.

32. Auer, S., Ermilov, I., Lehmann, J., Martin, M. (2015) LODStats. http://aksw.org/Projects/LODStats.html. Accessed 1 April 2015.

33. Bizer, C. (2008) DBpedia Mobile. http://wiki.dbpedia.org/DBpediaMobile. Accessed 31 March 2015.

34. Pietriga, E. (2007) IsaViz: A Visual Authoring Tool for RDF. www.w3.org/2001/11/IsaViz/. Accessed 31 March 2015.

CHAPTER 5

■ ■ ■

Semantic Web Services

In this service-oriented world, online services are important parts of web offerings. Online shopping, flight booking, hotel booking, navigation, public transport services, government services, community services, and media services are parts of our daily lives. However, the range of service offerings is widening. In the information technology (IT) industry, for example, there is also an endless variety of services. In the more and more popular cloud computing environments, the fundamental service models are Infrastructure as a Service (IaaS), such as Amazon EC2 and Google Cloud Storage; Platform as a Service (PaaS), such as WHM, Microsoft Azure, and the Google App Engine; and Software as a Service (SaaS), such as Hosted Exchange, GoogleApps, and NetSuite. Further services in the IT industry contain, but are not limited to, Database as a Service (DBaaS), Graph as a Service (GaaS), Storage as a Service (STaaS), Test Environment as a Service (TEaaS), API as a Service (APIaaS), Network as a Service (NaaS), and Unified Communications as a Service (UCaaS). Web services often have web sites that provide e-commerce, navigation with dynamic maps, remote control of a physical device, and so on. The mainstream XML-based standards for web service interoperability specify the syntax only, rather than the semantic meaning of messages. Semantic Web technologies can enhance service-oriented environments with well-defined, rich semantics. Semantic Web services leverage Semantic Web technologies to automate services and enable automatic service discovery, composition, and execution across heterogeneous users and domains.

Semantic Web Service Modeling

Web services are programs programmatically accessible over standard Internet protocols, using reusable components [1]. Web services are distributed and encapsulate discrete functionality. *Semantic Web Services* (*SWS*) make web service characteristics machine-interpretable via semantics. Semantic Web Services aim to combine web services and Semantic Web technologies with the aim of automating service-related tasks, such as discovery, composition, etc. [2]. Semantic Web Services can address some of the limitations of conventional web services, such as syntactic descriptions and the need for manual inspection of web service usability, usage, and integration. The life cycle of Semantic Web Services includes the service description or annotation, the advertisement, the discovery, the selection, the composition, and the execution of services, using four types of semantics: data semantics, functional semantics, Quality of Service (QoS) semantics, and execution semantics. The usage process of Semantic Web Services includes the following [3]:

- *Publication*: Making the description of service capability available

- *Discovery*: Locating different services suitable for a given task

- *Selection*: Choosing the most appropriate services among the available ones

- *Composition*: Combining services to achieve a goal

- *Mediation*: Solving data, protocol, and process mismatches

- *Execution*: Invoking services following programmatic conventions

Semantic Web Services have three different types of properties: functional, behavioral, and nonfunctional properties. *Functional properties* define the capabilities of a web service. *Behavioral properties* provide a way to achieve the required functionality through interaction with other services. *Nonfunctional properties* set the constraints over the functional and behavioral properties or add metadata about the service. For instance, assume we have a flight booking service wherein the functionality is the actual booking, which might be constrained by using a secure connection when security is a nonfunctional property. The communication and integration of service-based Semantic Web applications are provided by WSDL, an XML description language for web services, SOAP, an XML-based message format to exchange arbitrary XML data between services and clients, and UDDI, a data model and API for web service registries. In other words, the service consumer finds the service through the UDDI registry, which points to the WSDL description of the web service, as well as to the actual service, which communicates with the consumer using SOAP.

Typical Semantic Web services have three phases (publishing, searching, and binding), as well as three entities (the service requester, the service provider, and the service registry). For example, a service provider can publish the description of a service to the UDDI service registry in the form of an advertisement, which includes the profile of the service provider (company name and address), a service profile, such as service name and category, and the service interface definition URL (WSDL description).

Communication with XML Messages: SOAP

The *Simple Object Access Protocol* (*SOAP*) is a syntax for sending and receiving XML messages with web services. Each SOAP message contains a *SOAP envelope* that wraps the message, *a data encoding description*, and the *SOAP body* that contains the application-specific message for the back-end application (see Figure 5-1).

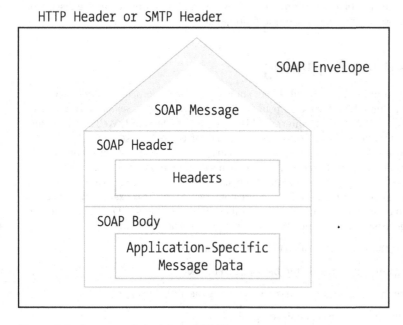

Figure 5-1. Structure of a web-based SOAP message

The root element of a SOAP message is the Envelope element, which is the container of the Header and Body elements (see Listing 5-1). The Body element can optionally contain a Fault element, which is used only if a fault occurs in the web service.

Listing 5-1. Structure of a SOAP Message

```
<?xml version="1.0"?>
<soap:Envelope xmlns:soap="http://www.w3.org/2001/12/soap-envelope">

  <soap:Header>
  </soap:Header>

  <soap:Body>

    <soap:Fault>
    </soap:Fault>

  </soap:Body>

</soap:Envelope>
```

The SOAP envelope always contains the namespace declaration pointing to http://www.w3.org/ 2001/12/soap-envelope. The Header element, an optional child element of the Envelope element, can provide information not directly related to the message itself, such as the maximum time requirement of the SOAP request. The Header element uses the same XML namespace as the Envelope element. The mustUnderstand Boolean attribute of the Header element can explicitly state (mustUnderstand="true") that the SOAP agent processing the message must "understand" the header block. If the header is not understood, a SOAP fault is returned. The role attribute can specify the SOAP message forwarder or processor.

■ **Note** SOAP supports predefined and custom roles that can be used in the Header element and the Fault element. SOAP messages are processed by three types of nodes: the sender, the forwarder (not always used, corresponds to the next role), and the last node that actually processes the SOAP message (corresponds to the ultimateReceiver role). The URI of the next role is http://www.w3.org/2003/05/soap-envelope/role/ next, while the URI of the ultimateReceiver role is http://www.w3.org/2003/05/soap-envelope/role/ ultimateReceiver.

The relay attribute determines whether a header block can be relayed if not processed.

The Body element, which is a mandatory element, contains the main part of the SOAP message to be processed by either the client or the web service, such as a service element and its parameters nested inside it. If you declare a Fault element within the Body element, it can perform actions if an error occurs when processing the SOAP message. The Fault element has two mandatory child elements (Code and Reason) and three optional child elements (Node, Role, and Detail) (see Listing 5-2).

Listing 5-2. SOAP Fault Structure

```
<env:Fault>
  <env:Code>
    <env:Value>env:Sender</env:Value>
    <env:Subcode>
        <env:Value>env:Sender</env:Value>
        <env:Subcode>
        </env:Subcode>
    </env:Subcode>
  </env:Code>
  <env:Reason>
   <env:Text>Incorrect Input Data</env:Text>
  </env:Reason>
  <env:Node>http://example.com/theNodeWhichFailed</env:Node>
  <env:Role>
    http://www.w3.org/2003/05/soap-envelope/role/ultimateReceiver
  </env:Role>
</env:Fault>
```

The Value element is a sub-element of the Code element. The Value element can have one of five values. The VersionMismatch attribute indicates that a root element was found in the SOAP message that was not a valid Envelope element. The MustUnderstand attribute value is returned if any header child element could not have been processed. If the encoding of the header element (the encodingStyle attribute value) cannot be processed, the fault to be returned is the value of the DataEncodingUnknown attribute. The Sender attribute value is used if the sender sent an incorrectly written SOAP message with missing or invalid data. The Receiver attribute value is returned if the receiver of the SOAP message failed to process the message, such as if the database the web service relies on is unavailable. If you need separate code blocks for error handling, you can optionally add the Subcode element to the Code element.

The Reason element contains one or more Text elements that provide the reason of the fault. The natural language of the description can be specified by the lang attribute on the Text element as an ISO language code. The optional Node element contains a URI that identifies the node where the fault has occurred. The Role element contains the role of the node in which the fault has occurred. The Detail element has child elements providing additional information about the fault that occurred. These child elements use your custom namespace.

Web Services Description Language (WSDL)

The *Web Service Description Language* (*WSDL*, pronounced "Wiz'-dul") is an XML-based interface definition language to describe the functionality of web services as collections of *network endpoints*, or *ports*, suitable for message exchange [4]. Ports are defined by associating a network address with a reusable binding, and the collections of ports define the *WSDL services*. The abstract, typed definitions of exchanged data form the *WSDL messages*. The collections of *operations* supported by one or more endpoints are the *port types*. The protocol and data format specifications provide a reusable *binding*, which is a concrete protocol and data format specification for a particular port type enabling WSDL to describe a public interface to web services. The file extension of WSDL files is .wsdl, while the Internet media type is application/wsdl+xml. A WSDL 2.0 file contains the following elements:

- The description element is the root element, which contains all other WSDL elements.

- The types element is the specification of the data types exchanged between the client and the web service described by default using XML Schema.

- The interface element enumerates the operations of the web service, the messages exchanged for each input and output operation, as well as the fault messages.

- The binding element describes how the web service is accessed over the network, usually binding the web service to the HTTP protocol.

- The service element declares where the web service can be accessed on the network, i.e., the URL of the service.

- The optional documentation element can contain a human-readable description of the web service.

- The optional import element can import XML Schemas or other WSDL files.

As a result, the skeleton WSDL document looks as shown in Listing 5-3.

Listing 5-3. Skeleton WSDL Document

```
<description>
  <types>
  </types>
  <interface>
  </interface>
  <binding>
  </binding>
  <service>
  </service>
</description>
```

The first part of all WSDL files is the definition of the service or services within the description root element, which also includes the standard namespace declarations, as well as the targetNamespace, the logical namespace for information about the service (see Listing 5-4).

Listing 5-4. XML Prolog and Namespace Declarations in WSDL

```
<?xml version="1.0" encoding="UTF-8"?>
<description ↵
 xmlns="http://www.w3.org/ns/wsdl" ↵
 xmlns:tns="http://www.example.com/wsdl" ↵
 xmlns:whttp="http://www.w3.org/ns/wsdl/http" ↵
 xmlns:wsoap="http://www.w3.org/ns/wsdl/soap" ↵
 targetNamespace="http://www.example.com/wsdl">
```

The xmlns attribute sets the default namespace of the description element to the standard WSDL namespace, http://www.w3.org/ns/wsdl. The default namespace is applied to all elements throughout the WSDL document that do not explicitly declare another namespace. The xmlns:tns attribute declares a namespace URI identical to the value of the targetNamespace (the namespace of your web service this schema is intended to target), providing a mechanism to refer to the target namespace via this namespace prefix (tns). The xmlns:stns attribute can be used to declare the Schema Target Namespace URI, which is the URI of the namespace of the XML Schema used for the web service types on the types element. The xmlns:wsoap declares the WSDL SOAP URI used in the bindings element. The xmlns:soap can be used to point to the SOAP URI of the SOAP version used by the web service described by the WSDL document. The xmlns:wsdlx declares the WSDL Extensions URI.

Complex data types are required in WSDL documents, to define web service requests and responses (see Listing 5-5). A web service typically has an input type, an output type, and sometimes a fault type. If the web service has more than one operation, each operation might have its own input type, output type, and fault type. The data types can be declared in any language as long as it is supported by the API of your web service, but most commonly, they are specified using XML Schema. This document section can be omitted if you use simple data types only.

Listing 5-5. Abstract Types in WSDL

```
<types>
  <xs:schema xmlns="http://www.example.com/wsdl" ↵
   xmlns:xs="http://www.w3.org/2001/XMLSchema" ↵
   targetNamespace="http://www.example.com/wsdl">
    <xs:element name="request"> … </xs:element>
    <xs:element name="response"> … </xs:element>
  </xs:schema>
</types>
```

The operations supported by your web service can be described by the interface element (see Listing 5-6). Each operation represents an interaction between the client and the service. The client can only call one operation per request. The fault element defines a fault that can be sent back to the client, which can be used by multiple operations. The operation element describes a method or procedure.

Listing 5-6. Abstract Interfaces in WSDL

```
<interface name="Interface1">
  <fault name="Fault1" element="tns:response" />
  <operation name="Operation1" pattern="http://www.w3.org/ns/wsdl/in-out">
    <input messageLabel="Message1" element="tns:request" />
    <output messageLabel="Message2" element="tns:response" />
  </operation>
</interface>
```

The next part defines how the operation should be performed, by declaring protocol and data format specifications for the operations and messages. This is done by "binding" the web service to the protocol through which it is accessible, using the binding element. The value of the name attribute on the binding element is referenced by the service element (see Listing 5-7). The interface attribute refers to the name of the interface element defined in the same WSDL file (using the prefix of the same document's target namespace). The type attribute defines the message format, to which the interface is bound.

Listing 5-7. Binding over HTTP in WSDL

```
<binding name="HttpBinding" interface="tns:Interface1" ↵
 type="http://www.w3.org/ns/wsdl/http">
  <operation ref="tns:Operation1" whttp:method="GET" />
</binding>
```

SOAP bindings can be specified by the wsoap:protocol attribute (see Listing 5-8). The fault element, when present, declares a fault, which can be sent back by the web service through the binding. The fault is defined in the interface element the binding refers to. The ref attribute on the operation element declares an operation defined in the interface element the binding refers to. The wsoap:mepDefault attribute specifies SOAP's default Message Exchange Pattern (MEP).

Listing 5-8. Binding with SOAP in WSDL

```
<binding name="SoapBinding" interface="tns:Interface1" ↵
 type="http://www.w3.org/ns/wsdl/soap" ↵
 wsoap:protocol="http://www.w3.org/2003/05/soap/bindings/HTTP/" ↵
 wsoap:mepDefault="http://www.w3.org/2003/05/soap/mep/request-response">
<operation ref="tns:Operation1" />
</binding>
```

The last part specifies the port address or addresses of the binding. The service element is the container of the network endpoints, or ports, through which the web service can be reached (see Listing 5-9).

Listing 5-9. Offering Endpoints for Both Bindings

```
  <service name="Service1" interface="tns:Interface1">
    <endpoint name="HttpEndpoint" binding="tns:HttpBinding" ↵
    address="http://www.example.com/rest/"/>
    <endpoint name="SoapEndpoint" binding="tns:SoapBinding" ↵
    address="http://www.example.com/soap/"/>
  </service>
</description>
```

The name attribute on the service element describes the name of the web service. The interface attribute specifies the interface element, to which the service is related. The address attribute of the endpoint element declares the web address of the service.

Semantic Annotations for WSDL (SAWSDL)

Semantic Annotations for Web Service Description Language (*SAWSDL*) is a standard to specify how web service data bindings can be mapped to formal models [5]. SAWSDL offers a repeatable way to connect RDF or OWL to Semantic Web Services with fixed data bindings, making it easier to programmatically find service data that meets application needs. The description of additional semantics for WSDL components is provided by SAWSDL through a set of extension attributes for the Web Services Description Language and XML Schema definition language. The namespace prefixes for SAWSDL are sawsdl, pointing to www.w3.org/ns/sawsdl, and sawsdlrdf, which refers to www.w3.org/ns/sawsdl#.

The interfaces in WSDL documents can be annotated using modelReference, which provides a reference to a concept or concepts in a semantic model that describe the WSDL interface (see Listing 5-10).

Listing 5-10. SAWSDL Model Reference for a WSDL Interface

```
<wsdl:interface name="Order" sawsdl:modelReference="http://yourbookshop.com/textbooks">
  …
</wsdl:interface>
```

WSDL operations can also be annotated using modelReference, referring to a concept in a semantic model to provide a high-level description of the operation, by specifying behavioral aspects or further semantic definitions for the operation (see Listing 5-11).

Listing 5-11. SAWSDL Model Reference for a WSDL Operation

```
<wsdl:operation name="order" pattern="http://www.w3.org/ns/wsdl/in-out"↵
  sawsdl:modelReference="http://www.example.com/purchaseorder#RequestPurchaseOrder">
  <wsdl:input element="OrderRequest" />
  <wsdl:output element="OrderResponse" />
</wsdl:operation>
```

Another example for the implementation of SAWSDL's model reference is fault annotation pointing to a high-level description of the fault, which may include further semantic annotations as well (see Listing 5-12).

Listing 5-12. SAWSDL Model Reference for a WSDL Fault

```
<wsdl:interface name="Order">
  <wsdl:fault name="ItemUnavailableFault" element="AvailabilityInformation" ↵
    sawsdl:modelReference="http://www.example.com/purchaseorder#ItemUnavailable" />
  ...
</wsdl:interface>
```

Assume we have an online shop with a Semantic Web Service interface. The WSDL description of the service can be annotated with SAWSDL, as shown in Listing 5-13.

Listing 5-13. SAWSDL Annotations in the WSDL File of a Semantic Web Service

```
<wsdl:description↵
  targetNamespace="http://www.example.com/wsdl/order#"↵
  xmlns="http://www.w3.org/2002/ws/sawsdl/spec/wsdl/order#"↵
  xmlns:wsdl="http://www.w3.org/ns/wsdl"↵
  xmlns:xs="http://www.w3.org/2001/XMLSchema"↵
  xmlns:sawsdl="http://www.w3.org/ns/sawsdl">
  <wsdl:types>
    <xs:schema targetNamespace="http://www.example.com/wsdl/order#"↵
      elementFormDefault="qualified">
      <xs:element name="OrderRequest" ↵
        sawsdl:modelReference="http://example.com/purchaseorder#OrderRequest"↵
        sawsdl:loweringSchemaMapping="http://www.example.com/mapping/lower.xml">
        <xs:complexType>
          <xs:sequence>
            <xs:element name="customerNo" type="xs:integer" />
            <xs:element name="orderItem" type="item" minOccurs="1" maxOccurs="unbounded" />
          </xs:sequence>
        </xs:complexType>
      </xs:element>
      <xs:complexType name="item">
        <xs:all>
          <xs:element name="UPC" type="xs:string" />
        </xs:all>
        <xs:attribute name="quantity" type="xs:integer" />
      </xs:complexType>
      <xs:element name="OrderResponse" type="confirmation" />
```

```
      <xs:simpleType name="confirmation" ↵
       sawsdl:modelReference="http://www.example.com/purchaseorder#OrderConfirmation">
        <xs:restriction base="xs:string">
          <xs:enumeration value="Confirmed" />
          <xs:enumeration value="Pending" />
          <xs:enumeration value="Rejected" />
        </xs:restriction>
      </xs:simpleType>
    </xs:schema>
  </wsdl:types>
  <wsdl:interface name="Order" sawsdl:modelReference="http://example.com/textbooks">
    <wsdl:operation name="order" pattern="http://www.w3.org/ns/wsdl/in-out"↵
     sawsdl:modelReference="http://www.example.com/purchaseorder#RequestPurchaseOrder">
      <wsdl:input element="OrderRequest" />
      <wsdl:output element="OrderResponse" />
    </wsdl:operation>
  </wsdl:interface>
</wsdl:description>
```

The loweringSchemaMapping on the OrderRequest element points to a mapping, which shows how the elements within the order request can be mapped from semantic data in the model to the actual execution format of the WS, for example, string or integer. In other words, loweringSchemaMapping lowers the data from the semantic model to XML. In contrast, LiftingSchemaMapping lifts data from XML to a semantic model.

XML Schema documents can be similarly annotated with SAWSDL.

Web Ontology Language for Services (OWL-S)

As an extension of the Web Ontology Language (OWL), *Web Ontology Language for Services* (*OWL-S*) facilitates the automation of web service tasks, such as discovery, composition, interoperation, execution, and execution monitoring [6]. OWL-S focuses on web service capabilities as well as functional and nonfunctional properties. OWL-S represents web service behavior based on *situation calculus*, a formal logic for representing and reasoning dynamic domains expressed in second-order logic. As an upper ontology language, OWL-S is suitable for describing web services through a Service class. Each entity of the Service class is a ServiceProfile.

OWL-S organizes a service description into four conceptual areas: the service model, the profile, the grounding, and the service. The *process model* describes how a client can interact with the service, including the sets of inputs, outputs, preconditions, and service execution results. The *service profile* describes the tasks performed by the service as human-readable data, including service name, service description, implementation limitations, quality of service, publisher, and contact information. The *grounding* provides all the details required by the client to interact with the service, including communication protocols, message formats, and port numbers. For grounding, the most commonly used language is WSDL. Because OWL-S atomic processes correspond to WSDL operations, the inputs and outputs of OWL-S atomic processes correspond to WSDL messages, while the input and output types of OWL-S atomic processes correspond to WSDL abstract types. The *service* binds the other parts into a unit that can be searched, published, and invoked.

■ **Note**   The different parts of the service can be reused and connected in various ways. For instance, the service provider might connect the process model with several profiles, in order to provide customized advertisements to different markets.

Using OWL-S, software agents can *automatically discover web services* to fulfill a specific need with certain quality constraints. OWL-S also allows software agents to *automatically read the description of inputs and outputs of web services* and invoke the service. Furthermore, OWL enables *automatic execution of complex tasks* that involve the coordinated invocation of various web services, based exclusively on the high-level description of the objective.

The ServiceProfile superclass of OWL-S is suitable for the different high-level service descriptions. The basic information provided by ServiceProfile links a profile instance to a service instance. The presents property can be used to express the relation between a service instance and a profile instance. The presentedBy property expresses that a profile is related to a service.

The serviceName, textDescription, and contactInformation OWL-S properties provide descriptions primarily for human consumption. Only one value is allowed for the first two properties, while an arbitrary number of contact persons can be provided. The value of serviceName is the name of the service that can be used as a service identifier. The textDescription provides a short service description, covering the service offering, the service prerequisites, and additional information to be shared with the receivers. The contactInformation declares contact persons using widely deployed vocabularies, such as FOAF, vCard, or Schema.

The service functionality, required conditions, and the expected and unexpected results can be defined with OWL-S properties such as hasInput and hasOutput datatype properties and the hasPrecondition and hasResult object properties, all of which are subproperties of the hasParameter object property. Additional profile attributes, such as the guaranteed service quality, can be expressed by serviceParameter, an optional property list for the profile description. The value of the serviceParameter property is an instance of the ServiceParameter class.

The service category can be expressed using ServiceCategory, usually by referring to a definition in an external vocabulary. The categoryName property declares the name of the service category either as a string literal or the URI of the property used as a process parameter. The value of taxonomy defines the taxonomy scheme as the URI of the taxonomy. The value property explicitly refers to a taxonomy value. The property value of code is the code associated with a taxonomy. The serviceParameterName is the name of the parameter as a literal or URI. The sParameter points to the parameter value in an external ontology.

The serviceClassification and serviceProduct properties specify the provided service type and the products that are handled by the service. In other words, serviceClassification is a mapping between the service profile and a service ontology, while serviceProduct is a mapping between a service profile and a product ontology.

To represent services as processes, OWL-S 1.1 defines Process (a subclass of ServiceModel). The Parameter class has the Input and Output subclasses to describe process parameters (see Listing 5-14).

Listing 5-14. Input and Output Are Subclasses of Parameter

```
<owl:Class rdf:ID="Input">
  <rdfs:subClassOf rdf:resource="#Parameter" />
</owl:Class>

<owl:Class rdf:ID="Output">
  <rdfs:subClassOf rdf:resource="#Parameter" />
</owl:Class>
```

Process parameters are typically expressed as SWRL variables (see Listing 5-15), because SWRL is a language specifically designed for expressing OWL rules [7].

Listing 5-15. A Process Parameter as a SWRL Variable

```
<owl:Class rdf:about="#Parameter" rdf:ID="/parameterType/">
  <rdfs:subClassOf rdf:resource="&swrl;#Variable" />
</owl:Class>
```

Each parameter has a type with a URI value that specifies the type of a class or datatype (see Listing 5-16). The type can be used, for example, to evaluate a credit card number for an e-commerce service.

Listing 5-16. Parameter Type Specified by a URI

```
<owl:Class rdf:ID="Parameter">
  <rdfs:subClassOf>
    <owl:Restriction>
      <owl:onProperty rdf:resource="#parameterType" />
      <owl:minCardinality rdf:datatype="&xsd;#nonNegativeInteger">1</owl:minCardinality>
    </owl:Restriction>
  </rdfs:subClassOf>
</owl:Class>
```

A process has at least two agents, namely TheClient and TheServer. Further agents can be listed using the hasParticipant property (see Listing 5-17).

Listing 5-17. Process Agents in OWL-S

```
<owl:ObjectProperty rdf:ID="hasParticipant">
  <rdfs:domain rdf:resource="#Order" />
</owl:ObjectProperty>

<owl:ObjectProperty rdf:ID="hasClient">
  <rdfs:subPropertyOf rdf:resource="#hasContract" />
</owl:ObjectProperty>

<process:Parameter rdf:ID="TheClient">
<process:Parameter rdf:ID="TheServer">
```

If a process has a precondition, the process cannot be performed unless the precondition is true. Preconditions can be express in OWL-S, as shown in Listing 5-18.

Listing 5-18. Precondition Definition

```
<owl:ObjectProperty rdf:ID="hasPrecondition">
  <rdfs:domain rdf:resource="#Order" />
  <rdfs:range rdf:resource="#Payment" />
</owl:ObjectProperty>
```

Inputs and outputs specify the data transformation of the service process. The input specifies the information required for process execution, while the output provides the transformed data (see Listing 5-19).

Listing 5-19. The hasInput, hasOutput, and hasLocal Subproperties of hasParameter

```
<owl:ObjectProperty rdf:ID="hasParameter">
  <rdfs:domain rdf:resource="#Order" />
  <rdfs:range rdf:resource="#Status" />
</owl:ObjectProperty>

<owl:ObjectProperty rdf:ID="hasInput">
  <rdfs:subPropertyOf rdf:resource="#validCard" />
  <rdfs:range rdf:resource="#Input" />
</owl:ObjectProperty>
```

```
<owl:ObjectProperty rdf:ID="hasOutput">
  <rdfs:subPropertyOf rdf:resource="#orderPlaced" />
  <rdfs:range rdf:resource="#Ordering" />
</owl:ObjectProperty>

<owl:ObjectProperty rdf:ID="hasLocal">
  <rdfs:subPropertyOf rdf:resource="#ordered" />
  <rdfs:range rdf:resource="#Local" />
</owl:ObjectProperty>
```

The output and the state change (effect) together are called a result (see Listing 5-20).

Listing 5-20. A Result

```
<owl:Class rdf:ID="Result">
  <rdfs:label>Result</rdfs:label>
</owl:Class>

<owl:ObjectProperty rdf:ID="hasResult">
  <rdfs:label>hasResult</rdfs:label>
  <rdfs:domain rdf:resource="#Order" />
  <rdfs:range rdf:resource="#Ordering" />
</owl:ObjectProperty>
```

If a result is declared, the output and effect conditions can be expressed using the four ResultVar (scoped to a particular result) or Local variables (bound in preconditions and used in the result conditions): inCondition, withOutput, hasEffect, and hasResultVar (see Listing 5-21). The inCondition property specifies the condition under which the result occurs. The withOutput and hasEffect properties determine what happens when the declared condition is true. The hasResultVar property declares the variables bound in the inCondition property.

Listing 5-21. Output and Effect Conditions

```
<owl:ObjectProperty rdf:ID="inCondition">
  <rdfs:label>inCondition</rdfs:label>
  <rdfs:domain rdf:resource="#Order" />
  <rdfs:range rdf:resource="#Payment" />
</owl:ObjectProperty>

<owl:ObjectProperty rdf:ID="hasResultVar">
  <rdfs:label>hasResultVar</rdfs:label>
  <rdfs:domain rdf:resource="#Order" />
  <rdfs:range rdf:resource="#Ordering" />
</owl:ObjectProperty>

<owl:ObjectProperty rdf:ID="withOutput">
  <rdfs:label>withOutput</rdfs:label>
  <rdfs:domain rdf:resource="#Order" />
  <rdfs:range rdf:resource="#Output" />
</owl:ObjectProperty>

<owl:ObjectProperty rdf:ID="hasEffect">
  <rdfs:label>hasEffect</rdfs:label>
```

```
    <rdfs:domain rdf:resource="#Order" />
    <rdfs:range rdf:resource="#Ordering" />
</owl:ObjectProperty>
```

While OWL-S is suitable for its primary purpose by describing service offers and requirements, owing to its limited expressiveness, unrelated operations are not supported.

Web Service Modeling Ontology (WSMO)

The *Web Service Modeling Ontology* (*WSMO*, pronounced "Wizmo") is a conceptual model for Semantic Web Services, covering the core Semantic Web Service elements as an ontology using the WSML formal description language and the WSMX execution environment [8]. WSMO is derived from and based on the Web Service Modeling Framework (WSMF) [9]. WSMO enables partial or full automation of discovery, selection, composition, mediation, execution, and monitoring tasks involved in web services. The four main components of WSMO are the *goals*, the *mediators*, the *web service descriptions*, and the *ontologies* that are represented as top-level elements (see Figure 5-2).

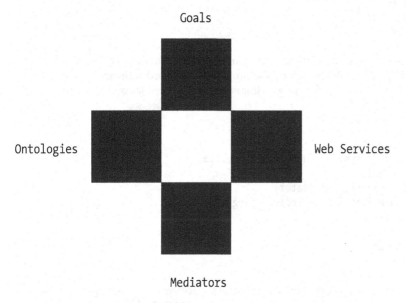

Figure 5-2. *Top-level WSMO elements*

Similar to OWL-S, WSMO also defines a mapping to WSDL, but with an ontology-based grounding, which prevents the loss of ontological descriptions throughout the service usage process. Whereas OWL-S does not have the concept of mediator, and mediation is a byproduct of orchestration or is derived from translation axioms, in WSMO, mediators are core conceptual elements.

WSMO has a goal-based approach to service description, which can be used when searching for services based on goals. The goals are the wishes of the client to be fulfilled by the service. Mediators are connectors between components that provide interoperability between different ontologies and resolve structural, semantic, and conceptual mismatches.

There are four types of WSMO mediators: mediators that link two goals, mediators that import ontologies and resolve possible representation mismatches between ontologies, mediators that link web services to goals, and mediators that link two web services. The Semantic Web Service descriptions can cover functional and usage descriptions. The functional descriptions describe the capabilities of the service, while the usage description describes the interface. The ontologies provide the formal description of the information used by all other components.

WSMO elements are described by nonfunctional properties, using the Dublin Core Metadata Set (Contributor, Coverage, Creator, Description, Format, Identifier, Language, Publisher, Relation, Rights, Source, Subject, Title, Type) for complete item description and resource management (see Listing 5-22).

Listing 5-22. Core WSMO Nonfunctional Properties Expressed Using Dublin Core in an Example Ontology

```
ontology <"http://www.example.com/holidayplanner">
  nonFunctionalProperties
    dc:title hasValue "Holiday Planner Example Ontology"
    dc:creator hasValue "Leslie Sikos"
    dc:subject hasValues {"Trip", "Itinerary", "Stop", "Ticket"}
    dc:description hasValue "Our Holiday Packages"
    dc:publisher hasValue "Leslie Sikos"
    dc:date hasValue "2015-02-21"
    dc:format hasValue "text/html"
  endNonFunctionalProperties
```

The service class can be used to describe services both from the client's and the service provider's point of view, featuring general metadata with nonfunctional properties, imported ontologies (if any), mediators, service capability, service interface, functions, axioms, and ontology instances (see Listing 5-23).

Listing 5-23. The Definition of the service Class

```
Class service
     hasNonFunctionalProperties type nonFunctionalProperties
     importsOntology type ontology
     usesMediator type {ooMediator, wwMediator}
     hasCapability type capability multiplicity = single-valued
     hasInterface type interface
     hasFunction type function
     hasInstance type instance
     hasAxiom type axiom
```

Nonfunctional properties can express much more than general service metadata, as they cover Quality of Service (QoS) information for availability and stability, such as Accuracy, NetworkRelatedQoS, Performance, Reliability, Robustness, Scalability, Security, Transactional, and Trust, as well as other financial, ownership, and versioning information (Financial, Owner, Version). For example, a service provider can describe student discounts or pensioner concession criteria using nonfunctional WSMO properties.

Beyond the nonfunctional properties, the ontology definitions can contain imported ontologies (importsOntology). To handle heterogeneities, you can define mediators using usesMediators (see Listing 5-24).

Listing 5-24. Defining a Mediator

```
usesMediators {<<http://www.example.com/externalMediator.wsml>>}
```

The entity sets of the knowledge domain of the ontology can be defined using concept. For a vacation booking service, for example, you have to define the concept of country and its properties, such as ISO country code (see Listing 5-25).

Listing 5-25. Defining Entity Sets for the Domain

```
concept country subConceptOf {cnt:country, geo:country}
  nonFunctionalProperties
    dc:description hasValue "Country Codes"
  endNonFunctionalProperties
  isoCode ofType xsd:string
  nonFunctionalProperties
    dc:description hasValue "ISO 3166 Country Code"
  endNonFunctionalProperties
```

The relationships between concepts can be defined using relation (see Listing 5-26).

Listing 5-26. Defining Relations between Concepts[10]

```
relation equalDistance
        nonFunctionalProperties
          dc:description hasValue "Computes equality of a distance"
        endNonFunctionalProperties
        d1 ofType distance
        d2 ofType distance
        definedBy
          forAll ?x,?y ( equalDistance[d1 hasValue ?x, d2 hasValue ?y] equivalent ↩
          kilometers(?x,?k1) and kilometers(?y,?k2) and ?k1=?k2).

relation lessThanDistance
        nonFunctionalProperties
          dc:description hasValue "Computes -less than- for a distance"
        endNonFunctionalProperties
        d1 ofType distance
        d2 ofType distance
        definedBy
          forAll ?x,?y ( equalDistance[d1 hasValue ?x, d2 hasValue ?y] equivalent ↩
          kilometers(?x,?k1) and kilometers(?y,?k2) and ?k1<?k2).

relation moreThanDistance
        nonFunctionalProperties
          dc:description hasValue "Computes -more than- for a distance"
        endNonFunctionalProperties
        d1 ofType distance
        d2 ofType distance
        definedBy
          forAll ?x,?y ( equalDistance[d1 hasValue ?x, d2 hasValue ?y] equivalent ↩
          kilometers(?x,?k1) and kilometers(?y,?k2) and ?k1>?k2).
```

Algorithms can be added to your WSMO ontology by defining functions. For instance, if your vacation booking service supports distances expressed in kilometers and miles, you can write functions to convert distances from one unit to the other (see Listing 5-27).

135

Listing 5-27. Defining Functions in WSMO[10]

```
function kilometers
        nonFunctionalProperties
          dc:description hasValue "Expressing a distance in kilometers"
        endNonFunctionalProperties
        d ofType distance
        range ofType xsd:float
        definedBy
          forAll ?x,?y (kilometers[d hasValue ?d, result hasValue ?y] equivalent ↵
            ?d[amount hasValue ?a, units hasValue ?u] and ((?u="Kilometers" and ?y=?a) or ↵
            (?a="Miles" and ?y=?a*1.609344))).

function miles
        nonFunctionalProperties
          dc:description hasValue "Expressing a distance in miles"
        endNonFunctionalProperties
        d ofType distance
        range ofType xsd:float
        definedBy
          forAll ?x,?y (miles[d hasValue ?d, result hasValue ?y] equivalent ↵
            ?d[amount hasValue ?a, units hasValue ?u] and ((?u="Miles" and ?y=?a) or ↵
            (?a="Kilometers" and ?y=?a/1.609344))).
```

Ontology instances can be defined using `instance`. In a flight booking service, for example, you can define destination countries offered by your service, as shown in Listing 5-28.

Listing 5-28. An Instance in a WSMO Ontology

```
instance Australia memberOf country
  isoCode hasValue "AU"^^xsd:string
```

Logical statements (axiomatic expressions) of an ontology can be defined by axiom (see Listing 5-29).

Listing 5-29. An Instance in a WSMO Ontology

```
axiom validDistance
      nonFunctionalProperties
        dc:description hasValue "The distance must be larger than 0km or 0m."
      endNonFunctionalProperties
      definedBy
        constraint
          ?D[amount hasValue ?A, units hasValue ?U] memberOf distance and ?A < 0 and not ↵
          (U="Kilometers" or U="Miles").
```

The functional capabilities of a service can be expressed using the `capability` class, which covers precondition, assumption, post-condition, and effect (state change) axioms, and variables shared among preconditions, post-conditions, assumptions, and effects (see Listing 5-30).

Listing 5-30. The Definition of the capability Class in WSMO

```
Class capability
      hasNonFunctionalProperties type nonFunctionalProperties
      importsOntology type ontology
      usesMediator type {ooMediator, wgMediator}
      hasSharedVariables type sharedVariables
      hasPrecondition type axiom
      hasAssumption type axiom
      hasPostcondition type axiom
      hasEffect type axiom
```

For example, if you use a government service to register pensioners, the effect of the service execution is that the user becomes a pensioner.

The *web service interface* describes operational competence of a web service using the interface class in two ways: through choreography and orchestration (see Listing 5-31). *Choreography* expresses web service capability from the interaction point of view, in other words, it models all service interactions, including the invariant elements of the state description (*state signature*), the *state* described by an instance set, and state changes (*guarded transitions*). *Orchestration* expresses web service capability from the functionality point of view.

Listing 5-31. Choreography and Orchestration Defined for the interface Class

```
Class interface
      hasNonFunctionalProperties type nonFunctionalProperties
      importsOntology type ontology
      usesMediator type ooMediator
      hasChoreography type choreography
      hasOrchestration type orchestration
```

The purpose of a web service can be expressed by the goal class (see Listing 5-32). For example, the goal of a service can be a user registration, a ticket purchase, or a room reservation.

Listing 5-32. The Definition of the goal Class in WSMO

```
Class goal sub-Class wsmoTopLevelElement
      importsOntology type ontology
      usesMediator type {ooMediator, ggMediator}
      requestsCapability type capability multiplicity = single-valued
      requestsInterface type interface
```

MicroWSMO and WSMO-Lite

MicroWSMO is an extension of hRESTS [11] designed for semantic annotations through SAWSDL extensions such as *model* (indicates that a link is a model reference) and *lifting* (lowering links to the respective data transformations) [12]. hRESTS provides a WSDL equivalent for RESTful services, making it possible to annotate the HTML markup of the service description. An example is shown in Listing 5-33.

Listing 5-33. Annotated Service Description

```
<div class="service">
  <p><span class="label">Dream Holidays</span> is a ↵
    <a rel="model" href="/BookingService/"> hotel room reservation</a> service.
  </p>
  <p class="operation" …>
  </p>
</div>
```

These annotations can be used by microWSMO to refer to elements of the same lightweight service modeling ontology as *WSMO-Lite*, which fills the annotations with concrete service semantics. WSMO-Lite is not bound to a particular service description format and allows the creation of matching stacks for SOAP and REST.

Web Service Modeling Language (WSML)

The *Web Service Modeling Language* (*WSML*) is a formal language for axiomatic expressions that provides the conceptual syntax and semantics for the elements of WSMO, the Web Service Modeling Ontology [13]. WSML can be used to formally describe WSMO elements as ontologies, Semantic Web services, goals, and mediators. WSML is based on mathematical logic, such as description logic and first-order logic, as well as logic programming.

WSML has two syntaxes: the *conceptual syntax* and the *logical expression syntax.* The conceptual syntax is used for the ontology, goal, web service, and mediator modeling. Logical expressions refine the ontology, goal, web service, and mediator definitions, using a logical language. The conceptual syntax has a frame-like style by which classes, relations, and instances, as well as their attributes, are specified in a single syntactic construct. However, attribute names are global in WSML. Argument lists are separated by commas and surrounded by curly brackets. Statements start with a keyword and can be spread over multiple lines. WSML implements the RDF namespace mechanism. The WSML keywords are defined at the namespace www.wsmo.org/wsml/wsml-syntax# and commonly abbreviated with the prefix wsml. WSML identifiers can be data values, Internationalized Resource Identifiers (IRIs, which are URIs that can contain Unicode characters such as Chinese ideographs, Japanese kanji, Cyrillic characters, etc.), or anonymous identifiers. The basic data types are string, integer, and decimal. Data values are based on the XML Schema datatypes but expressed with a different syntax (see Listing 5-34).

Listing 5-34. The Date "22 February 2015" in WSML

```
_date(2015,2,22)
```

There are three syntactical shortcuts for string, integer, and decimal data types. String data values can be written between double quotation marks (see Listing 5-35). Double quotation marks inside a string should be escaped using \.

Listing 5-35. A String in Double Quotation Marks

```
dc#title hasValue "Your Amigo"
```

Integer values can be written without declaring the number type. For example, 5 is a shortcut for _integer("5"). If a decimal symbol is present, the number is assumed to be a decimal number. For example, 22.5 is a shortcut for _decimal("22.5").

IRIs start with an underscore and are written in double quotes (see Listing 5-36).

Listing 5-36. A Full IRI in WSML

```
_"http://example.org/YourOntology#YourTerm"
```

IRIs can be abbreviated as a *serialized Qualified Name* (*sQName*), which combines the namespace prefix and the local entity name separated by #. In Listing 5-35, for example, dc#title corresponds to http://purl.org/dc/elements/1.1#title, foaf#name abbreviates http://xmlns.com/foaf/0.1/name, xsd#string refers to http://www.w3.org/2001/XMLSchema#string, and schema#Person corresponds to http://schema.org/Person. WSML defines two IRIs, one for universal truth (http://www.wsmo.org/wsml/wsml-syntax#true) and another one for universal falsehood (http://www.wsmo.org/wsml/wsml-syntax#false).

The third WSML identifier type, the anonymous identifier, represents a globally unique IRI.

The optional *namespace references* can be defined at the top of WSML documents, below the WSML variant identification. The namespace reference block is preceded by the namespace keyword. All namespace references, except for the default namespace, consist of the prefix and the IRI that identifies the namespace (see Listing 5-37).

Listing 5-37. Namespace Declarations in WSML

```
namespace {_"http://www.yourdefaultns.com/yourOntology/term#", ↵
  dc _"http://purl.org/dc/elements/1.1#", ↵
  foaf _"http://xmlns.com/foaf/0.1/", ↵
  xsd _"http://www.w3.org/2001/XMLSchema#", ↵
  wsml _"http://www.wsmo.org/wsml-syntax#"}
```

WSML headers might contain nonfunctional properties, may import ontologies, and may use mediators. Nonfunctional property blocks are delimited by the nonFunctionalProperties and endNonFunctionalProperties keywords that can be abbreviated as nfp and endnfp. The list of attribute values within the block contains the attribute identifier, the hasValue keyword, and the attribute value, which can be any kind of identifier (data value, IRI, anonymous identifier, or a comma-separated list). The Dublin Core properties are recommended for nonfunctional property definitions; however, terms of other external vocabularies are also allowed (see Listing 5-38).

Listing 5-38. A Nonfunctional Property Block in WSML

```
nonFunctionalProperties
  dc#title hasValue "WSML Example"
  dc#subject hasValue "training"
  dc#description hasValue "WSML non-functional property examples"
  dc#contributor hasValue {_"http://lesliesikos.com/datasets/sikos.rdf#sikos"}
  dc#date hasValue _date("2015-02-22")
  dc#format hasValue "text/html"
  dc#language hasValue "en-AU"
endNonFunctionalProperties
```

In the header, ontologies can optionally be imported using the importsOntology keyword, by declaring the namespace IRI (see Listing 5-39).

Listing 5-39. Importing Ontologies

```
importsOntology {_"http://purl.org/dc/elements/1.1#", _"http://schema.org/Person"}
```

Mediators can be optionally defined in the header with the usesMediator keyword to link different WSML elements (ontologies, goal, and web services) and resolve heterogeneities between the elements (see Listing 5-40).

Listing 5-40. Using a Mediator

```
usesMediator _"http://example.com/importMediator"
```

Web Services Business Process Execution Language (WS-BPEL)

Business processes require sophisticated exception management, enterprise collaboration, task sharing, and end-to-end control. The *Web Services Business Process Execution Language* (*WS-BPEL*), often abbreviated as *BPEL (Business Process Execution Language)*, is an XML-based standard language for specifying web service actions for business processes. BPEL is suitable for *Service-Oriented Architectures* (*SOA*), and is implemented by industry giants such as Oracle and based on earlier execution languages, such as IBM's Web Service Flow Language (WSFL) and Microsoft's XLang. The ten original design goals of BPEL are the following:

1. Define business processes that interact with external entities through web service operations and that manifest themselves as web services. Both the operations and the web services are defined using WSDL 1.1.

2. Define business processes based on an XML serialization. Do not define a graphical representation of processes or provide any particular design methodology for processes.

3. Define a set of web service orchestration concepts to be used by external (abstract) and internal (executable) views of a business process.

4. Provide hierarchical as well as graph-like controls.

5. Provide data manipulation functions for process data and control flow.

6. Support an identification mechanism for process instances that allows the definition of instance identifiers at the application message level.

7. Support the implicit creation and termination of process instances as the basic life cycle mechanism.

8. Define a long-running transaction model based on compensation actions and scoping to support failure recovery for parts of long-running business processes.

9. Use web services as the model for process decomposition and assembly.

10. Build on web services standards.

In order to define logic for service interactions, BPEL defines business process behavior through web service orchestration. BPEL processes transfer information using the web service interfaces. BPEL can model web service interactions as executable business processes, as abstract business processes, or through the behavior of processes. The BPEL programming language supports

- Message sending and receiving

- XML and WSDL typed variables

- A property-based message correlation mechanism

- An extensible language plug-in model to allow writing expressions and queries in multiple languages[1]

- Structured-programming constructs, such as `if-then-elseif-else`, `while`, `sequence`, and `flow`

- Logic in local variables, fault-handlers, compensation-handlers, and event-handlers

- Scopes to control variable access

Some of the popular BPEL engines are Apache ODE, BizTalk Server, Oracle BPEL Process Manager, SAP Exchange Infrastructure, Virtuoso Universal Server, and WebSphere Process Server.

Semantic Web Service Software

Developers can use *semantic execution environments* such as WSMX and IRS to provide automatic discovery, composition, selection, mediation, and invocation of Semantic Web Services. The development of Semantic Web Services can be speeded up using purpose-built frameworks and plug-ins such as the Web Services Modeling Toolkit (WSMT) and the Semantic Automated Discovery and Integration plug-in for Protégé.

Web Service Modeling eXecution environment (WSMX)

The *Web Service Modeling eXecution environment* (*WSMX*) is the reference implementation of the Web Service Modeling Ontology using WSML as the internal language and WSMT for modeling [14]. It is an open source execution environment for business applications, with integrated web services available at `http://sourceforge.net/projects/wsmx/`, providing increased business processes automation and scalability. WSMX consumes semantic messages, discovers semantically annotated web services, and processes them. Between the back-end applications of requested services and the provided services, WSMX has a system interface, an administration interface, resource manager interfaces for mapping and datastore access, and a reasoner framework.

Internet Reasoning Service (IRS-III)

The *Internet Reasoning Service* (*IRS*) is the Open University's Semantic Web Services framework, which allows applications to semantically describe and execute Web services [15]. It supports the provision of semantic reasoning services within the context of the Semantic Web. The best-known implementation of the Internet Reasoning Service is IRS-III.

Web Services Modeling Toolkit (WSMT)

The *Web Services Modeling Toolkit* (*WSMT*) is a lightweight framework for rapid Semantic Web Service development and deployment available at `http://sourceforge.net/projects/wsmt/`. It also collects existing SWS tools within one application. The Web Services Modeling Toolkit can be integrated into the WSMX and IRS-III execution environments.

The Web Services Modeling Toolkit is primarily designed for Java programmers developing software in Integrated Development Environments such as Eclipse or NetBeans. The Toolkit aims to help developers of Semantic Web Services using the WSMO paradigm. Java developers can combine the Web Services Modeling

---

[1]BPEL has native XPath 1.0 support.

Toolkit with other plug-ins, such as the Eclipse Web Tools Platform (WTP), which provides tools with XML and WSDL support for creating Semantic Web Services and describes them semantically using WSMO. The Web Services Modeling Toolkit supports the creation of common document types used in Semantic Web Services through editing, validation, testing, and deployment. The Toolkit features a text editor, a form-based editor, and a validator for WSML and provides different views for reasoning and discovery.

Because mappings between two ontologies are created at design time and applied automatically at runtime in order to perform instance transformation, the Web Services Modeling Toolkit provides guidance for ontology-ontology mappings. WSMT mappings are expressed in the Abstract Mapping Language (AML), which is then transformed to WSML. The Toolkit features an AML text editor and a visual editor, an AML validator, and provides mapping and testing view for AML.

Semantic Automated Discovery and Integration (SADI)

Semantic Automated Discovery and Integration (*SADI*) is a lightweight set of Semantic Web Service design patterns (https://code.google.com/p/sadi/). It was primarily designed for scientific service publication and is especially useful in bioinformatics. Powered by web standards, SADI implements Semantic Web technologies to consume and produce RDF instances of OWL-DL classes, where input and output class URIs resolve to an OWL document through HTTP GET. SADI supports RDF/XML and Notation3 serializations. The SADI design patterns provide automatic discovery of appropriate services, based on user needs, and can automatically chain these services into complex analytical workflows. SADI is available as a plug-in for the Protégé ontology editor, the IO Informatics Knowledge Explorer to graph visualization, as well as Taverna, an open-source workflow design and enactment workbench.

UDDI Semantic Web Service Listings

Universal Description, Discovery and Integration (*UDDI*) is a platform-independent XML-based directory service for businesses offering web services. It describes web services and business processes programmatically in a single, open, and secure environment. UDDI is described in WSDL and communicates via SOAP. UDDI can be used to improve e-commerce interoperability between streamline online transactions. Similar to the White Pages or Yellow Pages of telephone books, UDDI allows business listings with business name, location, and offered products and/or web services. Any company can be added to the UDDI registry, regardless of the business size. Already listed enterprises include Microsoft, IBM, Ariba, HP, Compaq, American Express, SAP, and Ford, just to mention the most well-known ones. UDDI can help business owners to discover relevant businesses and decision makers to increase access to current customers and reach potential customers, expand offerings, and extend market reach.

Summary

In this chapter, you learned what Semantic Web Services are and how they can be described using WSDL, annotated using SAWSDL, and modeled using OWL-S, WSMO, MicroWSMO and WSMO-Lite, and WSML. You became familiar with the Semantic Web Service software, such as the WSMX and IIR-III execution environments, as well as the WSMT Toolkit and the SADI Protégé plug-in. You learned about the UDDI service listing used to dynamically look up and discover services provided by external business partners and service providers.

The next chapter will show you how to store triples and quads efficiently in purpose-built graph databases: triplestores and quadstores.

References

1. Domingue, J., Martin, D. (2008) Introduction to the Semantic Web Tutorial. The 7th International Semantic Web Conference, 26–30 October, 2008, Karlsruhe, Germany.

2. Facca, F. M., Krummenacher, R. (2008) Semantic Web Services in a Nutshell. Silicon Valley Semantic Web Meet Up, USA.

3. Stollberg, M., Haller, A. (2005) Semantic Web Services Tutorial. 3rd International Conference on Web Services, Orlando, FL, USA, 11 July 2005.

4. Chinnici, R., Moreau, J.-J., Ryman, A., Weerawarana, S. (eds.) (2007) Web Services Description Language (WSDL) Version 2.0 Part 1: Core Language. www.w3.org/TR/wsdl20/. Accessed 2 April 2015.

5. Farrell, J., Lausen, H. (eds.) (2007) Semantic Annotations for WSDL and XML Schema. www.w3.org/TR/sawsdl/. Accessed 2 April 2015.

6. Martin, D. et al. (2004) OWL-S: Semantic Markup for Web Services. www.w3.org/Submission/OWL-S/. Accessed 2 April 2015.

7. Horrocks, I. et al. (2004) SWRL: A Semantic Web Rule Language. Combining OWL and RuleML. www.w3.org/Submission/SWRL/. Accessed 2 April 2015.

8. Lausen, H., Polleres, A., Roman, D. (eds.) (2005) Web Service Modeling Ontology (WSMO). www.w3.org/Submission/WSMO/. Accessed 2 April 2015.

9. Fensel, D., Bussler, C. (2002) The Web Service Modeling Framework WSMF. www.swsi.org/resources/wsmf-paper.pdf. Accessed 2 April 2015.

10. Stollberg, M., Lausen, H., Polleres, A., Lara, R. (eds.) (2004) Locations Ontology. www.wsmo.org/2004/d3/d3.2/b2c/20041004/resources/loc.wsml.html. Accessed 4 April 2015.

11. Roman, D., Kopecký, J., Vitvar, T., Domingue, J., Fensel, D. (2014) WSMO-Lite and hRESTS: Lightweight semantic annotations for Web services and RESTful APIs. Web Semantics: Science, Services and Agents on the World Wide Web, http://dx.doi.org/10.1016/j.websem.2014.11.006.

12. Kopecký, J., Vitvar, T. (2008) MicroWSMO: Semantic Description of RESTful Services. http://wsmo.org/TR/d38/v0.1/20080219/d38v01_20080219.pdf. Accessed 4 April 2015.

13. de Bruijn, J. et al. (2005) Web Service Modeling Language (WSML). www.w3.org/Submission/WSML/. Accessed 2 April 2015.

14. DERI and STI2 (2008) Web Service Modelling eXecution environment. www.wsmx.org. Accessed 4 April 2015.

15. Domingue, J. et al. (2011) Internet Reasoning Service. http://technologies.kmi.open.ac.uk/irs/. Accessed 2 April 2015.

CHAPTER 6

■■■

Graph Databases

Graph models and algorithms are ubiquitous, due to their suitability for knowledge representation in e-commerce, social media networks, research, computer networks, electronics, as well as for maximum flow problems, route problems, and web searches. Graph databases are databases with Create, Read, Update, and Delete (CRUD) methods exposing a graph data model, such as property graphs (containing nodes and relationships), hypergraphs (a relationship can connect any number of nodes), RDF triples (subject-predicate-object), or quads (named graph-subject-predicate-object). Graph databases are usually designed for online transactional processing (OLTP) systems and optimized for transactional performance, integrity, and availability. Unlike relational and NoSQL databases, purpose-build graph databases, including triplestores and quadstores, do not rely on indices, because graphs naturally provide an adjacency index, and relationships attached to a node provide a direct connection to other related nodes. Graph queries are performed using this locality to traverse through the graph, which can be carried out with several orders of magnitude higher efficiency than that of relational databases joining data through a global index. In fact, most graph databases are so powerful that they are suitable even for Big Data applications.

Graph Databases

To leverage the power of the Resource Description Framework (RDF), data on the Semantic Web can be stored in *graph databases* rather than relational databases. A graph database is a database that stores RDF statements and implements graph structures for semantic queries, using nodes, edges, and properties to represent and retrieve data. A few graph databases are based on relational databases, while most are purpose-built from the ground up for storing and retrieving RDF statements.

There are two important properties of graph databases that determine efficiency and implementation potential. The first one is the *storage*, which can be native graph storage or a database engine that transforms an RDF graph to relational, object-oriented, or general-purpose database structures. The other main property is the *processing engine*. True graph databases implement so-called *index-free adjacency*, whereby connected nodes are physically linked to each other in the database. Because every element contains a direct pointer to its adjacent element, no index lookups are necessary. Graph databases store arbitrarily complex RDF graphs by simple abstraction of the graph nodes and relationships. Unlike other database management systems, graph databases do not use inferred connections between entities using foreign keys, as in relational databases, or other data, such as the ones used in MapReduce. The computational algorithms are implemented as *graph compute engines*, which identify clusters and answer queries.

One of the main advantages of graph databases over relational databases and NoSQL stores is *performance* [1]. Graph databases are typically thousands of times more powerful than conventional databases in terms of indexing, computing power, storage, and querying. In contrast to relational databases, where the query performance on data relations decreases as the dataset grows, the performance of graph databases remains relatively constant.

While relational databases require a comprehensive data model about the knowledge domain up front, graph databases are inherently *flexible*, because graphs can be extended with new nodes and new relationship types effortlessly, while subgraphs merge naturally to their supergraph.

Because graph databases implement freely available standards such as RDF for data modeling and SPARQL for querying, the storage is usually free of proprietary formats and third-party dependencies. Another big advantage of graph databases is the option to use arbitrary external vocabularies and schemas, while the data is available programmatically through Application Programming Interfaces (APIs) and powerful queries.

■ **Note** Some graph databases have limitations when it comes to storing and retrieving RDF triples or quads, because the underlying model not always covers the features of RDF well, as for example, using URIs as identifiers is not the default scenario, and the naming convention often differs from that of RDF. Most graph databases do not support SPARQL out of the box, although many provide a SPARQL add-on. The proprietary query languages introduced by graph database vendors are not standardized like SPARQL.

The widely adopted relational databases were originally designed to store data such as tabular structures in an organized manner. The irony of relational databases is that their performance is rather poor when handling ad hoc relationships. For example, the foreign keys of relational databases mean development and maintenance overhead, while they are vital for the database to work. Joining two tables in a relational database might increase complexity by mixing the foreign key metadata with business data. Even simple queries might be computationally complex. The handling of sparse tables in relational databases is poor. Regarding NoSQL databases, including key-value-, document-, and column-oriented databases, the relationship handling is not perfect either. Because NoSQL databases typically store sets of disconnected documents, values, or columns (depending on the type), they are not ideal for storing data interconnections and graphs.

The main parameters of graph databases are the load rate in triples/second or quads/second (sometimes combined with the indexing time) and the query execution time. Further features that can be used for comparing graph databases are licensing, source availability (open source, binary distribution, or both), scalability, graph model, schema model, API, proprietary query language and query method, supported platforms, consistency, support for distributed processing, partitioning, extensibility, visualizing tools, storage back end (persistency), language, and backup/restore options. The comparison of the most commonly used graph databases is summarized in Table 6-1.

Table 6-1. Comparison of Common Graph Databases [2]

	License	Platform	Language	Distribution	Cost	Transactional	Memory-Based	Disk-Based	Single-Node	Distributed	Graph Algorithms	Text-Based Query Language	Embeddable	Software	Datastore Type
MySQL	GPL/Proprietary	x86	C/C++	Bin	Free	X	-	X	X	-	-	SQL	X	X	X	SQLDB
Oracle	Proprietary	x86	C/C++	Bin	$180–$950	X	-	X	X	X	-	SQL	X	X	X	SQLDB
SQL Server	Proprietary	x86-Win	C++	Bin	$898–$8592	X	-	X	X	-	-	SQL	-	X	X	SQLDB
SQLite	Public Domain	x86	C	Src/Bin	Free	X	X	X	X	-	-	SQL	X	X	X	SQLDB
AllegroGraph	Proprietary	x86	Likely Java	Bin	Free-ish/$$$$	X	-	X	X	-	X	SPARQL/RDFS++/Prolog	-	X	X	GDB
ArangoDB	Apache	x86	C/C++/JS	Src/Bin	Free	-	-	X	X	-	-	AQL	-	X	X	GDB/KV/DOC
DEX	Proprietary	x86	C++	Bin	Free Personal/Commercial $$	X	-	X	X	-	X	Traversal	X	-	X	GDB
FlockDB	Apache	Java	Java/Scala/Ruby	Src	Free	-	-	X	X	X	-	-	-	X	X	GDB
GraphBase	Proprietary	Java	Java	Bin	Free, $15/mo, $20,000	?	-	X	X	-	-	Bounds	X	X	X	GDB
HyperGraphDB	LGPL	Java	Java	Src	Free	MVCC	X	X	X	X	-	HGQuery/Traversal	X	-	-	HyperGDB
InfiniteGraph	Proprietary	Java	Java/C++	Bin	Free Trial/$5,000	Both	-	X	X	X	-	Gremlin	X	X	X	GDB
InfoGrid	AGPL/Proprietary	Java	Java	Src/Bin	Free + Support	-	X	X	X	X	-	-	X	X	-	GDB
Neo4j	GPL/Proprietary	Java	Java	Src/Bin	Free, $6,000–$24,000	X	-	X	X	-	X	Cypher	X	X	X	GDB/NoSQL

(continued)

Table 6-1. (*continued*)

	License	Platform	Language	Distribution	Cost	Transactional	Memory-Based	Disk-Based	Single-Node	Distributed	Graph Algorithms	Text-Based Query Language	Embeddable	Software	Datastore	Type
OrientDB	Apache	Java	Java	Src/Bin	Free + Support	Both	X	X	X	X	–	Extended SQL/Gremlin	X	X	X	GDB/NoSQL
Titan	Apache	Java	Java	Src/Bin	Free + Support	Both	–	X	X	X	–	Gremlin	X	X	–	GDB
Bagel	BSD	Java	Java/Scala/Spark	Src	Free	–	X	–	X	X	X	–	X	–	–	BSP
BGL	Boost	x86/C++	C++	Src/Bin	Free	–	X	–	X	–	X	–	X	–	–	Library
Faunus	Apache	Java	Java	Src	Free + Support	Both	–	X	X	X	–	Gremlin	X	X	–	Hadoop
Gephi	GPL/CDDL	Java	Java/OpenGL	Src/Bin	Free	–	X	X	X	–	X	–	X	X	–	Toolkit
Giraph	Apache	Java	Java	Src	Free		X	;	X	X	X	–	X	–	–	BSP
GraphLab	Apache	x86	C++	Src	Free	–	X	X	X	X	X	–	X	–	–	BSP
Graph Stream	LGPL/CeCILL-C	Java	Java	Src/Bin	Free	–	X	–	X	–	X	–	X	–	–	Library
Hama	Apache	Java	Java	Src	Free	–	X	–	X	X	X	–	X	–	–	BSP
MTGL	BSD	x86/XMT	C++	Src	Free	–	X	–	X	–	X	–	X	–	–	Library
NetworkX	BSD	x86	Python	Src/Bin	Free	–	X	–	X	–	X	–	X	–	–	Library
PEGASUS	Apache	Java	Java	Src/Bin	Free	–	–	X	X	X	X	–	–	X	–	Hadoop
STINGER	BSD	x86/XMT	C	Src	Free	–	X	–	X	–	X	–	X	X	X	Library
uRiKA	Proprietary	XMT	Likely C++	Bin	$$$$	?	X	–	X	–	–	SPARQL	–	X	X	Appliance

148

While graph database vendors often compare their products to other graph databases, the de facto industry standard for benchmarking RDF databases is the Lehigh University Benchmark (LUBM), which is suitable for performance comparisons [3].

Triplestores

All graph databases designed for storing RDF triples are called *triplestores* or *subject-predicate-object databases*, however, the triplestores that have been built on top of existing commercial relational database engines (such as SQL-based databases) are typically not as efficient as the native triplestores with a database engine built from scratch for storing and retrieving RDF triples. The performance of native triplestores is usually better, due to the difficulty of mapping the graph-based RDF model to SQL or NoSQL queries.

The advantages of graph databases are derived from the advantageous features of RDF, OWL, and SPARQL. RDF data elements are globally unique and linked, leveraging the advantages of the graph structure. Adding a new schema element is as easy as inserting a triple with a new predicate. Graph databases also support ad hoc SPARQL queries. Unlike the column headers, foreign keys, or constraints of relational databases, the entities of graph databases are categorized with classes; predicates are properties or relationships; and they are all part of the data. Due to the RDF implementation, graph databases support automatic inferencing for knowledge discovery. The data stored in these databases can unify vocabularies, dictionaries, and taxonomies through machine-readable ontologies. Graph databases are commonly used in semantic data integration, social network analysis, and Linked Open Data applications.

Quadstores

It is not always possible to interpret RDF statements without a graph identifier. For example, if a given name is used as a subject, it is out of context if we do not state the person we want to describe. If, however, we add the web site address of the same person to each triple that describes the same person, all components become globally unique and dereferenceable. A *quad* is a subject-predicate-object triple coupled with a graph identifier. The identified graph is called a *named graph*.

For example, consider an LOD dataset description in a Turtle file registered on datahub.io, such as http://www.lesliesikos.com/datasets/sikos-void.ttl. To make RDF statements about the dataset graph, the subject is set to the file name and extension of the RDF file representing the graph (http://www.lesliesikos.com/datasets/sikos.rdf). This makes it possible to write RDF statements about the file, describing it as an LOD dataset (void:Dataset), adding a human-readable title to it using Dublin Core (dc:title), declaring its creator (dc:creator), and so on, as shown in Figure 6-1.

■ **Caution**   Notice the difference between http://www.lesliesikos.com/datasets/sikos.rdf and http://www.lesliesikos.com/datasets/sikos.rdf#sikos. The first example refers to a file; the second refers to a person described in the file.

If a graph database stores the graph name (representing the graph context or provenance information) for each triple, the database is called a *quadstore*.

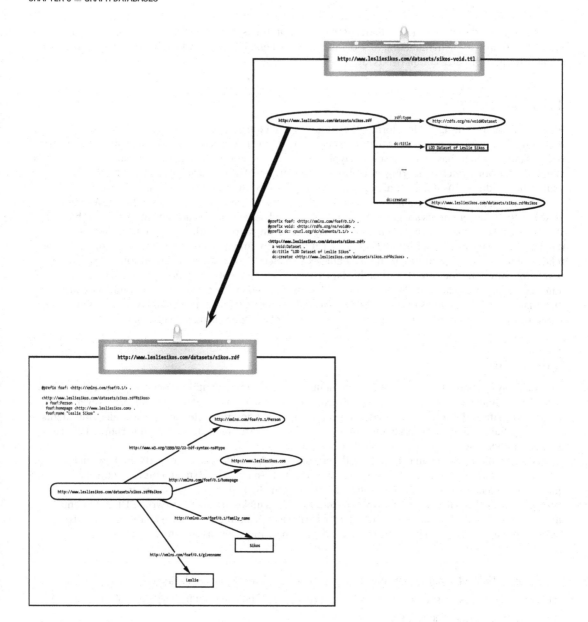

Figure 6-1. *Referencing from a named graph to another named graph*

The Most Popular Graph Databases

Some of the most widely deployed, high-performance graph databases are AllegroGraph, Neo4j, Blazegraph (formerly Big Data), OpenLink Virtuoso, Clark & Parsia's Stardog, BigOWLIM, 4Store, YARS2, Jena TDB, RDFox, Jena SDB, Mulgara, RDF Gateway, Kowari, and Sesame. However, not everyone uses a native graph database engine to store triples or quads. Some examples are Oracle Spatial and Graph with Oracle Database, Jena with PostgreSQL, and 3Store with MySQL 3.

AllegroGraph

AllegroGraph is an industry-leading graph database platform [4]. It can combine geospatial, temporal, and social network queries into a single query. It supports online backups, point-in-time recovery, replication, and warm standby. AllegroGraph supports automatic triple indexing, user-defined indices, as well as text indexing at the predicate level. Similar to other databases, AllegroGraph implements the ACID (Atomicity, Consistency, Isolation, and Durability) properties of transaction processing. Atomicity means that a transaction either completely fails or completely succeeds. Consistency means that every transaction takes the database as a whole from one consistent state to another, so the database can never be inconsistent. Isolation refers to the feature that all the transactions can handle data of other completed transactions and cannot rely on partial results of transactions running concurrently. Durability means that once the database system signals the successful completion of a transaction to the application, the changes made by the transaction will persist, even in the presence of hardware and software failures, except when a hard disk failure destroys the data.

All AllegroGraph clients (Java, Python, JavaScript, Lisp) are based on the REST protocol. AllegroGraph works with multiple programming languages and environments, such as Java in Sesame or Jena (through a command line or in an IDE such as Eclipse), Python, Ruby, C#, Clojure, JRuby, Scala, Perl, Lisp, and PHP. The graph database supports cloud hosting on Amazon EC2 for distributed computing. General graph traversal can be performed through JIG, a JavaScript-based interface. AllegroGraph also supports dedicated and public sessions. AllegroGraph works as an advanced graph database to store RDF triples and query the stored triples through various query APIs like SPARQL and Prolog. It supports RDFS++ reasoning with its built-in reasoner. AllegroGraph includes support for federation, social network analysis, geospatial capabilities, and temporal reasoning. AllegroGraph is available in three editions: the Free Version (the number of triples is limited to 5 million), the Developer Version (the number of triples is limited to 50 million), and the Enterprise Version (unlimited triples).

AllegroGraph can store not only triples or quads but also additional information, including the named graph (context) and the model (including a unique triple identifier and a transaction number), which makes it a *quintuplestore*. AllegroGraph is particularly efficient in representing and indexing geospatial and temporal data. It has 7 standard indices and 24 user-controlled indices. The standard indices are sets of sorted indices used to quickly identify a contiguous block of triples that are likely to match a specific query pattern. These indices are identified by names referring to their arrangement. The default set of indices are called spogi, posgi, ospgi, gspoi, gposi, gospi, and i, where

- s stands for the subject URI

- p stands for the predicate URI

- o stands for the object URI or literal

- g stands for the graph URI

- i stands for the triple identifier (unique within the triplestore)

Custom index arrangements are used to eliminate indices that are not needed for your application or to implement custom indices to match unusual triple patterns.

AllegroGraph supports full text indexing, free text indexing, and range indexing. Full text indexing makes it possible to search for Boolean expressions, expressions with wild cards, and phrases. Free text indexing powers free text searches, by which you can combine keyphrase searches with queries.

AllegroGraph has full RDF, SPARQL 1.0, and partial SPARQL 1.1 support, and includes an RDFS++ reasoner. Querying can be performed not only through SPARQL but also programmatically using Lisp, Prolog, or JavaScript. Prolog is implemented for rules with a usability layer called CLIF+, which makes it easy to combine rules and queries. AllegroGraph is very efficient in storing property graphs as well. AllegroGraph supports node typing, edge typing, node and edge attributes, as well as directed, undirected, restricted, and loop edges, attribute indexing, and ontologies. It supports traversals through adjacency lists and special indices.

AllegroGraph implements a variety of graph algorithms. For social network analysis, for example, it uses generators with a first-class function that processes a one-node input and returns all children, while the speed is guaranteed by neighborhood matrices or adjacency hash tables. AllegroGraph considers a variety of graph features, such as separation degrees (the distance between two nodes) and connection strength (the number of shortest paths between two nodes through predicates and rules).

All functionalities of AllegroGraph are available via the Lisp shell, and many from cshell, wget, and curl. Franz Inc. provides JavaScript, Prolog, and Lisp algorithms, Lisp and JavaScript scripting, REST/JSON protocol support, IDE integration, and admin tools for developers. You can import data from a variety of formats and export data by creating triple dumps from an AllegroGraph client.

WebView

WebView, AllegroGraph's HTTP-based graphical user interface (GUI) for user and repository management, is included in the AllegroGraph server distribution packages. To connect to WebView, browse to the AllegroGraph port of your server in your web browser. If you have a local installation of AllegroGraph, use localhost with the port number. The default port number is 10035. With WebView, you can browse the catalogs, repositories, and federations, manage repositories, apply Prolog rules and functions to repositories, perform RDFS++ reasoning on a repository, and import RDF data into a repository or a particular graph in a repository. WebView can display used namespaces and provides the option to add new namespaces. Telnet connections can be opened to AllegroGraph processes, which can be used for debugging. Local and remote repositories can be federated into a single point of access.

WebView supports triple index configuration and free text indexing setup for repositories. SPARQL and Prolog queries can be executed, saved, and reused, and queries can be captured as a URL for embedding in applications. WebView can visualize `construct` and `describe` SPARQL query results as graphs. The query results are connected to triples and resources, making it easy to discover connections. WebView can also be used to manage AllegroGraph users and user roles and repository access, as well as open sessions for commit and rollback.

Installing the AllegroGraph Server

There are two options to install the AllegroGraph server natively. The first option is to install AllegroGraph from the RPM (Red Hat Package Manager) package as an administrator on Red Hat, Fedora, or CentOS. The second option is to install the server by extracting files from a `.tar.gz` archive, which does not require administrative privileges. The third option is to deploy a VMware appliance, which is not recommended for performance reasons.

Installing the RPM Package

To install the AllegroGraph server from the RPM package, the following steps are required:

1. Download the `.rpm` file from the Franz web site at `http://franz.com/agraph/downloads/server`.

2. Install the RPM (see Listing 6-1)

    Listing 6-1. Installing the AllegroGraph Server from the RPM Package

    ```
    # rpm -i agraph-version_number.x86_64.rpm
    ```

    where `version_number` is the latest version you are about to install.

3. Run the configuration script as shown in Listing 6-2.

Listing 6-2. Run the Configuration

```
# /usr/bin/configure-agraph
```

The script will ask for directories to be used for storing the configuration file, the log files, data, settings, and server process identifiers, as well as the port number (see Listing 6-3).

Listing 6-3. Directory and Port Settings

```
Welcome to the AllegroGraph configuration program. This script will ↵
help you establish a baseline AllegroGraph configuration.

You will be prompted for a few settings.  In most cases, you can hit ↵
return to accept the default value.

Location of configuration file to create:
[/home/leslie/tmp/ag5.0/lib/agraph.cfg]:
Directory to store data and settings:
[/home/leslie/tmp/ag5.0/data]:
Directory to store log files:
[/home/leslie/tmp/ag5.0/log]:
Location of file to write server process id:
[/home/leslie/tmp/ag5.0/data/agraph.pid]:
Port:
[10035]:
```

▨ **Tip**   The default answers are usually adequate and can be reconfigured later, if necessary.

---

4.   If you are logged on as the root operator when running the script, you will be asked to create a non-root user account (see Listing 6-4).

Listing 6-4. Creating a Restricted User Account

```
User to run as:
[agraph]:

User 'agraph' doesn't exist on this system.
Create agraph user:
[y]:
```

5.   Add a user name and password for the AllegroGraph super-user (see Listing 6-5). This user is internal and not identical to the server logon account.

Listing 6-5. Creating the SuperUser Account

```
SuperUser account name:
[super]:
SuperUser account password:
```

You have to confirm the password by repeating it.

6. Set the instance timeout in seconds, i.e., the length of time a database will stay open without being accessed (see Listing 6-6). The default value is 604800 (one week in seconds).

Listing 6-6. Set Instance Timeout

```
Instance timeout seconds:
[604800]:
```

7. The configuration file is saved to the folder you specified in step 3 (see Listing 6-7).

Listing 6-7. The Configuration File Is Saved

```
/home/leslie/tmp/ag5.0/lib/agraph.cfg has been created.

If desired, you may modify the configuration.
```

8. The start and stop commands specific to your installation are displayed (see Listing 6-8).

Listing 6-8. Commands to Start and Stop the Server with Your Installation

```
You can start AllegroGraph by running:
/home/leslie/tmp/ag5.0/bin/agraph-control --config /home/leslie/tmp/
ag5.0/lib/agraph.cfg start

You can stop AllegroGraph by running:
/home/leslie/tmp/ag5.0/bin/agraph-control --config /home/leslie/tmp/
ag5.0/lib/agraph.cfg stop
```

9. If you use a commercial version, you have to install the license key purchased from Franz Inc. The license key includes the client name, defines the maximum number of triples that can be used, the expiration date, and a license code. To install your license key, copy the whole key content you received via e-mail, and paste it into the agraph.cfg configuration file.

■ **Note** The configuration script can also be run non-interactively by specifying --non-interactive on the configure-agraph command, along with additional arguments that provide answers to the questions the script would have asked. The arguments that require a path as their value are --config-file, --data-dir, --log-dir, and --pid-file. --runas-user expects a user, while --create-runas-user tells the script to create the user named in --runas-user, if it does not exist yet. The internal user that received super-user privileges can be declared using --super-user, which requires the user name as its value. The password for this user can be set as --super-password, followed by the password. If you don't want the password to be shown in the command line, you can specify a file that contains the super-user password with --super-password-file, followed by the path.

To verify the installation, open a browser and load the AllegroGraph WebView URL, which is the IP address of the server, followed by a semicolon (:) and the port number. For local installations, the IP address is substituted by localhost.

If you want to uninstall the server anytime later, you can use the erase argument on the rpm command, as shown in Listing 6-9, which won't remove other directories created by AllegroGraph.

Listing 6-9. Uninstalling AllegroGraph

```
# rpm --erase agraph
```

Installing the TAR Archive

The other option to install the AllegroGraph server is to extract the gzipped TAR (Tape Archive). This is a good choice for Ubuntu and other Linux users and does not require administrative privileges.

1. Download the .tar.gz file from http://franz.com/agraph/downloads/server.

2. Extract the archive using the tar command, as shown in Listing 6-10.

    Listing 6-10. Extracting the TAR Archive

    ```
    $ tar zxf agraph-version_number-linuxamd64.64.tar.gz
    ```

3. The command creates the agraph-version_number subdirectory, which includes install-agraph, the installation script. You must provide the path to a writable directory on which you want to install AllegroGraph, as shown in Listing 6-11.

    Listing 6-11. Run the Installation Script

    ```
    $ agraph-5.0/install-agraph /home/leslie/tmp/ag5.0

    Installation complete.
    Now running configure-agraph.
    ```

4. Answer the questions to configure your installation (similar to steps 3–6 for configuring the RPM installation). The last step reveals how you can start and stop your server.

5. Verify your installation by opening a browser and directing it to your server IP or localhost with the port number you specified during installation.

    To uninstall an older .tar.gz installation, delete the AllegroGraph installation directory, as shown in Listing 6-12.

    Listing 6-12. Removing the AllegroGraph Directory

    ```
    % rm -rf obsolete-allegrograph-directory/
    ```

Deploying the Virtual Machine

If you use a virtual 64-bit Linux to evaluate or use AllegroGraph, you need a virtual environment, and you have to deploy the virtual machine image file.

■ **Note**   Franz Inc. encourages native installations, rather than a virtual environment, even for evaluation.

---

1. Download the virtual environment you want to use, such as VMware Player for Windows or VMware Fusion for Mac OS, from `https://my.vmware.com/web/vmware/downloads`.

2. Download the virtual machine image file from `http://franz.com/agraph/downloads/`.

3. Unzip the image.

4. Run the VMware Player.

5. Click Open a Virtual Machine.

6. Browse to the directory where you unzipped the image file and open `AllegroGraph vx Virtual Machine.vmx` file, where x is the version of AllegroGraph.

7. Take ownership, if prompted.

8. Play Virtual Machine.

9. When prompted for Moved or Copied, select Copied.

10. Log in to the Linux Virtual Machine as the user `franz`, with the password `allegrograph`.

11. To start AllegroGraph, double-click the `agstart` shortcut on the Desktop and select Run in Terminal Window when prompted, or open a Terminal window and run the `agstart` command.

12. Launch FireFox and click AGWebView in the taskbar, or visit `http://localhost:10035`.

13. Log in to AllegroGraph as the `test` user, with the password `xyzzy`.

To stop AllegroGraph, double-click the agstop shortcut on the Desktop and select Run in Terminal Window when prompted, or open a Terminal window and run the `agstop` command.

Installing the AllegroGraph Client

AllegroGraph has clients for Java, Python, Clojure, Ruby, Perl, C#, and Scala [5]. One of the options for the Java client, for example, is to run it as an Eclipse project. The Jena client is a variant of the Java client. The Python client requires the `cjson` and `pycurl` libraries of Python on top of the core Python installation. You can check whether these packages are installed on your system, using the q parameter on the `rpm` command, as shown in Listing 6-13.

Listing 6-13. Checking Python Dependencies for AllegroGraph

```
rpm -q python python-cjson python-pycurl
```

If they are not installed, on most Linux systems you have to use yum (see Listing 6-14).

Listing 6-14. Installing Dependencies

```
sudo yum install python python-cjson python-pycurl
```

For Ubuntu systems, you need apt-get to install the required libraries (see Listing 6-15).

Listing 6-15. Installing Dependencies on Ubuntu

```
sudo apt-get install python python-cjson python-pycurl
```

Java API

After starting the server, you can use new AllegroGraphConnection(); from Java to connect to the default running server (see Listing 6-16). If you are using a port number other than the default 10035 port, you have to set the port number using setPort(port_number).

Listing 6-16. Connecting to the AllegroGraph Server Through the Java API

```java
import com.franz.agbase.*;
public class AGConnecting {
  public static void main(String[] args) throws AllegroGraphException {
    AllegroGraphConnection ags = new AllegroGraphConnection();
    try {
      System.out.println("Attempting to connect to the server on port" + ags.getPort());
      ags.enable();
    } catch (Exception e) {
      throw new AllegroGraphException("Server connection problem.", e);
    }
    System.out.println("Connected.");
    }
}
```

A triplestore can be created using the create method and closed with the closeTripleStore method, as shown in Listing 6-17. You can disconnect from an AllegroGraph server with ags.disable().

Listing 6-17. Creating an AllegroGraph Triplestore with the Java API

```java
import com.franz.agbase.*;
public class AGCreateTripleStore {
  public static void main(String[] args) throws AllegroGraphException {
    AllegroGraphConnection ags = new AllegroGraphConnection();
        try {
          ags.enable();
        } catch (Exception e) {
          throw new AllegroGraphException("Server connection problem.", e);
        }
    try {
      AllegroGraph ts = ags.create("newstore", AGPaths.TRIPLE_STORES);
      System.out.println("Triplestore created.");
      System.out.println("Closing triplestore…");
```

```
      ts.closeTripleStore();
    } catch (Exception e) {
      System.out.println(e.getMessage());
    }
    System.out.println("Disconnecting from the server…");
    ags.disable();
  }
}
```

There are two ways to open an AllegroGraph triplestore from Java: using the access method, which opens the store and, if it does not exist, it will be created, or the open method, which opens an existing store but gives an error if the triplestore does not exist. Let's open a triplestore and index all triples, as demonstrated in Listing 6-18.

Listing 6-18. Indexing all Triples of an AllegroGraph Triplestore

```
import com.franz.agbase.*;
import com.franz.agbase.AllegroGraph.StoreAttribute;
public class AGOpenTripleStore {
  public static void main(String[] args) throws AllegroGraphException {
  AllegroGraphConnection ags = new AllegroGraphConnection();
    try {
      ags.enable();
    } catch (Exception e) {
      throw new AllegroGraphException("Server connection problem.", e);
    }
    System.out.println("Opening triplestore…");
    ts = ags.open("existingstore", AGPaths.TRIPLE_STORES);
    System.out.println("Triple store opened with " + ts.numberOfTriples() + " triples.");
    try {
      System.out.println("Indexing triplestore…");
      ts.indexAllTriples();
    } catch (Exception e) {
      System.out.println(e.getLocalizedMessage());
    }
    ts.closeTripleStore(true);
    System.out.println("Disconnecting from the server.");
    ags.disable();
}
```

The default access mode is read+write. To open a triplestore in read-only mode, set the StoreAttribute to READ_ONLY (see Listing 6-19).

Listing 6-19. Open a Triplestore in Read-Only Mode

```
ts = new AllegroGraph(AGPaths.TRIPLE_STORES + "yourstore");
ts.setAttribute(StoreAttribute.READ_ONLY, true);
ags.open(ts);
```

Let's add a triple to our triplestore in N-triples. Once com.franz.agbase.* is imported and the connection to the server established, you can add a statement to the triplestore using addStatement (see Listing 6-20).

Listing 6-20. Adding an RDF Statement to the Triplestore

```
ts.addStatement("<http://www.lesliesikos.com/datasets/sikos.rdf#sikos>", ↵
                "<http://xmlns.com/foaf/0.1/homepage>", ↵
                "<http://www.lesliesikos.com>");
```

All triples of the default graph can be retrieved and displayed using the showTriples method (see Listing 6-21).

Listing 6-21. Listing All Triples

```
TriplesIterator cc = ts.getStatements(null, null, null);
AGUtils.showTriples(cc);
```

Triplestore information such as the number of triples or the list of namespaces used in a triplestore can be retrieved using showTripleStoreInfo (see Listing 6-22).

Listing 6-22. Displaying Triplestore Information

```
import com.franz.agbase.*;
public class AGTripleStoreInfo {
  public static void showTripleStoreInfo(AllegroGraph mystore) throws AllegroGraphException
{
    System.out.println("NumberOfTriples: " + ts.numberOfTriples());
    AGUtils.printStringArray("Namespace Registry: ", ts.getNamespaces());
  }
}
```

To run a simple SPARQL SELECT query to retrieve all subject-predicate-object triples (SELECT * {?s ?p ?o}), we create a SPARQLQuery object (sq) and display the results of the query using doSparqlSelect (see Listing 6-23).

Listing 6-23. Querying the Triplestore Through the Java API

```
import com.franz.agbase.*;
public class AGSparqlSelect {
  public static void main(String[] args) throws AllegroGraphException {
    AllegroGraphConnection ags = new AllegroGraphConnection();
    try {
      ags.enable();
    } catch (Exception e) {
      throw new AllegroGraphException("Server connection problem", e);
    }
    AllegroGraph ts = ags.renew("sparqlselect", AGPaths.TRIPLE_STORES);
    ts.addStatement("<http://www.lesliesikos.com/datasets/sikos.rdf#sikos>",↵
                    "<http://xmlns.com/foaf/0.1/homepage>", ↵
                    "<http://www.lesliesikos.com>");
    ts.addStatement("<http://www.lesliesikos.com/datasets/sikos.rdf#sikos>", ↵
                    "<http://xmlns.com/foaf/0.1/interest>", ↵
                    "<http://dbpedia.org/resource/Electronic_organ>");
    String query = "SELECT * {?s ?p ?o}";
    SPARQLQuery sq = new SPARQLQuery();
    sq.setTripleStore(ts);
```

```
    sq.setQuery(query);
    doSparqlSelect(sq);
  }
  public static void doSparqlSelect(SPARQLQuery sq) throws AllegroGraphException {
    if (sq.isIncludeInferred()) {
      System.out.println("\nQuery (with RDFS++ inference):");
    } else {
      System.out.println("\nQuery:");
    }
    System.out.println("  " + sq.getQuery());
    ValueSetIterator it = sq.select();
    AGUtils.showResults(it);
    }
}
```

Gruff

Gruff is a grapher-based triplestore browser, query manager, and editor for AllegroGraph [6]. Gruff provides a variety of tools for displaying cyclical graphs, creating property tables, and managing queries as SPARQL or Prolog code. In *graph view*, the nodes and relationships stored in AllegroGraph graphs can be visualized and manipulated using Gruff, as shown in Figure 6-2.

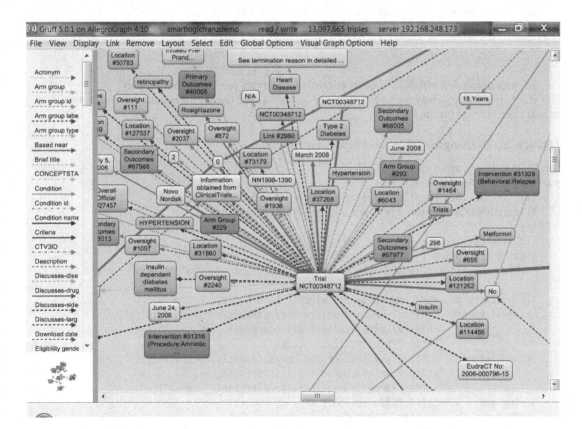

Figure 6-2. *Visualizing a graph stored in AllegroGraph using Gruff [7]*

The *query view* displays a view on which you can run a SPARQL or Prolog query and see the results in a table. The *graphical query view* makes it possible to plan a query visually as a diagram, by arranging the node boxes and link lines that represent triple patterns in the query. The triples patterns can contain variables as well as graph objects. The graphical query view supports hierarchies and filters and the automatic generation of SPARQL or Prolog queries. The *table view* displays a property table for a single node. Related nodes can be explored using hyperlinks, and property values can be edited directly. Each table row represents an RDF triple from the store.

Neo4j

Neo4j is one of the world's leading graph databases, which queries connected data a thousand times faster than relational databases [8]. Neo4j has a free "Community Edition" and a commercial "Enterprise Edition," both supporting property graphs; native graph storage and processing; ACID, a high-performance native API; its own graph query language, Cypher; and HTTPS (via plug-in). The advanced performance and scalability features that are available only in the Enterprise Edition are the Enterprise Lock Manager, a high-performance cache; clustering; hot backup; and advanced monitoring. Neo4j can be used as a triplestore or quadstore by installing an add-on called neo-rdf.

Installation

The Neo4j server is available in two formats under Windows: `.exe` and `.zip`. Neo4j can be installed using the `.exe` installer, as follows:

1. Download the latest Neo4j Server executable installation file from `www.neo4j.org/download`.

2. Double-click the `.exe` file.

3. Click Next and accept the agreement.

4. Start the Neo4j Server by clicking Neo4j Community under Start button ➤ All Programs ➤ Neo4j Community ➤ Neo4j Community

   By default, the `C:\Users\username\Documents\Neo4j\default.graphdb` database will be selected, which can be changed (see Figure 6-3).

Figure 6-3. *Neo4j ready to be started*

5. Click the Start button, which creates the necessary files in the background in the specified directory.

6.   Access Neo4j by visiting http://localhost:7474 in your browser (see Figure 6-4).

Figure 6-4. Neo4j started

The sidebar of the Neo4j web interface on the left provides convenient clickable access to information about the current Neo4j database (node labels, relationship types, and database location and size), saved scripts (see Figure 6-5), and information such as documentation, guides, a sample graph application, reference, as well as the Neo4j community resources.

Figure 6-5. The web interface of Neo4j

The Neo4j web interface provides command editing and execution on the top (starting with $:), including querying with Neo4j's query language, Cypher. If you write complex queries or commands, or commands you want to use frequently, you can save them for future use. By default, the command editor is a single-line editor suitable for short queries or commands only. If you need more space, you can switch to multiline editing with Shift+Enter, so that you can write commands spanning on multiple lines or write multiple commands without executing them one by one (see Figure 6-6).

```
1  CREATE (TheMatrix:Movie {title:'The Matrix', released:1999, tagline:'Welcome to the Real World'})
2  CREATE (Keanu:Person {name:'Keanu Reeves', born:1964})
3  CREATE
4    (Keanu)-[:ACTED_IN {roles:['Neo']}]->(TheMatrix),
5    (Carrie)-[:ACTED_IN {roles:['Trinity']}]->(TheMatrix),
6    (Laurence)-[:ACTED_IN {roles:['Morpheus']}]->(TheMatrix),
```

Figure 6-6. *Writing Cypher commands*

In multiline editing, you can run queries with Ctrl+Enter. Previously used commands can easily be retrieved using the command history. In the command line editor, you can use client-side commands as well, such as `:help`, which opens the Neo4j Help. The main part of the browser window displays the content, query answers, etc., depending on the commands you use. Each command execution results in a result frame (subwindow), which is added to the top of a stream to create a scrollable collection in reverse chronological order. Each subwindow can be maximized to full screen or closed with the two icons on the top right of the subwindow you hover your mouse over. Similar subwindows are used for data visualization as well. The stream can be cleared with the `:clear` command.

The web interface of Neo4j provides advanced visualization options. The nodes and relationships can be displayed with identifiers or labels in the color of your choice. The colors, line width, font size, and bubble size of graph visualizations can be changed arbitrarily through CSS style sheets, as shown in Figure 6-7.

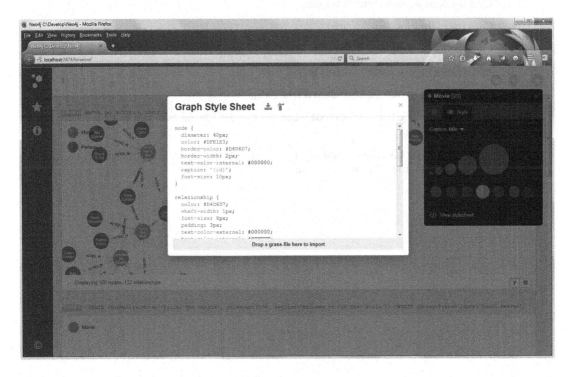

Figure 6-7. *Graph visualization options in Neo4j*

Java API

Neo4j has a Native Java API and a Cypher Java API. To demonstrate the native Java API of Neo4j, let's develop a Java application in Eclipse.

1. If you don't have Eclipse installed, follow the instructions discussed in Chapter 4.

2. Visit http://www.neo4j.org/download and under the Download Community Edition button, select Other Releases.

3. Under the latest release, select the binary of your choice for Linux or Windows.

4. Extract the archive.

5. In Eclipse, create a Java project by selecting File ➤ New ➤ Java Project.

6. Right-click the name of the newly created project and select Properties (or select File ➤ Properties).

7. Select Java Build Path and click the Libraries tab.

8. Click Add Library... on the right.

9. Select User Library as the library type.

10. Click the Next ➤ button on the bottom.

11. Click User Libraries... on the right.

12. Click the New... button.

13. Add a name to your library, such as NEO4J_JAVA_LIB.

14. Click the Add external JARs... button on the right.

15. Browse to your Neo4j directory (neo4j-community-version_number) and go to the lib subdirectory.

16. Select all the .jar files (for example, with Ctrl+A) and click Open, which will add the files to your project library (see Figure 6-8).

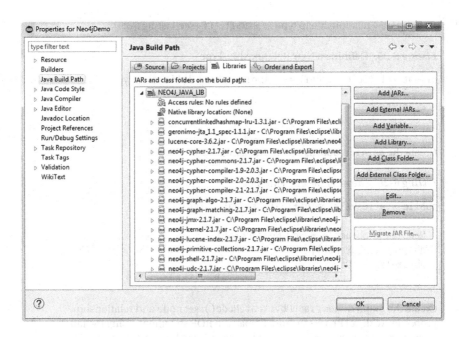

Figure 6-8. *The Neo4j software library*

17. Click OK.

18. Click Finish.

19. Once you click OK, the Neo4j software library will be added to your Eclipse project.

Let's create a simple graph with nodes, a relationship between the nodes, node properties, and relationship properties.

1. Initialize the database as shown in Listing 6-24.

Listing 6-24. Initializing the Database

```java
import org.neo4j.graphdb.GraphDatabaseService;
import org.neo4j.graphdb.Node;
import org.neo4j.graphdb.Relationship;
import org.neo4j.graphdb.RelationshipType;
import org.neo4j.graphdb.Transaction;
import org.neo4j.graphdb.factory.GraphDatabaseFactory;

public class Neo4jDemo
{
  private static final String DB_PATH = "target/neo4jdemodb";
  GraphDatabaseService graphDb;
  Node firstNode;
  Node secondNode;
  Relationship relationship;

}
```

2. Define a new relationshSeip type as WEBSITE_OF (see Listing 6-25).

    Listing 6-25. Defining a New Relationship Type

    ```
    private static enum RelTypes implements RelationshipType
    {
      WEBSITE_OF
    }
    ```

3. Create the main method, as shown in Listing 6-26.

    Listing 6-26. Creating the main Method

    ```
    public static void main(final String[] args)
    {
      Neo4jDemo dbsample = new Neo4jDemo();
      dbsample.createDb();
      dbsample.shutDown();
    }
    ```

4. Create the graph nodes graphDb.createNode(); set node and relationship
    properties with setProperty; and display the RDF statement, using the label
    of the subject and the predicate, and the URI of the object (see Listing 6-27).
    The simple RDF statement will describe the relationship between the machine-
    readable description of a person and the URL of his/her web site.

    Listing 6-27. Creating Nodes and Setting Properties

    ```
    void createDb()
    {

     graphDb = new GraphDatabaseFactory().newEmbeddedDatabase(DB_PATH);

      try ( Transaction tx = graphDb.beginTx() )
      {
        firstNode = graphDb.createNode();
        firstNode.setProperty("uri", "http://dbpedia.org/resource/Leslie_
        Sikos");
        firstNode.setProperty("label", "Leslie Sikos");
        secondNode = graphDb.createNode();
        secondNode.setProperty("uri", "http://www.lesliesikos.com");
        secondNode.setProperty("label", "website address");
        relationship = firstNode.createRelationshipTo(secondNode, RelTypes.
        WEBSITE_OF);
        relationship.setProperty("uri", "http://schema.org/url");
        relationship.setProperty("label", "website");

        System.out.print(secondNode.getProperty("uri") + " is the ");
        System.out.print(relationship.getProperty("label") + " of ");
        System.out.print(firstNode.getProperty("label"));

        tx.success();
      }
    }
    ```

5. Shut down the Neo4j database once you have finished (see Listing 6-28).

    Listing 6-28. Shutting Down Neo4j

    ```
    void shutDown()
    {
      System.out.println();
      System.out.println("Shutting down database…");
      graphDb.shutdown();
    }
    ```

6. Run the application (see Listing 6-29) to display the RDF statement we created in the database (see Figure 6-9).

    Listing 6-29. Final Code for Creating a Database with Nodes and Properties, and Displaying Stored Data

    ```
    import org.neo4j.graphdb.GraphDatabaseService;
    import org.neo4j.graphdb.Node;
    import org.neo4j.graphdb.Relationship;
    import org.neo4j.graphdb.RelationshipType;
    import org.neo4j.graphdb.Transaction;
    import org.neo4j.graphdb.factory.GraphDatabaseFactory;

    public class Neo4jDemo
    {
      private static final String DB_PATH = "target/neo4jdemodb";
      GraphDatabaseService graphDb;
      Node firstNode;
      Node secondNode;
      Relationship relationship;

      private static enum RelTypes implements RelationshipType
      {
        WEBSITE_OF
      }

      public static void main(final String[] args)
      {
        Neo4jDemo dbsample = new Neo4jDemo();
        dbsample.createDb();
        dbsample.shutDown();
      }

      void createDb()
      {

        graphDb = new GraphDatabaseFactory().newEmbeddedDatabase(DB_PATH);

        try ( Transaction tx = graphDb.beginTx() )
        {
          firstNode = graphDb.createNode();
    ```

```
        firstNode.setProperty("uri", "http://dbpedia.org/resource/Leslie_
        Sikos");
        firstNode.setProperty("label", "Leslie Sikos");
        secondNode = graphDb.createNode();
        secondNode.setProperty("uri", "http://www.lesliesikos.com");
        secondNode.setProperty("label", "website address");
        relationship = firstNode.createRelationshipTo(secondNode,
        RelTypes.WEBSITE_OF);
        relationship.setProperty("uri", "http://schema.org/url");
        relationship.setProperty("label", "website");
        System.out.print(secondNode.getProperty("uri") + " is the ");
        System.out.print(relationship.getProperty("label") + " of ");
        System.out.print(firstNode.getProperty("label"));
        tx.success();
      }
    }

    void shutDown()
    {
      System.out.println();
      System.out.println("Shutting down database…");
      graphDb.shutdown();
    }
  }
```

Figure 6-9. *A Neo4j application in Eclipse*

4Store

4Store is an efficient, scalable, and stable RDF database available for Linux systems such as Arch Linux, Debian, Ubuntu, Fedora, and CentOS, as well as Mac OS and FreeBSD [9]. To install 4Store on Linux, follow these steps:

1. Download the installer from `http://www.4store.org`.

2. Prepare your system to be used with 4Store by configuring it to look for libraries in `/usr/local/lib` and/or `/usr/local/lib64`. On most systems, you have to create a file called `/etc/ld.so.conf.d/local.conf` to achieve this, which contains these two paths, each on a separate line. You have to run `/sbin/ldconfig` as root. Once completed, the `$PKG_CONFIG_PATH` environmental variable should include the correct paths for locally installed packages.[1] Check whether your Linux distribution includes all the dependencies, namely `raptor`, `rasqal`, `glib2`, `libxml2`, `pcre`, `avahi`, `readline`, `ncurses`, `termcap`, `expat`, and `zlib`.

3. Build your 4Store from Tarballs or Git. For the first option, extract the files from the `.tar.gz` archive with `tar xvfz 4store-version.tar.gz`. Change the working directory to the `4store-version` directory with `cd`. Run `./configure`, and then run `make`. For the second option, change directory using `cd` to the directory that Git cloned, and run `sh autogen.sh`. The rest of the installation is the same as in the steps for the first option.

■ **Note**   Creating your build from Git might require additional dependencies.

---

4. Install 4Store by running `make install` as root.

If you want to install 4Store on a Mac, download the most recent version, open the `.dmg`, and install the 4Store application by dragging it into the `Applications` folder.

Once installed, you can run the 4Store application, which gives you a command line. You can create a triplestore using the command `4s-backend-setup triplestorename`, start the triplestore using `4s-backend triplestorename`, and run a SPARQL endpoint using `4s-httpd -p portnumber triplestorename`. The web interface will be available in your browser at `http://localhost:portnumber`.

The simplest command to import data from an RDF file is to use `4s-import`, specifying the database name to import the data to and the source RDF, as shown in Listing 6-30.

Listing 6-30. Importing Data from an RDF File to 4Store

```
4s-import your4store external.rdf
```

To import data programmatically, you can choose from a variety of options, depending on the language you prefer. In Ruby, for example, you can use `4store-ruby` (`https://github.com/moustaki/4store-ruby`), a Ruby interface to 4Store working over HTTP. For accessing the SPARQL server, you need HTTP PUT calls only, which are supported by most modern programming languages without installing a store-specific package. Purpose-built software libraries, however, make the HTTP requests easier. In Ruby, for instance, you can use `rest-client` (`https://github.com/rest-client/rest-client`), as shown in Listing 6-31. If you don't have `rest-client` installed, you can install it normally, e.g., `sudo gem install rest-client`.

---

[1]Assuming that your Linux distribution does not package recent versions of Raptor and Rasqal.

Listing 6-31. Using rest-client

```
#!/usr/bin/env ruby
require 'rubygems'
require 'rest_client'

filename = '/social.rdf'
graph    = 'http://yourgraph.com'
endpoint = 'http://localhost:8000'

response = RestClient.put endpoint + graph, File.read(filename), :content_type => ↵
 'application/rdf+xml'
puts "Response #{response.code}:
#{response.to_str}"
```

To run the script from the command line, use the ruby command with the filename as a parameter, such as ruby `loadrdf24store.rb`. Now, if you visit `http://localhost:portnumber/status/size/` in your browser, the new triples added from the RDF file should be listed.

Let's run a SPARQL query programmatically and process the results as XML, to list the RDF types of your dataset.

1. Install the XML parser Nokogiri for Ruby as gem `install nokogiri`.

2. Load all the required libraries (see Listing 6-32).

    Listing 6-32. Loading Required Libraries

    ```
    #!/usr/bin/env ruby
    require 'rubygems'
    require 'rest_client'
    require 'nokogiri'
    ```

3. Create a string for storing the SPARQL query and another one to store the endpoint (see Listing 6-33).

    Listing 6-33. Creating the Query and Endpoint Strings

    ```
    query = 'SELECT DISTINCT ?type WHERE { ?thing a ?type . } ORDER BY ?type'
    endpoint = 'http://localhost:8000/sparql/'
    ```

4. Using Nokogiri, process the XML output of the SPARQL query (see Listing 6-34).

    Listing 6-34. Processing the SPARQL Query Output

    ```
    response = RestClient.post endpoint, :query => query
    xml = Nokogiri::XML(response.to_str)
    ```

5. Find all the RDF types in the XML output and display them with puts, as shown in Listing 6-35.

Listing 6-35. Finding the RDF Types of the Output

```
xml.xpath('//sparql:binding[@name = "type"]/sparql:uri', 'sparql' =>
'http://www.w3.org/2005/sparql-results#').each do |type|
  puts type.content
end
```

6. Save the script as a Ruby file and run it using the `ruby` command with the file name as the parameter, such as `ruby rdf-types.rb`.

Oracle

Oracle is an industry-leading database. *Oracle Spatial and Graph*, Oracle's RDF triplestore/quadstore and ontology management platform, provides automatic partitioning and data compression, as well as high-performance parallel and direct path loading with the Oracle Database and loading through Jena [10].

Oracle Spatial and Graph supports parallel SPARQL and SQL querying and RDF graph update with SPARQL 1.1, SPARQL endpoint web services, SPARQL/Update, Java APIs with open source Apache Jena and Sesame, SQL queries with embedded SPARQL graph patterns, as well as SQL insert and update. It also supports ontology-assisted table data querying with SQL operators. Oracle Spatial and Graph features native inferencing with parallel, incremental, and secure operation for scalable reasoning with RDFS, OWL 2, SKOS, user-defined rules, and user-defined inference extensions. It has reasoned plug-ins for PelletDB and TrOWL. The semantic indexing of Oracle Spatial and Graph is suitable for text mining and entity analytics with integrated natural language processors. The database also supports R2RML direct mapping of relational data to RDF triples. For spatial RDF data storage and querying, Oracle supports GeoSPARQL as well.

Oracle Spatial and Graph can be integrated with the Apache Jena and Sesame application development environments, along with the leading Semantic Web tools for querying, visualization, and ontology management.

Blazegraph

Blazegraph is the flagship graph database product of SYSTAP, the vendor of the graph database previously known as Bigdata. It is a highly scalable, open source storage and computing platform [11]. Suitable for Big Data applications and selected for the Wikidata Query Service, Blazegraph is specifically designed to support big graphs, offering Semantic Web (RDF/SPARQL) and graph database (tinkerpop, blueprints, vertex-centric) APIs. The robust, scalable, fault-tolerant, enterprise-class storage and query features are combined with high availability, online backup, failover, and self-healing.

Blazegraph features an ultra-high performance RDF graph database that supports RDFS and OWL Lite reasoning, as well as SPARQL 1.1 querying. Designed for huge amounts of information, the Blazegraph RDF graph database can load 1 billion graph edges in less than an hour on a 15-node cluster. Blazegraph can be implemented in single machine mode (Journal), in high-availability replication cluster mode (HAJournalServer), or in horizontally sharded cluster mode (BlazegraphFederation). Blazegraph can execute distributed jobs by reading data not only from a local file system but also from the Web or the *Hadoop Distributed File System* (HDFS). The storage indexing is designed for very large datasets with up to 50 billion edges on a single machine, but Blazegraph can scale even larger graphs when implemented in a horizontally scaled architecture. Beyond high availability, the HAJournalServer also provides replication, online backup, and horizontal query scaling. BlazegraphFederation features fast, scalable parallel indexed storage and incremental cluster size growth. Both platforms support fully concurrent readers with snapshot isolation.

Blazegraph provides APIs for both Sesame and Blueprint. Blazegraph can be deployed as a server and accessed via a lightweight REST API. Blazegraph is released with Java wrappers, including a Sesame wrapper and a Blueprints wrapper. Blazegraph also has several enterprise deployment options, including a high-availability architecture and a dynamic-sharding scale-out architecture for very large graphs.

Summary

In this chapter, you learned about the power of graph databases and their advantages over mainstream relational and NoSQL databases. You now understand the concept of triples and quads, and the two main graph database types used for Semantic Web applications: the triplestores and the quadstores. You are now familiar with the most popular graph databases and know how to install and configure AllegroGraph, Neo4j, and 4Store and use their APIs for programmatic database access. You know the visualization options of AllegroGraph and Neo4j for displaying, analyzing, and manipulating graph nodes and links.

The next chapter will show you how to query structured datasets with SPARQL, the primary query language for RDF, and graph datastores, using proprietary query languages. You will learn how to write queries to answer complex questions based on the knowledge represented in Linking Open Data (LOD) datasets.

References

1. Cudré-Mauroux, P., Enchev, I., Fundatureanu, S., Groth, P., Haque, A., Harth, A., Keppmann, F. L., Miranker, D., Sequeda, J., Wylot, M. (2013) NoSQL Databases for RDF: An Empirical Evaluation. Lecture Notes in Computer Science 2013, 8219:310–325, http://dx.doi.org/10.1007/978-3-642-41338-4_20.

2. McColl, R., Ediger, D., Poovey, J., Campbell, D., Bader, D. A. (2014) A performance evaluation of open source graph databases. In: Proceedings of the first workshop on Parallel programming for analytics applications, pp 11–18, New York, NY, http://dx.doi.org/10.1145/2567634.2567638.

3. Heflin, J. (2015) SWAT Projects—the Lehigh University Benchmark (LUBM). http://swat.cse.lehigh.edu/projects/lubm/. Accessed 8 April 2015.

4. Franz, Inc. (2015) AllegroGraph RDFStore Web 3.0's Database. http://franz.com/agraph/allegrograph/. Accessed 10 April 2015.

5. Franz, Inc. (2015) AllegroGraph Client Downloads. http://franz.com/agraph/downloads/clients. Accessed 10 April 2015.

6. Franz, Inc. (2015) Gruff: A Grapher-Based Triple-Store Browser for AllegroGraph. http://franz.com/agraph/gruff/. Accessed 10 April 2015.

7. Franz, Inc. (2015) http://franz.com/agraph/gruff/springview3.png. Accessed 10 April 2015.

8. Neo Technology Inc. (2015) Neo4j, the World's Leading Graph Database. http://neo4j.com. Accessed 10 April 2015.

9. Garlik (2009) 4store—Scalable RDF storage. www.4store.org. Accessed 10 April 2015.

10. Oracle (2015) Oracle Spatial and Graph. www.oracle.com/technetwork/database/options/spatialandgraph/overview/index.html. Accessed 10 April 2015.

11. SYSTAP LLC (2015) Blazegraph. www.blazegraph.com/bigdata. Accessed 10 April 2015.

CHAPTER 7

Querying

While machine-readable datasets are published primarily for software agents, automatic data extraction is not always an option. Semantic Information Retrieval often involves users searching for the answer to a complex question, based on the formally represented knowledge in a dataset or database. While Structured Query Language (SQL) is used to query relational databases, querying graph databases and flat Resource Description Framework (RDF) files can be done using the SPARQL Protocol and RDF Query Language (SPARQL), the primary query language of RDF, which is much more powerful than SQL. SPARQL is a standardized language capable of querying local and online RDF files, Linked Open Data (LOD) datasets, and graph databases; constructing new RDF graphs, based on the information in the queried graphs; adding new RDF statements to or deleting triples from a graph; inferring logical consequences; and federating queries across different repositories. SPARQL can query multiple data sources at once, to dynamically merge the smaller graphs into a large supergraph. While graph databases often have a proprietary query language (often based on or extending SPARQL), most publicly available datasets have a SPARQL endpoint, from which you can run SPARQL queries. As for the developers, many Semantic Web software tools provide a SPARQL application programming interface (API) for programmatic access.

SPARQL: The Query Language for RDF

As mentioned before, the primary *query language* of RDF is *SPARQL* (pronounced "sparkle," a recursive acronym for *SPARQL Protocol and RDF Query Language*), which can be used to retrieve and manipulate information stored in RDF or in any format that can be retrieved as RDF [1]. The output can be a result set or an RDF graph.

Structure and Syntax

SPARQL uses a Notation3-like syntax. The URIs can be written in full between the less than (<) and greater than (>) characters (see Listing 7-1) or abbreviated using the namespace mechanism with the PREFIX keyword (see Listing 7-2).

Listing 7-1. Full URI Syntax in SPARQL

```
<http://example.com>
```

Listing 7-2. Using the Namespace Mechanism in SPARQL

```
PREFIX schema: <http://schema.org/>
```

After declaring the Schema.org namespace (`http://schema.org/`), for example, `http://schema.org/Person` can be abbreviated as `schema:Person`. The *default namespace* of a SPARQL query can be set by using the `PREFIX` directive with no prefix (e.g., `PREFIX : <http://yourdefaultnamespace.com/>`), so that you can use empty prefixes in your queries, such as `?a :knows ?b`. Similar to N3, the URI `http://www.w3.org/1999/02/22-rdf-syntax-ns#type` or `rdf:type` can be abbreviated as a. Literals can be written with or without a language tag and typing. Plain string literals are delimited by quotation marks, such as `"a plain literal"`, while plain literals including a language tag end in the @ sign and the standard language code, such as `"Wagen"@de` (the word *car* in German). Typed literals are written analogously to the typed literals in RDF, as, for example, `"55"^^xsd:integer` (55 is an integer number rather than two meaningless characters in a string literal). Frequently used typed literals can be abbreviated such that `"true"^^xsd:boolean` corresponds to `true`, while integer and decimal numbers are automatically assumed to be of type `xsd:integer` or `xsd:decimal`, respectively. As a consequence, `"5"^^xsd:integer` can be abbreviated as 5, while `"13.1"^^xsd:decimal` can be written as 13.1.

Each SPARQL query has a head and a body. The head of a SPARQL query is an expression for constructing the answer for the query. The evaluation of a query against an RDF graph is performed by checking whether the body is matched against the graph, which results in a set of bindings for the variables in the body. These bindings are processed using relational operators such as projection and distinction to generate the output for the query. The body can be a simple triple pattern expression or a complex RDF graph pattern expression containing triple patterns, such as subject-predicate-object RDF triples, where each subject, predicate, or object can be a variable. The body can also contain conjunctions, disjunctions, optional parts, and variable value constraints (see Figure 7-1).

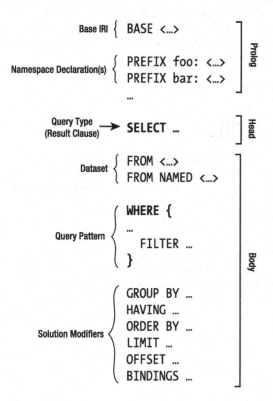

Figure 7-1. *The structure of SPARQL queries*

The BASE directive, the namespace declarations (PREFIX), the dataset declaration (FROM, FROM NAMED), and the query modifiers (GROUP BY, HAVING, ORDER BY, LIMIT, OFFSET, BINDINGS) are optional. The BASE directive and the list of prefixes are used to abbreviate URIs. The BASE keyword defines the base URI against which all relative URIs in the query are resolved. The list of prefixes can contain an arbitrary number of PREFIX statements. The prefix abbreviation pref preceding the semicolon represents the prefix URI, which can be used throughout the SPARQL query, making it unnecessary to repeat long URIs (standard namespace mechanism). The FROM clause specifies the default graph to search. The FROM NAMED clause can be used to specify a named graph to query. In some cases, as, for example, when the SPARQL endpoint used for the query is dedicated to the LOD dataset from which you want to retrieve data, the FROM clause is optional and can be safely omitted. The WHERE clause specifies the patterns used to extract the desired results. The query modifiers, such as ORDER BY or LIMIT, if present, are in the last part of the query.

SPARQL 1.0 and SPARQL 1.1

The first version of SPARQL, SPARQL 1.0, was released in 2008 [2]. SPARQL 1.0 introduced the SPARQL grammar, the SPARQL query syntax, the RDF term constraints, the graph patterns, the solution sequences and solution modifiers, and the four core query types (SELECT, CONSTRUCT, ASK, and DESCRIBE). SPARQL 1.0 has been significantly extended with new features in SPARQL 1.1 [3].

For example, SPARQL 1.1 supports *aggregation*. To perform aggregation, first you have to segregate the results into groups, based on the expression(s) in the GROUP BY clause. Then, you evaluate the projections and aggregate functions in the SELECT clause, to get one result per group. Finally, the aggregated results have to be filtered in a HAVING clause.

The *SPARQL 1.1 Update language* supports graph update operations (INSERT DATA, DELETE DATA, DELETE/INSERT, LOAD, CLEAR) and graph management operations (CREATE, DROP, COPY, MOVE, and ADD) [4]. The INSERT DATA operation adds some triples written inline in the request into the graphstore. The DELETE DATA operation is used to remove RDF triples, if the respective graphs in the graphstore contain them. The DELETE/INSERT operation can be used to remove triples from, or add triples to, the graphstore, based on bindings for a query pattern specified in a WHERE clause. The LOAD operation reads an RDF document from an internationalized resource identifier (IRI) and inserts its triples into the specified graph in the graphstore. The CLEAR operation removes all the triples in the specified graph(s) in the graphstore. The CREATE operation creates a new graph in the graphstore. The DROP operation removes a graph and all of its contents. The COPY operation modifies a graph to contain a copy of another graph. In other words, it inserts all data from an input graph into a destination graph. The MOVE operation moves all of the data from one graph into another graph. The ADD operation reproduces all data from one graph into another graph. It is also possible to update RDF graphs through a protocol known as the *SPARQL 1.1 Uniform HTTP Protocol* [5].

The *SPARQL 1.1 Service Description* specification [6] provides a method for discovering information about SPARQL services, such as the supported extension functions, and details of the default dataset. It also has a vocabulary for describing SPARQL services, which has the namespace IRI http://www.w3.org/ns/sparql-service-description# and the prefix sd. In Semantic Web applications, it is not always possible to explicitly write graph structures for graph pattern matching, and that is why SPARQL 1.1 defines semantic entailment relations called *entailment regimes* [7]. These standard semantic entailment relations can be used in applications that rely on RDF statements inferred from explicitly given assertions, so that the graph pattern matching is performed using semantic entailment relations instead of explicitly given graph structures. SPARQL 1.1 supports additional serialization formats for the query output, including JSON [8], CSV, and TSV [9], beyond the formats supported by SPARQL 1.0, such as XML [10]. Beyond the four core SPARQL query types introduced in SPARQL 1.0, SPARQL 1.1 also supports reasoning queries and federated queries, as you will see in the next section.

Query Types

The optional namespace declarations are followed by the *query*. The four core query types in SPARQL are the SELECT, the ASK, the CONSTRUCT, and the DESCRIBE queries. SELECT queries provide a value selection for the variables matching the query patterns. The yes/no queries (ASK queries) provide a Boolean value. CONSTRUCT queries create new RDF data from the above values, as well as resource descriptions. DESCRIBE queries return a new RDF graph containing matched resources. The most frequently used SPARQL queries are the SELECT queries.

Beyond the basic query types, SPARQL 1.1 also supports reasoning through REASON queries and executes queries distributed over different SPARQL endpoints (*federated queries*), using the SERVICE keyword [11].

Pattern Matching

The query output result clause is followed by the *pattern matching*. Two different pattern types can be used in SPARQL queries: the *triple patterns* and the *graph patterns*. The SPARQL triple patterns are similar to the subject-predicate-object triples of RDF, but they can also include *variables*. This makes it possible to select RDF triples from an RDF graph that match your criteria described in the pattern. Any or all subject, predicate, or object values can be variables, all of which are identified by a question mark[1] preceding the string, such as ?name. To match an exact RDF triple, you have to write the subject-predicate-object names followed by a ., such as shown in Listing 7-3.

Listing 7-3. Exact RDF Triple Matching in SPARQL

```
ex:Person schema:familyName "Sikos" .
```

To match one variable, you have to substitute the appropriate triple component (the subject, the predicate, or the object) with a variable (see Listing 7-4).

Listing 7-4. Matching One Variable in SPARQL

```
?person schema:familyName "Sikos" .
```

A variable is not limited to any part of the triple pattern. You can substitute any triple components (the subject, the predicate, or the object) with variables (see Listing 7-5).

Listing 7-5. Matching Multiple Variables in SPARQL

```
?person schema:familyName ?name .
```

Even all components can be variables. For instance, the triple pattern ?subject ?object ?name will match all triples in your RDF graph. Sometimes, much more complex selection rules are required than what you can express in a single triple pattern. A collection of triple patterns is called a *graph pattern* and is delimited by curly braces (see Listing 7-6).

Listing 7-6. A Graph Pattern in SPARQL

```
{
  ?who schema:name ?name.
  ?who iswc:research_topic ?research_topic.
  ?who foaf:knows ?others.
}
```

---

[1] Alternatively, the dollar sign ($) can be used.

Graph patterns can be used for matching optional parts, creating a union of patterns, nesting, filtering values of possible matchings, and choosing the data source to be matched by the pattern. As a result, a graph pattern will find all resources with all the desired properties written in the pattern. Graph patterns make it possible to write complex queries, because each returned resource can be substituted into all occurrences of the variable, in case the same variable is used in multiple triple patterns. This leads to a truly sophisticated selection unknown to the conventional Web, whereby you cannot use multiple filtering in searches beyond some basic operators, such as AND, OR, or XOR. However, SPARQL supports filter functions too, including logical (!, &&, ||, =, !=, <, <=, >, and >=) and mathematical operations (+, -, *, /), as well as comparisons (=, !=, >, <). SPARQL has built-in tests for checking web addresses, blank graph nodes, literals, and bounds (isURI, isBlank, isLiteral, bound), accessors such as str, datatype, and lang (see Listing 7-7), and other functions, such as sameTerm, langMatches, and regex, for checking same terms, language matching, and writing regular expressions.

Listing 7-7. Language Checking in SPARQL

```
lang(?title)="en"
```

Beyond the SPARQL 1.0 operators and functions, SPARQL 1.1 also supports existence-checking functions (EXISTS, NOT EXISTS), both of which can be used as part of a graph pattern (such as in Listing 7-8, to find persons who do not have an e-mail address) as well as in FILTER expressions.

Listing 7-8. Existence Checking in a Graph Pattern

```
SELECT ?person
WHERE
{
  ?person rdf:type foaf:Person .
  NOT EXISTS { ?person foaf:mbox ?email }
}
```

SPARQL 1.1 also has additional functions, such as COUNT, SUM, AVG, MIN, MAX, SAMPLE, and GROUP_CONCAT. Furthermore, SPARQL 1.1 supports *property paths* that allow triple patterns to match arbitrary-length paths through a graph. Predicates are combined with operators similar to regular expressions (see Table 7-1).

Table 7-1. Property Path Constructs in SPARQL 1.1

Construct	Meaning
path1/path2	Forwards path (path1 followed by path2)
^path1	Backwards path (object to subject)
path1|path2	Either path1 or path2
path1*	path1, repeated zero or more times
path1+	path1, repeated one or more times
path1?	path1, optionally
path1{m,n}	At least m and no more than n occurrences of path1
path1{n}	Exactly n occurrences of path1
path1{m,}	At least m occurrences of path1
path1{,n}	At most n occurrences of path1

Solution Modifiers

The last optional part of the SPARQL queries are the *solution modifiers*. Once the output of the pattern has been computed (in the form of a table of values of variables), solution modifiers allow you to modify these values, applying standard classical operators such as projection,[2] DISTINCT (removes duplicates), ORDER (sorting mechanism), and LIMIT (sets the maximum number of results returned).

SELECT Queries

The most common SPARQL queries are the SELECT queries. The SELECT clause specifies data items (variable bindings) to be returned by the SPARQL query. Even through LOD datasets can contain thousands or even millions of RDF triples, you can select those items that meet your criteria. For example, from a writer's dataset, you can list those writers who lived in the 20th century or those who are American. SPARQL supports joker characters, so you can select all variables mentioned in the query, using SELECT *. If you want to eliminate potential duplicates, use the DISTINCT keyword after SELECT, such as SELECT DISTINCT ?var. SELECT queries are often used to extract triples through specific variables and expressions. For example, assume we need a query to extract all names mentioned in someone's FOAF file declared using foaf:name. The abbreviation of the namespace requires a PREFIX declaration. The query is a SELECT query, which uses a variable for the names (?name), and a WHERE clause with a triple pattern to find all subjects (?person) and objects (?name) linked with the foaf:name predicate (see Listing 7-9).

Listing 7-9. A SELECT Query to Find Subjects and Objects Linked with a Declared Predicate

```
PREFIX foaf:  <http://xmlns.com/foaf/0.1/>
SELECT ?name
WHERE {
  ?person foaf:name ?name .
}
```

If we need all those people from an FOAF file who have an e-mail address specified, we have to declare two predicates, one for the name (foaf:name) and another for the e-mail address (foaf:mbox), while all the subjects (?person) and objects (?name, ?email) are variables (see Listing 7-10).

Listing 7-10. A SELECT Query to Find Subjects and Objects Linked with Two Different Predicates

```
PREFIX foaf:  <http://xmlns.com/foaf/0.1/>
SELECT ?name ?email
WHERE {
  ?person foaf:name ?name .
  ?person foaf:mbox ?email .
}
```

The output will contain all the names and e-mail addresses.

---

[2] Only those expressions that consist of aggregates and constants can be projected in SPARQL query levels using aggregates. The only exception is using GROUP BY with one or more simple expressions consisting of one variable only, which variable can be projected from that level.

> ■ **Note**   If the persons are described using `Schema.org/Person`, the names can be expressed using the `givenName` and `familyName` properties, and the e-mail address using the `email` property, while the namespace has to be modified to `http://schema.org/`.

The results of the SELECT queries are typically displayed as a table of values (in HTML, XML, or JSON).

Filtering

If we have to extract all those landlocked countries from DBpedia that have a population larger than 5 million, we need the FILTER keyword in the WHERE clause (see Listing 7-11).

Listing 7-11. A SELECT Query with a Filter to Extract All Landlocked Countries from DBpedia with More Than 5 Million Inhabitants

```
PREFIX rdfs: <http://www.w3.org/2000/01/rdf-schema#>
PREFIX type: <http://dbpedia.org/class/yago/>
PREFIX prop: <http://dbpedia.org/property/>
SELECT ?country_name ?population
WHERE {
    ?country a type:LandlockedCountries ;
             rdfs:label ?country_name ;
             prop:populationEstimate ?population .
    FILTER (?population > 5000000) .
}
```

The Boolean condition(s) provided will filter out the unwanted query results, in this case, all those landlocked countries that have fewer than 5 million inhabitants.

> ■ **Note**   The preceding example uses the ; shortcut to separate triple patterns sharing the same subject `?country`.

ASK Queries

If you need the answer to a yes/no question, you can use the ASK query in SPARQL. For instance, you can query DBpedia to find out whether the Amazon is longer than the Nile (see Listing 7-12).

Listing 7-12. An ASK Query in SPARQL

```
PREFIX prop: <http://dbpedia.org/property/>
ASK
{
  <http://dbpedia.org/resource/Amazon_River> prop:length ?amazonLength .
  <http://dbpedia.org/resource/Nile> prop:length ?nileLength .
  FILTER(?amazon > ?nile) .
}
```

The result of ASK queries is either `true` or `false`. In our example, the output is `true`.

CONSTRUCT Queries

SPARQL can be used not only to retrieve information from datasets but also to create new graphs, or to reshape existing RDF graphs by adding new triples. Such queries are called CONSTRUCT queries. Assume you want to extend your family tree description by adding a grandmother. To do so, you have to identify the gender and parent-child relationships of the other family members (see Listing 7-13).

Listing 7-13. Preparing a CONSTRUCT Query

```
:Ben    :hasParent  :Christina ;
        :gender     :male .
:Luke   :hasParent  :Linda ;
        :gender     :male .
:Christina :hasParent :Anna ;
        :gender     :female .
:Linda  :hasParent :Anna ;
        :gender     :female .
:Anna   :gender     :female .
```

The next step is to run a CONSTRUCT query to create new triples based on the preceding ones, to specify who is whose grandmother (see Listing 7-14).

Listing 7-14. A CONSTRUCT Query

```
PREFIX : <http://samplefamilytreeonto.com/>

CONSTRUCT { ?p :hasGrandmother ?g . }

WHERE {?p      :hasParent ?parent .
       ?parent :hasParent ?g .
       ?g      :gender    :female .}
```

The newly constructed triples describe the relationship between the two grandchildren and their grandmother (see Listing 7-15).

Listing 7-15. A CONSTRUCT Query Generates New Triples

```
:Ben
      :hasGrandmother :Anna .

:Luke
      :hasGrandmother :Anna .
```

DESCRIBE Queries

The DESCRIBE queries describe the resources matched by the given variables. For example, if you run a DESCRIBE query on a dataset of countries (see Listing 7-16), the output will be all the triples related to the queried country (see Listing 7-17).

Listing 7-16. A DESCRIBE Query

```
DESCRIBE ?country
```

Listing 7-17. The Output of a DESCRIBE Query

```
ex:Hungary a geo:Country;
ex:continent geo:Europe;
ex:flag <http://yourwebsite.com/img/flag-hun.png> ;
…
```

Federated Queries

In SPARQL 1.1, queries can issue a query on another SPARQL endpoint during query execution. These queries are called *federated queries*, in which the remote SPARQL endpoint is declared by the SERVICE keyword, which sends the corresponding part of the query to the remote SPARQL endpoint. For example, if the remote SPARQL endpoint is DBpedia's endpoint, a federated query can be written as shown in Listing 7-18.

Listing 7-18. A Federated Query in SPARQL 1.1

```
SELECT DISTINCT ?person
WHERE {
  SERVICE <http://dbpedia.org/sparql> { ?person a <http://schema.org/Person> . }
} LIMIT 10
```

A sample output of this query is shown in Listing 7-19, identifying ten persons from DBpedia.

Listing 7-19. Federated Query Result Example

```
---------------------------------------------------------
| person                                                |
=========================================================
| <http://dbpedia.org/resource/%C3%81ngel_Gim%C3%A9nez> |
| <http://dbpedia.org/resource/Aaron_Lines>             |
| <http://dbpedia.org/resource/Abel_Lafleur>            |
| <http://dbpedia.org/resource/Ada_Maimon>              |
| <http://dbpedia.org/resource/Adam_Krikorian>          |
| <http://dbpedia.org/resource/Albert_Constable>        |
| <http://dbpedia.org/resource/Alex_Reid_(actress)>     |
| <http://dbpedia.org/resource/Alex_Reid_(art_dealer)>  |
| <http://dbpedia.org/resource/Alex_Reid_(fighter)>     |
| <http://dbpedia.org/resource/Alex_Reid_(footballer)>  |
---------------------------------------------------------
```

REASON Queries

In SPARQL 1.1, reasoning can be performed by executing a SPARQL query with the REASON keyword, followed by a rule set in an ontology or declarative language (declared as a URL to a rule delimited by <> or inline N3 rules between curly braces), and a combination of an OVER and a WHERE clause to define the triples for reasoning.

For example, to list all the acquaintances of Leslie Sikos from two different datasets, you can write a federated query with reasoning, as shown in Listing 7-20, regardless of whether Leslie Sikos listed them as acquaintances or other people stated that they know him.

Listing 7-20. Find Acquaintances Regardless of the Relationship Direction

```
REASON {
  { ?x foaf:knows ?y } => { ?y foaf:knows ?x }
}
OVER {
  :LeslieSikos foaf:knows ?person .
}
WHERE {
  {
    SERVICE <http://examplegraph1.com/sparql> { :LeslieSikos foaf:knows ?person . }
  } UNION {
    SERVICE <http://examplegraph2.com/sparql> { :LeslieSikos foaf:knows ?person . }
  }
}
```

URL Encoding of SPARQL Queries

In order to provide the option for automated processes to make SPARQL queries, SPARQL can be used over HTTP, using the SPARQL Protocol (abbreviated by the *P* in SPARQL). SPARQL endpoints can handle a SPARQL query with parameters of an HTTP GET or POST request. The query is URL-encoded to escape special characters and create the query string as the value of the query variable. The parameters are defined in the standardized SPARQL Protocol [12]. As an example, take a look at the default DBpedia SPARQL endpoint (http://dbpedia.org/sparql/) query shown in Listing 7-21.

Listing 7-21. A URL-Encoded SPARQL Query

```
http://dbpedia.org/sparql?default-graph-uri=http%3A%2F%2Fdbpedia.org&query=select+distinct+
%3FConcept+where+{[]+a+%3FConcept}+LIMIT+100&format=text%2Fhtml&timeout=30000&debug=on
```

■ **Note** The second parameter (default-graph-uri) is DBpedia's proprietary implementation, which extends the standard URL-encoded SPARQL query.

Graph Update Operations

In SPARQL 1.1, new RDF triples can be added to a graph, using the INSERT DATA operation. If the destination graph does not exist, it is created. As an example, assume there are two RDF statements about a book in a graph, title and format (see Listing 7-22).

Listing 7-22. Data Before the INSERT DATA Operation

```
@prefix dc: <http://purl.org/dc/elements/1.1/> .
@prefix schema: <http://schema.org/> .

<http://www.lesliesikos.com/mastering-structured-data-on-the-semantic-web/> dc:title ↵
  "Mastering Structured Data on the Semantic Web" .
<http://www.lesliesikos.com/mastering-structured-data-on-the-semantic-web/> ↵
  schema:bookFormat schema:Paperback .
```

To add two new triples to this graph about the author and the language the book was written in, you can use the INSERT DATA operation, as shown in Listing 7-23. Because the subject is the same for both triples, it has to be declared just once in a semicolon-separated list.

Listing 7-23. Adding New Triples to a Graph, Using the INSERT DATA Operation

```
PREFIX dc: <http://purl.org/dc/elements/1.1/>
PREFIX schema: <http://schema.org/>

INSERT DATA
{
  <http://www.lesliesikos.com/mastering-structured-data-on-the-semantic-web/> dc:creator ↵
  "Leslie Sikos" ;
  schema:inLanguage "English" .
}
```

As a result, the graph will contain four triples about the book, as demonstrated in Listing 7-24.

Listing 7-24. Data After the INSERT DATA Operation

```
@prefix dc: <http://purl.org/dc/elements/1.1/> .
@prefix schema: <http://schema.org/> .

<http://www.lesliesikos.com/mastering-structured-data-on-the-semantic-web/> dc:title ↵
 "Mastering Structured Data on the Semantic Web" .
<http://www.lesliesikos.com/mastering-structured-data-on-the-semantic-web/> ↵
 schema:bookFormat schema:Paperback .
<http://www.lesliesikos.com/mastering-structured-data-on-the-semantic-web/> dc:creator ↵
 "Leslie Sikos" .
<http://www.lesliesikos.com/mastering-structured-data-on-the-semantic-web/> dc:inLanguage ↵
 "English" .
```

SPARQL 1.1 also supports the removal of RDF triples, using the DELETE DATA operation. For example, to remove the book format and the language of the book from Listing 7-24, you declare the prefixes, use the DELETE DATA operation, and list the statements to remove (see Listing 7-25).

Listing 7-25. Removing Triples from a Graph, Using the DELETE DATA Operation

```
PREFIX schema: <http://schema.org/>
PREFIX dc: <http://purl.org/dc/elements/1.1/>

DELETE DATA
{
  <http://www.lesliesikos.com/mastering-structured-data-on-the-semantic-web/> ↵
  schema:bookFormat schema:Paperback ; dc:inLanguage "English" .
}
```

Graph Management Operations

In SPARQL 1.1, RDF statements can be copies from the default graph to a named graph using the COPY operation. As an example, assume we have the triples shown in Listing 7-26.

Listing 7-26. Data Before Copying

```
# Default Graph

@prefix foaf:  <http://xmlns.com/foaf/0.1/> .

<http://examplegraph.com/Leslie> a foaf:Person .
<http://examplegraph.com/Leslie> foaf:givenName "Leslie" .
<http://examplegraph.com/Leslie> foaf:mbox  <mailto:leslie@examplegraph.com> .

# Graph http://examplenamedgraph.com

<http://examplenamedgraph.com/Christina> a foaf:Person .
<http://examplenamedgraph.com/Christina> foaf:givenName "Christina" .
```

All triples of the default graph can be copied to the named graph with the COPY operation, as shown in Listing 7-27.

Listing 7-27. A COPY DEFAULT TO Operation SPARQL 1.1

```
COPY DEFAULT TO <http:/examplenamedgraph.com>
```

The result of the COPY DEFAULT TO operation is shown in Listing 7-28.

Listing 7-28. Data After the COPY DEFAULT TO Operation

```
# Default Graph

@prefix foaf:  <http://xmlns.com/foaf/0.1/> .

<http://examplegraph.com/Leslie> a foaf:Person .
<http://examplegraph.com/Leslie> foaf:givenName "Leslie" .
<http://examplegraph.com/Leslie> foaf:mbox  <mailto:leslie@examplegraph.com> .

# Graph http://examplenamedgraph.com

@prefix foaf:  <http://xmlns.com/foaf/0.1/> .

<http://examplegraph.com/Leslie> a foaf:Person .
<http://examplegraph.com/Leslie> foaf:givenName "Leslie" .
<http://examplegraph.com/Leslie> foaf:mbox  <mailto:leslie@examplegraph.com> .
```

■ **Note**   The original content of the named graph is lost by the COPY operation.

Similarly, RDF statements can be moved from the default graph to a named graph, using the MOVE operation. For example, assume you have the data shown in Listing 7-29.

Listing 7-29. Data Before the MOVE DEFAULT TO Operation

```
# Default Graph

@prefix foaf:  <http://xmlns.com/foaf/0.1/> .

<http://examplegraph.com/Nathan> a foaf:Person .
<http://examplegraph.com/Nathan> foaf:givenName "Nathan" .
<http://examplegraph.com/Nathan> foaf:mbox  <mailto:nathan@examplegraph.com> .

# Graph http://examplenamedgraph.com

@prefix foaf:  <http://xmlns.com/foaf/0.1/> .

<http://examplenamedgraph.com/Peter> a foaf:Person .
<http://examplenamedgraph.com/Peter> foaf:givenName "Peter" .
```

To move all RDF statements from the default graph into a named graph, you can use the MOVE operation, as shown in Listing 7-30.

Listing 7-30. A MOVE DEFAULT TO Operation

```
MOVE DEFAULT TO http://examplenamedgraph.com
```

■ **Note**   The original content of the named graph is lost by the MOVE operation (see Listing 7-31).

Listing 7-31. Data After the MOVE DEFAULT TO Operation

```
# Default Graph

# Graph http://examplenamedgraph.com

@prefix foaf:  <http://xmlns.com/foaf/0.1/> .

<http://examplegraph.com/Nathan> a foaf:Person .
<http://examplegraph.com/Nathan> foaf:givenName "Nathan" .
<http://examplegraph.com/Nathan> foaf:mbox  <mailto:nathan@examplegraph.com> .
```

RDF statements can be inserted from an input graph to a destination graph, using the ADD operation. Listing 7-32 shows sample RDF triples to be added from the default graph to a named graph.

Listing 7-32. Data Before the ADD Operation

```
# Default graph
@prefix foaf:  <http://xmlns.com/foaf/0.1/> .

<http://examplegraph.com/Michael> a foaf:Person .
<http://examplegraph.com/Michael> foaf:givenName "Michael" .
<http://examplegraph.com/Michael> foaf:mbox  <mailto:mike@examplegraph.com> .
```

```
# Graph http://examplenamedgraph.com
@prefix foaf:  <http://xmlns.com/foaf/0.1/> .

<http://examplenamedgraph.com/Jemma> a foaf:Person .
```

The ADD operation in Listing 7-33 performs the task.

Listing 7-33. An ADD Operation in SPARQL 1.1

```
ADD DEFAULT TO <http://examplenamedgraph.com>
```

As a result, the default graph is merged to the named graph (see Listing 7-34).

Listing 7-34. The Result of an ADD Operation

```
# Default graph
@prefix foaf:  <http://xmlns.com/foaf/0.1/> .

<http://examplegraph.com/Michael> a foaf:Person .
<http://examplegraph.com/Michael> foaf:givenName "Michael" .
<http://examplegraph.com/Michael> foaf:mbox  <mailto:mike@examplegraph.com> .

# Graph http://examplenamedgraph.com
@prefix foaf:  <http://xmlns.com/foaf/0.1/> .

<http://examplenamedgraph.com/Jemma> a foaf:Person .

<http://examplegraph.com/Michael> a foaf:Person .
<http://examplegraph.com/Michael> foaf:givenName "Michael" .
<http://examplegraph.com/Michael> foaf:mbox <mailto:mike@example> .
```

Proprietary Query Engines and Query Languages

While most Semantic Web platforms and graph databases have SPARQL support through a SPARQL query engine such as Apache Jena's ARQ or AllegroGraph's sparql-1.1, some vendors provide their own query language. Many of these query languages are partially compatible with, or similar to, SPARQL but are often incompatible with other Semantic Web software products beyond the ones they are released with.

SeRQL: The Sesame RDF Query Language

Sesame supports not only SPARQL but also *SeRQL* (pronounced "circle"), the *Sesame RDF Query Language* [13]. Regardless of whether you have a connection to a local or remote Sesame repository, you can perform a SeRQL query on a `SesameRepository` object, retrieve the result as a table, and display the values (see Listing 7-35).

Listing 7-35. A SeRQL Query, Using the Sesame Repository API

```
String query = "SELECT * FROM {x} p {y}";
QueryResultsTable resultsTable = myRepository.performTableQuery(QueryLanguage.SERQL, query);

int rowCount = resultsTable.getRowCount();
int columnCount = resultsTable.getColumnCount();
```

```
for (int row = 0; row < rowCount; row++) {
    for (int column = 0; column < columnCount; column++) {
        Value value = resultsTable.getValue(row, column);

        if (value != null) {
            System.out.print(value.toString());
        }
        else {
            System.out.print("null");
        }

        System.out.print("\t");
    }

    System.out.println();
}
```

■ **Note**   Some repository operations require elevated privileges, so you might have to log on to the
SesameService before obtaining the repository object. For instance, if you do not have read access to a
repository, you will get an AccessDeniedException.

If you have to change a lot of RDF triples in your repository, you can use the Sesame Graph API in
combination with SeRQL CONSTRUCT queries. For instance, if we have a repository that describes the
manuscript of a book with many triples, and the book has been published since the last update of the
repository, there are many obsolete property values (draft) for the PublicationStatus property from the
Publishing Status Ontology (PSO) that should be changed to published. Rather than changing the property
values manually for each affected triple, we derive the new triples from the existing PublicationStatus
statements, changing the object of these statements from draft to published (see Listing 7-36).

Listing 7-36. Changing Multiple Property Values, Using the Sesame Graph API

```
myRepository.addGraph(QueryLanguage.SERQL, ↵
"CONSTRUCT {X} <http://purl.org/spar/pso/PublicationStatus> {\"published\"} " + ↵
"FROM {X} <http://purl.org/spar/pso/PublicationStatus> {\"draft\"}");
```

Now all the triples are updated with the new property value; however, these triples are duplicated.
The original triples with the obsolete property value have to be removed from the graph. To do so, we select
all PublicationStatus triples with the object draft (the old value) and remove these triples from the
repository (see Listing 7-37).

Listing 7-37. Removing All Triples with the Obsolete Property Value

```
myRepository.removeGraph(QueryLanguage.SERQL, ↵
"CONSTRUCT * " + "FROM {X} <http://purl.org/spar/pso/PublicationStatus> {\"draft\"}";
```

■ **Note**   This workaround is needed only because SeRQL does not support update operations. Another option
to update a Sesame repository is using the SAIL API.

CQL: Neo4j's Query Language

Neo4j has a proprietary query language called *Cypher Query Language* (*CQL*), a declarative pattern-matching language with an SQL-like, very simple, and human-readable syntax [14]. The most frequently used Neo4j CQL commands and clauses are CREATE (to create nodes, relationships, and properties), MATCH (to retrieve data about nodes, relationships, and properties), RETURN (to return query results), WHERE (to provide conditions to filter retrieval data), DELETE (to delete nodes and relationships), REMOVE (to delete properties of nodes and relationships), ORDER BY (to sort retrieval data), and SET (to add or update labels). The most frequently used Neo4j CQL functions are String (to work with String literals), Aggregation (to perform some aggregation operations on CQL Query results), and Relationship (to get details of Relationships such as startnode and endnode). The data types of Neo4j CQL are similar to the Java programming language. The datatypes are used to define properties of nodes and relationships, such as boolean, byte, short, int, long, float, double, char, and string.

The MATCH command identifies a node through the node name and the node label. The MATCH command expects the node name and the label name as the arguments in curly brackets separated by a colon (see Listing 7-38).

Listing 7-38. MATCH Command Syntax

```
MATCH
(
   node-name:label-name
)
```

The RETURN clause is used in CQL, with the MATCH command, to retrieve data about nodes, relationships, and properties from a Neo4j graph database. The RETURN clause can retrieve some or all properties of a node and retrieve some or all properties of nodes and associated relationships. The arguments of the RETURN clause are the node name(s) and property name(s) (see Listing 7-39).

Listing 7-39. RETURN Clause Syntax

```
RETURN
   node-name.property1-name, … node-name. propertyn-name
```

For example, to retrieve all property data of the Fac node representing a university's faculties, you can combine the MATCH command with the RETURN clause, as shown in Listing 7-40.

Listing 7-40. Retrieving All Faculty Data

```
MATCH (fac: Fac)
RETURN fac.facno,fac.fname,fac.location
```

The number of rows returned by the command will be identical to the number of faculties of the university stored in the database.

Similar to SPARQL, Neo4j's CQL uses the WHERE clause to get the desired data (see Listing 7-41). Rather than using the WHERE clause with the SELECT command, however, in CQL, you use it with SELECT's CQL equivalent, MATCH.

Listing 7-41. The Syntax of the WHERE Clause in CQL

```
WHERE condition boolean_operator additional_condition
```

The first argument provides the condition, consisting of a property name, a comparison operator, and a value. The property name is the name of a graph node or the name of a relationship. The comparison operator is one of = (equal to), <> (not equal to), < (less than), > (greater than), <= (less than or equal to), or >= (greater than or equal to). The value is a literal value, such as a number, a string literal, etc. The second and third arguments (the Boolean operator and multiple conditions) are optional. The Boolean operator can be AND, OR, NOT, or XOR.

To sort rows in ascending order or descending order, use the ORDER BY clause with the MATCH command (similar to SPARQL's ORDER BY on the SELECT queries). The ORDER BY clause contains the list of properties used in sorting, optionally followed by the DESC keyword (when sorting in descending order).

Identify Datasets to Query

To access data from LOD datasets, you can perform a semantic search, browse dataset catalogs, or run queries directly from a dedicated query interface. For searching machine-readable data, you can use *semantic search engines* such as Sindice (http://sindice.com) or FactForge (http://factforge.net). Third-party *data marketplaces* such as http://datamarket.com can find open data from secondary data sources and consume or acquire data for data seekers.

To retrieve information from datasets, you can run SPARQL queries on purpose-built access points called *SPARQL endpoints* (as mentioned earlier) that usually provide a web interface and, optionally, an API. The automatic discovery of the SPARQL endpoint for a given resource is not trivial; however, *dataset catalogs* such as http://datahub.io and http://dataportals.org can be queried for a SPARQL endpoint with a given URI. Because a prerequisite for all LOD datasets to be added to the LOD Cloud Diagram is to provide a dedicated SPARQL endpoint, Datahub registries often include a SPARQL endpoint URL.

Another approach for identifying SPARQL endpoints is using the VoID standardized vocabulary, which is specifically designed for describing datasets. In VoID files, the descriptions are provided as URLs, which can be canonically derived from a URI.

Public SPARQL Endpoints

Many SPARQL endpoints are publicly available and typically have a default LOD dataset set for querying. Your SPARQL queries will run on the default graph of the endpoint, unless you refer to named graphs in your queries. For example, DBpedia's SPARQL endpoint is http://dbpedia.org/sparql/, which runs queries on DBpedia by default.

■ **Note**   DBpedia offers two other interfaces to its SPARQL endpoint. The first is called *SPARQL Explorer* and is available at http://dbpedia.org/snorql/. The second is the *DBpedia Query Builder* available at http://querybuilder.dbpedia.org, which can be used to build your own queries. Because the dataset is the same in each case, the SPARQL query results are identical on all three interfaces.

SPARQL endpoints dedicated to a particular dataset can be domain-specific. Since the Web of Data is highly distributed, there is no SPARQL endpoint to query the entire Semantic Web (like Google searches on the conventional Web). However, the most frequently used public SPARQL endpoints can query extremely large datasets containing millions or even billions of triples, which are suitable to answer complex questions (see Table 7-2).

Table 7-2. Popular Public SPARQL Endpoints

Service/Dataset	SPARQL Endpoint
Datahub/CKAN	http://semantic.ckan.net/sparql
DBpedia	http://dbpedia.org/sparql/
GeoNames	http://geosparql.org/
Linked Open Commerce	http://linkedopencommerce.com/sparql/
Linked Open Data Cloud	http://lod.openlinksw.com/sparql
LinkedGeoData	http://linkedgeodata.org/sparql
Sindice	http://sparql.sindice.com/
URIBurner	http://uriburner.com/sparql

Setting Up Your Own SPARQL Endpoint

If you publish your LOD dataset on your server, you might want to set up a dedicated SPARQL endpoint to provide easy access to it. There are a couple of free, open source, and commercial products available, not all of which have a full SPARQL 1.1 support, but most have a complete SPARQL 1.0 support. Some products are standalone SPARQL endpoints that you can install on your web server, while others are more comprehensive products that provide a SPARQL endpoint as a feature. The most widely deployed SPARQL endpoints are OpenLink Virtuoso, Fuseki, D2R, 4store SPARQL Server, and PublishMyData.

OpenLink Virtuoso

OpenLink Virtuoso is by far the most widely deployed SPARQL endpoint. Among others, Virtuoso is implemented as the SPARQL endpoint for DBpedia and DBpedia Live, LinkedGeoData, Sindice, the BBC, BioGateway, data.gov, CKAN, and the LOD Cloud Cache.

The Virtuoso SPARQL Query Editor provides the default LOD dataset associated with a particular installation, which can be overridden when querying named graphs. For example, the default dataset of the DBpedia SPARQL endpoint is http://dbpedia.org, as shown in Figure 7-2. This is obviously different in each installation of Virtuoso, but the interface is usually very similar, if not identical.

The Query Text is a multiline text area in which you can write your SPARQL queries. This textarea usually contains a skeleton query, which you can easily modify by overwriting, removing, or adding SPARQL code. Under the textarea, you can select the output format, optionally the maximum time after which the query execution will stop, and the rigorous check of the query. Some installations offer a set of sample queries as a drop-down list. You typically have two buttons as well: one to run the query you wrote (Run Query) and another to clear the textarea (Reset).

The output format drop-down might vary somewhat from installation to installation, but generally, you have options such as HTML, Spreadsheet, XML, JSON, JavaScript, Turtle, RDF/XML, N-Triples, CSV, TSV, and CXML. Some of the output formats might not be available, due to configuration or missing components. For example, the CXML data exchange format suitable for faceted view, which can be displayed by programs such as Microsoft Pivot, require the Virtuoso Universal Server (Virtuoso Open Source does not contain some required functions), the ImageMagick plug-in, the QRcode plug-in (before version 0.6; after version 0.6 it is optional), and the sparql_cxml VAD package to be installed, in order to get this option.

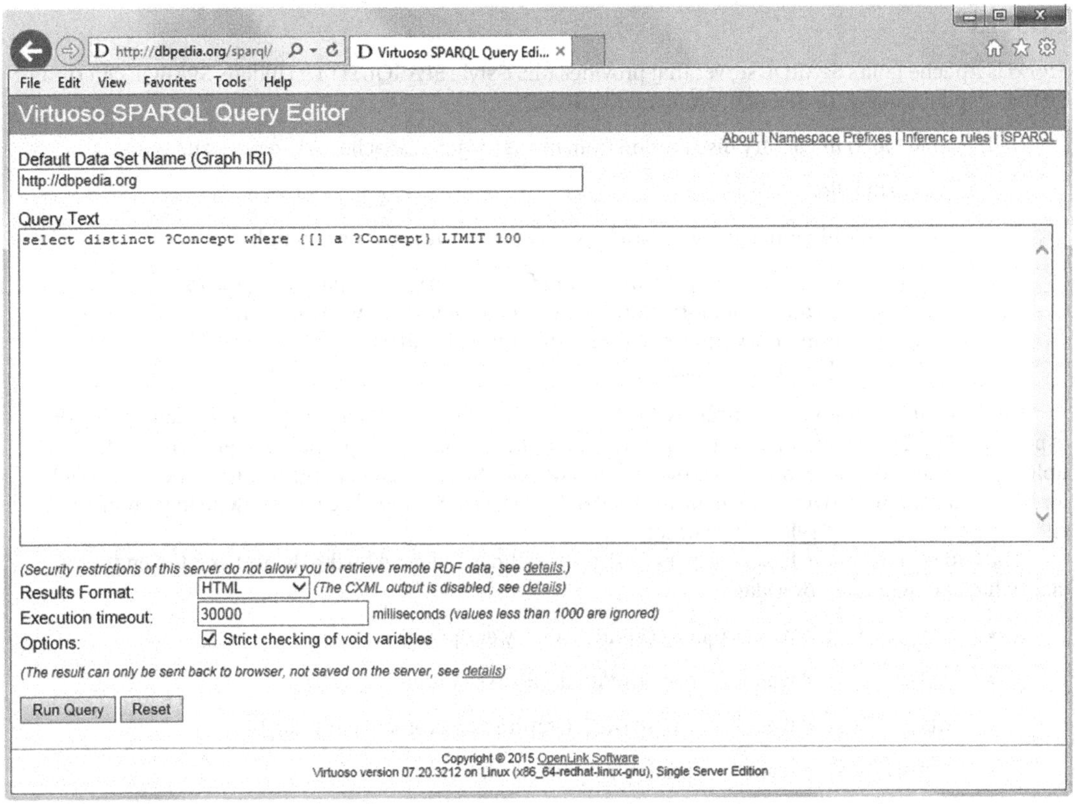

Figure 7-2. *A Virtuoso SPARQL endpoint*

To install the OpenLink Virtuoso SPARQL Endpoint, follow these steps:

1. Download Virtuoso Open Source from `http://virtuoso.openlinksw.com/dataspace/doc/dav/wiki/Main/VOSDownload` or the commercial edition of Virtuoso from `http://virtuoso.openlinksw.com/download/`.

2. For the commercial Windows Open Source Edition, run the installer; otherwise, create a build.

3. Verify the installation and the configuration of the environmental variables by running the `virtuoso -?` Command.

4. Start the Virtuoso server with `virtuoso-start.sh`.

5. Verify the connection to the Virtuoso Server, using `isql localhost` (if using the default DB settings), `isql localhost:1112` (assuming demo database), or visit `http://<virtuoso-server-host-name>:[port]/conductor` in your browser

6. Open the SPARQL endpoint at `http://<virtuoso-server-host-name>:[port]/sparql`.

7. Run a test query such as `SELECT DISTINCT * WHERE {?s ?p ?o} LIMIT 50`.

Fuseki

Fuseki is Apache Jena's SPARQL server that provides REST-style SPARQL HTTP Update, SPARQL Query, and SPARQL Update, using the SPARQL protocol over HTTP.

1. Download the binary distribution from `https://jena.apache.org/download/`.

2. Unzip the file.

3. Set file permission using the `chmod +x fuseki-server s-*` command.

4. Run the server by executing the command `fuseki-server --update --mem /ds`, which creates an in-memory, non-persistent dataset. If you want to create an empty, in-memory (non-persistent) dataset and load a file into it, use `--file=FILE` instead of `--mem`.

The default port number of Fuseki is 3030, which can be overridden by the port argument in the form `--port=number`. Fuseki not only supports SPARQL 1.1 queries, SPARQL 1.1 update operations, and file upload to a selected dataset but also provides validators for SPARQL Query and SPARQL Update, as well as for RDF serializations. To open the control panel of Fuseki, visit `http://localhost:3030` in your browser, click `Control Panel`, and select the dataset.

The URI scheme of the Fuseki server consists of the host, followed by the dataset and the endpoint, all of which are separated by a slash.

- `http://host/dataset/query` (SPARQL query endpoint)

- `http://host/dataset/update` (SPARQL UPDATE endpoint)

- `http://host/dataset/data` (SPARQL Graph Store Protocol endpoint)

- `http://host/dataset/upload` (file upload endpoint)

To load some RDF data into the default graph of the server, use the `s-put` command, as shown in Listing 7-42.

Listing 7-42. Load RDF Data into the Default Graph of Fuseki

```
s-put http://localhost:3030/ds/data default books.ttl
```

To retrieve data from the default graph of the server, use the `s-get` command (see Listing 7-43).

Listing 7-43. Retrieving Data, Using `s-get`

```
s-get http://localhost:3030/ds/data default
```

The default graph of the server can be queried with SPARQL, using the .../query endpoint employing the `s-query` command, as demonstrated in Listing 7-44.

Listing 7-44. SPARQL Querying with Fuseki

```
s-query --service http://localhost:3030/ds/query 'SELECT * {?s ?p ?o}'
```

A SPARQL UPDATE query can be executed using the .../update endpoint with `s-update`. As an example, let's clear the default graph, as shown in Listing 7-45.

Listing 7-45. A SPARQL UPDATE Query with Fuseki

```
s-update --service http://localhost:3030/ds/update 'CLEAR DEFAULT'
```

To use SPARQL 1.1 Query from Java applications, you can use the `QueryExecutionFactory.`
`sparqlService` of Apache Jena's SPARQL query engine, ARQ. For the programmatic access of
SPARQL Update, use `UpdateExecutionFactory.createRemote`. SPARQL HTTP can be used through
`DatasetAccessor`.

D2R

The *D2R Server* is a tool for publishing relational databases as Linked Data, providing access to the database
content through a browser interface and querying the database using SPARQL. D2R performs on-the-fly
transformation of SPARQL queries to SQL queries via a mapping. Among others, D2R is used as the SPARQL
endpoint of Dailymed, a comprehensive, up-to-date dataset of marketed drugs in the United States. The D2R
Server can be installed as follows:

1. Download the server from `http://d2rq.org`.

2. Run the server in one of the following ways:

   - From the command line (for development or testing), with the syntax shown in
     Listing 7-46.

     Listing 7-46. Running D2R From the Command Line

     ```
     d2r-server [--port port] [-b serverBaseURI][--fast] [--verbose]
     [--debug] mapping-file.ttl
     ```

     Because the default port number is 2020, the default server URI is
     `http://localhost:2020`. The `fast` argument can optionally be used for
     performance optimization, the `verbose` argument for detailed logging, and
     debug for full logging. Optionally, you can declare the name of the D2RQ
     mapping file to use. If the mapping file is not provided, the database connection
     must be specified on the command line, so that a default mapping will be used.

   - Deploy the D2R Server web application into a servlet container, such as Apache
     Tomcat or Jetty (for production).

     a) Ensure that the mapping file includes a configuration block,
        setting the base URI in the form `http://servername/webappname/`.
        The `d2r:Server` instance in this file configures the D2R server
        (see Listing 7-47).

     Listing 7-47. D2R Configuration File Example

     ```
     @prefix d2r: <http://example.com/d2r-server/config.rdf#> .
     @prefix meta: <http://exampe.com/d2r-server/metadata#> .

     <> a d2r:Server;
       rdfs:label "My D2R Server";
       d2r:baseURI <http://localhost:2020/>;
       d2r:port 2020;
       d2r:vocabularyIncludeInstances true;

       d2r:sparqlTimeout 300;
       d2r:pageTimeout 5;
     ```

```
meta:datasetTitle "My Dataset" ;
meta:datasetDescription "This dataset contains Semantic Web ↵
  publication resources." ;
meta:datasetSource "The dataset covers publications from all related ↵
  datasets such as XY." ;

meta:operatorName "John Smith" ;
      .
```

The d2r:Server instance supports a variety of configuration properties. The human-readable server name can be provided using rdfs:label. The base URI of the server can be declared using d2r:baseURI (the equivalent of the –b command line parameter). The port number of the server can be added as d2r:port (same as --port in the command line). By default, the RDF and HTML representations of vocabulary classes are also list instances, and the property representations are also list triples using the property. The d2r:vocabularyIncludeInstances configuration property accepts the false Boolean value to override this behavior. To specify automatic detection of mapping file changes, one can use the d2r:autoReloadMapping property. The default value is true. The maximum number of entities per class map can be set using d2r:limitPerClassMap. The default value is 50, and the limit can be disabled with the property value set to false. The maximum number of values from each property bridge can be configured using d2r:limitPerPropertyBridge. The default value is 50, and the limit can be disabled with the property value set to false. The timeout of the D2R server's SPARQL endpoint can be set in seconds as the property value of the d2r:sparqlTimeout property. If you want to disable the timeout for the SPARQL endpoint, set the value to 0. The timeout for generating resource description pages can be similarly set in seconds, using the d2r:pageTimeout, which can also be disabled by setting the value to 0. The default resource metadata template can be overridden using d2r:metadataTemplate, which specifies a literal value for the path name, either absolute or relative to the location of the server configuration file. The default dataset metadata template can be overridden by the value of d2r:datasetMetadataTemplate. The d2r:disableMetadata property enables the automatic creation and publication of all dataset and resource metadata, which accepts a Boolean value. The true value is assumed if the d2r:disableMetadata property is omitted.

b)   The name of the configuration file declared as the configFile param in /webapp/WEB-INF/web.xml has to be changed to the name of your configuration file. The recommended location of the mapping file is the /webapp/WEB-INF/ directory.

c)   In the main directory of the D2R server, run ant war, which creates the d2rq.war file (requires Apache Ant).

d)   The name of your web application can optionally be changed by renaming the file to webappname.war.

e)   Deploy the .war file into your servlet container, such as by copying it into the webapps directory of Tomcat.

4store SPARQL Server

4store provides a SPARQL HTTP protocol server, which can answer SPARQL queries using the SPARQL HTTP query protocol. To run 4store's SPARQL server, use the `4s-httpd` command with the port number and KB name as shown in Listing 7-48.

Listing 7-48. Running 4store's HTTP Server

```
4s-httpd -p port_number 4store_KB_name
```

■ **Note**   Multiple 4store KBs have to run on separate ports.

Once the server is running, the overview page can be accessed in the web browser at `http://localhost:port_number/status/`, and the SPARQL endpoint at `http://localhost:port_number/sparql/` with an HTML interface at `http://localhost:port_number/test/`. From the command line, you can query the SPARQL server using the sparql-query tool available at `https://github.com/tialaramex/sparql-query`.

PublishMyData

PublishMyData is a commercial Linked Data publishing platform. Because it is a *Software as a Service* (SaaS) in the cloud, you don't have to install anything to use it. Beyond the SPARQL endpoint, PublishMyData provides RDF data hosting, a Linked Data API, and customizable visualizations. It supports SPARQL 1.1. To submit a SPARQL query from your code, issue an HTTP GET request to the SPARQL endpoint, as demonstrated in Listing 7-49.

Listing 7-49. SPARQL Query on PublishMyData

```
http://example.com/sparql?query=URL-encoded_query
```

For instance, to run the query `SELECT * WHERE {?s ?p ?o} LIMIT 10` and get the results in JSON, the URL to be used will have the structure shown in Listing 7-50.

Listing 7-50. URL-Encoded SPARQL Query with PublishMyData

```
http://example.com/sparql.json?query=SELECT+%2A+WHERE+%7B%3Fs+%3Fp+%3Fo%7D+LIMIT+10
```

For demonstrating programmatic access, let's use JavaScript to request data from the SPARQL endpoint (see Listing 7-51).

Listing 7-51. Using jQuery to Request Data Through the SPARQL Endpoint

```
<!DOCTYPE html>
<html>
  <head>
    <script src="http://code.jquery.com/jquery-1.9.1.min.js"></script>
  </head>
  <body>
    <script type="text/javascript">
      var siteDomain = "example.com";
      var query = "SELECT * WHERE {?s ?p ?o} LIMIT 10";
```

```
      var url = "http://" + siteDomain + "/sparql.json?query=";
      url += encodeURIComponent(query);
      $.ajax({
        dataType: 'json',
        url: url,
        success: function(data) {
        alert('success: ' + data.results.bindings.length + ' results');
        console.log(data);
        }
      });
    </script>
  </body>
</html>
```

When requesting the SPARQL output as JSON, a callback parameter can be passed, so that the results will be wrapped in the function, which can prevent cross-domain issues when running JavaScript under older browsers (see Listing 7-52).

Listing 7-52. Using a Callback Function

```
http://example.com/sparql.json?callback=myCallbackFunction&query=SELECT+%2A+WHERE+%7B%3Fs ↵
+%3Fp+%3Fo%7D+LIMIT+10
```

Alternatively, you can make a JSON-P request with jQuery and can omit the callback parameter from the URL by setting the dataType to jsonp, as shown in Listing 7-53.

Listing 7-53. Using JSON-P for SPARQL Querying

```
queryUrl = 'example.com/sparql.json?query=SELECT+%2A+WHERE+%7B%3Fs+%3Fp+%3Fo%7D+LIMIT+10'

$.ajax({
  dataType: 'jsonp',
  url: queryUrl,
  success: function(data) {
  // callback code
  alert('success!');
  }
});
```

You can also use Ruby to request data from the PublishMyData SPARQL endpoint, as shown in Listing 7-54.

Listing 7-54. Make a Request to the PublishMyData SPARQL Endpoint in Ruby

```
require 'rest-client'
require 'json'

query = 'SELECT * WHERE {?s ?p ?o} LIMIT 10'
site_domain = "example.com"
url = "http://\#example.com/sparql.json"
```

```
results_str = RestClient.get url, {:params => {:query => query}}
results_hash = JSON.parse results_str
results_array = results_hash["results"]["bindings"]

puts "Total number of results: \#{results_array.length}"
```

The request in this case is written as JSON, and the result will be put in a Hash table.

Summary

In this chapter, you learned the foundations of SPARQL, the standardized query language of RDF. You are now familiar with the query types and know how to write SPARQL queries to answer complex questions, display all nodes of an RDF graph with a particular feature, filter results, or add new triples to a dataset. By now you also recognize the most popular SPARQL endpoint interfaces and know how to set up your own endpoint.

The next chapter will show you how to handle high-volume, high-velocity datasets, leverage Semantic Web technologies in Big Data applications, and add structured data to your site, so that it will be considered for inclusion in the Google Knowledge Graph.

References

1. The W3C SPARQL Working Group (2013) SPARQL 1.1 Overview. W3C Recommendation. World Wide Web Consortium. www.w3.org/TR/sparql11-overview/. Accessed 6 March 2015.

2. Prud'hommeaux, E., Seaborne, A. (2008) SPARQL Query Language for RDF. www.w3.org/TR/rdf-sparql-query/. Accessed 18 April 2015.

3. Harris, S., Seaborne, A. (2013) www.w3.org/TR/sparql11-query/. Accessed 18 April 2015.

4. Gearon, P., Passant, A., Polleres, A. (eds.) (2013) SPARQL 1.1 Update. www.w3.org/TR/sparql11-update/. Accessed 18 April 2015.

5. Ogbuji, C. (ed.) (2013) SPARQL 1.1 Graph Store HTTP Protocol. W3C Recommendation. World Wide Web Consortium. www.w3.org/TR/sparql11-http-rdf-update/. Accessed 6 March 2015.

6. Williams, G. T. (ed.) SPARQL 1.1 Service Description. www.w3.org/TR/sparql11-service-description/. Accessed 18 April 2015.

7. Glimm, B., Ogbuji, C. (eds.) (2013) SPARQL 1.1 Entailment Regimes. www.w3.org/TR/sparql11-entailment/. Accessed 18 April 2015.

8. Seaborne, A. (ed.) (2013) SPARQL 1.1 Query Results JSON Format. www.w3.org/TR/sparql11-results-json/. Accessed 18 April 2015.

9. Seaborne, A. (ed.) (2013) SPARQL 1.1 Query Results CSV and TSV Formats. www.w3.org/TR/sparql11-results-csv-tsv/. Accessed 18 April 2015.

10. Hawke, S. (ed.) (2013) SPARQL Query Results XML Format (Second Edition). www.w3.org/TR/rdf-sparql-XMLres/. Accessed 18 April 2015.

11. Prud'hommeaux, E., Buil-Aranda, C. (eds.) (2013) SPARQL 1.1 Federated Query. `www.w3.org/TR/sparql11-federated-query/`. Accessed 18 April 2015.

12. Feigenbaum, L., Williams, G. T., Clark, K. G., Torres, E. (eds.) (2013) SPARQL 1.1 Protocol. W3C Recommendation. World Wide Web Consortium. `www.w3.org/TR/sparql11-protocol/`. Accessed 9 March 2015.

13. Broekstra, J., Ansell, P., Visser, D., Leigh, J., Kampman, A., Schwarte, A. et al. (2015) The SeRQL query language. `http://rdf4j.org/sesame/2.7/docs/users.docbook?view#chapter-serql`. Accessed 22 April 2015.

14. Neo Technology, Inc. (2015) Intro to Cypher. `http://neo4j.com/developer/cypher-query-language/`. Accessed 22 April 2015.

CHAPTER 8

■ ■ ■

Big Data Applications

The sustainability of huge and ever-growing data pools using different formats that cannot be processed with traditional software tools is the next big challenge for web designers, Internet marketers, and software engineers and requires new technologies and practices. One of the approaches to cope with Big Data is to use Semantic Web technologies, especially machine-interpretable metadata and Linked Data. Implementing the Resource Description Framework (RDF) and RDF-based standards ensures that data and its meaning are encapsulated, and concepts and relationships can be managed while connecting diverse data from various data sources. Graph representations, such as Facebook's Open Graph, add context to and visualize Big Data for data analysis. The Service-Oriented Architecture (SOA) infrastructure over Big Data makes it possible to update Big Data in real time. Data can be automatically classified, relationships associated, and new relationships found, so that data can be collected and integrated without worrying about schemas and data descriptions, yet providing a data description. Big Data applications on the Semantic Web include, but are not limited to, next-generation Search Engine Result Pages, social media graphs, analysis of natural language content, publishing factual data about massive world events, interlinking BBC's online content, as well as high-performance data storage and processing.

Big Semantic Data: Big Data on the Semantic Web

Big Data refers to any high-volume, high-velocity datasets too large and complex to process using traditional data processing tools, applications, and database systems. Representing petabytes of data, such datasets store billions of hidden values unavailable for efficient and automatic machine processing. Big Data is characterized by four *V*s:

- **Volume**: Huge amounts of data stored in, and retrieved from, massive datasets. The challenge is to achieve a reasonable processing speed, especially in real-time applications.

- **Velocity**: High-rate data flow. The challenge is the streaming data processing.

- **Variety**: Different forms of data. The challenge is to deal with the different data structures, data formats, and serializations.

- **Veracity**: Uncertainty of data. The challenge is to handle trust issues, determine accuracy, and cope with poor data quality.

One of the promising approaches to address the issues associated with Big Data is to implement Semantic Web technologies in order to build systems that can efficiently handle Big Data and evolve with the growing data processing needs.

Google Knowledge Graph and Knowledge Vault

One of the best known Big Data applications on the Semantic Web is the *Google Knowledge Graph*, which was introduced in 2012. The Google Knowledge Graph is a semantic knowledge base to enhance traditional Search Engine Result Pages (SERPs) with semantic search information gathered from a wide variety of sources. The data sources used by the Knowledge Graph include pages indexed by Google, objects on GoogleMaps, public data sources such as Wikipedia, LOD datasets such as DBpedia, the CIA World Factbook, and the FDA datasets, as well as subject-specific resources such as Weather Underground and World Bank, for meteorological information and economic statistics, respectively. The result of a Knowledge Graph search is not only relevant information far more accurate that what you would find with traditional searches but also related information, such as similar resources people search for the most. For example, if you search for Leonardo da Vinci, you not only get facts about him and his famous works like *Mona Lisa* and *The Last Supper*, but Google will also suggest other notable painters of the same era, such as Jan van Eyck, Dürer, Raphael, and Michelangelo (see Figure 8-1).

Figure 8-1. *The Google Knowledge Graph finds data resources related to your search phrase [1]*

Similarly, if searching for the title of an action movie, the results will include similar movies, while searching for a particular inventor will disclose additional inventors, with similar research fields and awards. The Knowledge Graph contains more than half a billion objects and over 18 billion facts about relationships between different objects that help software agents "understand" the meaning of the search keywords, and these figures are constantly growing.

Depending on the search phrase used, the search results retrieved from the Google Knowledge Graph are represented in two ways. The first one, called the *Google Knowledge Panel*, is displayed on the right-hand side of the Search Engine Result Pages, next to the organic search results. Searching for persons or brand names typically results in a Knowledge Panel, as shown in Figure 8-2.

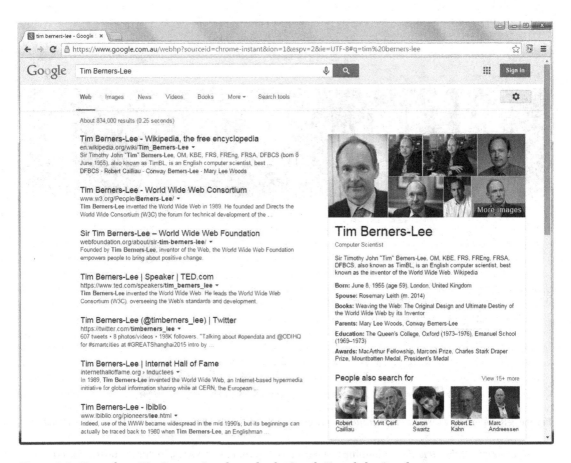

Figure 8-2. *Facts about Tim Berners-Lee shown by the Google Knowledge Panel*

If the object has a social media presence on Facebook, YouTube, Twitter, Instagram, Google+, etc., links to those pages will also be displayed. The most related links are shown under "People also search for," which can be extended by clicking the "View more" link. If you search for a living musician, you might also see "Upcoming events" on the Knowledge Panel, containing the venue and date of upcoming concerts.

The second type of data representation for data retrieved from the Google Knowledge Graph is the Google Knowledge Carousel, which shows entities related to the search phrase. For instance, if you search for Clint Eastwood's filmography, Google will provide the organic results, a Knowledge Panel on Clint Eastwood, as well as a Knowledge Carousel about his most famous movies, such as *The Good, the Bad and the Ugly, Unforgiven, The Outlaw Josey Wales, Gran Torino, A Fistful of Dollars, Dirty Harry*, and so on (see Figure 8-3). The Carousel is also used when you click certain link types on the Knowledge Panel. For example, if you click an upcoming concert of a musician displayed on the Knowledge Panel, all the upcoming concerts of the musician will be shown on a Carousel at the top.

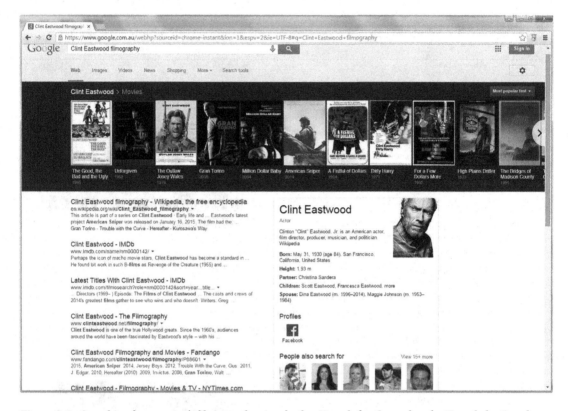

Figure 8-3. *Searching for an actor's filmography gives both a Knowledge Carosel and a Knowledge Panel*

The *Google Knowledge Vault* combines data from conventional web sites, including unstructured text, DOM trees, and tables, as well as structured data from Freebase. It is a large database of automatically extracted structured data. The amount of information users can retrieve depends on the structure and correctness of the queries.

The Knowledge Vault derives much of its data from the Knowledge Graph and the sources thereof, as well as harvesting its own data, ranking its reliability and compiling all results into a database of over 1.6 billion facts collected by machine learning algorithms. There are no more ambiguous natural language queries about Jaguar (car make or animal) or Taj Mahal (monument, musician, or casino), as Google knows exactly what is the difference between these "things."

Get Your Company, Products, and Events into the Knowledge Graph

If you describe your company, products, services, or events on your web site using controlled vocabulary terms, either as HTML5 Microdata or JSON-LD, they will be considered to be included in the Google Knowledge Graph. The Schema.org terms can be used to define features and relationships such as the surname of a person (http://schema.org/familyName), the genre of a music album (http://schema.org/music/artist/album), or the opening hours of a store (http://schema.org/openingHours). The more precise category you use, the better. For example, if you have a concert, use http://schema.org/MusicEvent rather than http://schema.org/Event, or if you have a soccer match, use http://schema.org/SportsEvent instead of http://schema.org/Event. Event organizers, for example, can describe upcoming events by adding structured data to the markup as a separate code block in JSON-LD, so that Google might include them on the Knowledge Graph (see Listing 8-1). The vocabulary is defined using @context and @type, as discussed earlier, in Chapter 3.

Listing 8-1. JSON-LD Annotation of a Band in the Markup

```
<script type="application/ld+json">
  {
    "@context"   : "http://schema.org",
    "@type"      : "MusicEvent",
    "name"       : "Nice Band Live",
    "startDate"  : "2015-09-18T20:00",
    "url"        : "http://www.nicebandexample.com/tour/150918",
    "location"   : {
                     "@type"   : "Place",
                     "name"    : "The Oval",
                     "address" : "1234 Blackwood Plaza",
                     "sameAs"  : "http://www.xyzoval.com"
                   },
    "performer" : {
                     "@type"   : "MusicGroup",
                     "name"    : "Nice Band",
                     "sameAs"  : "http://www.nicebandexample.com"
                   },
    "offers"    : {
                     "@type" : "Offer",
                     "url"   : "http://www.exampleticketseller.com"
                   }
  }
</script>
```

Similarly, online retailers and shops can describe products using Schema.org terms. To identify which properties you can use, go to http://schema.org/Book and check the property list. Here, we added the web site of the book with url, defined the author by referring to the corresponding DBpedia page, declared the available formats (paperback and e-book) using Schema.org terms, among other properties (see Listing 8-2).

Listing 8-2. JSON-LD Annotation of a Product Description

```
<script type="application/ld+json">
  {
    "@context": "http://schema.org",
    "@type": "Book",
    "url": "http://www.lesliesikos.com/web-standards-mastering-html5-css3-and-xml-second- ↵
     edition/",
    "author": "http://dbpedia.org/resource/Leslie_Sikos",
    "bookFormat": "http://schema.org/Paperback",
    "bookFormat": "http://schema.org/EBook",
    "datePublished": "2014-12-24",
    "image": "http://www.lesliesikos.com/img/web-design-book.jpg",
    "inLanguage": "English",
    "isbn": "1484208846",
```

```
    "name": "Web Standards: Mastering HTML5, CSS3, and XML",
    "numberOfPages": "524",
    "offers": {
      "@type": "Offer",
      "availability": "http://schema.org/InStock",
      "price": "39.89",
      "priceCurrency": "USD"
    },
    "publisher": "http://dbpedia.org/resource/Apress",
    "about": "http://dbpedia.org/resource/Web_design"
  }
</script>
```

Product offerings can be annotated using GoodRelations, covering properties such as the web page of the advertisement on eBay or Gumtree, the accepted payment methods, the item price and currency, the category of the product, the official vendor web page describing the product, and the description of the product (see Listing 8-3).

Listing 8-3. JSON-LD Annotation of a Product Offering in the Markup

```
{
  "@context": {
    "gr": "http://purl.org/goodrelations/v1#",
    "pto": "http://www.productontology.org/id/",
    "schema": "http://schema.org/",
    "xsd": "http://www.w3.org/2001/XMLSchema#",
    "schema:url": {
      "@type": "@id"
    },
    "gr:acceptedPaymentMethods": {
      "@type": "@id"
    },
    "gr:hasBusinessFunction": {
      "@type": "@id"
    },
    "gr:hasCurrencyValue": {
      "@type": "xsd:float"
    }
  },
  "@id": "http://www.ebay.com/itm/ExampleAd-Giant-TCR-Advanced-1-Road-Bike-/21621444051",
  "@type": "gr:Offering",
  "gr:acceptedPaymentMethods": "gr:Cash",
  "gr:description": "Want to sell my Giant TCR Advanced 1 Road Bike as I'm moving ↵
    interstate",
  "gr:hasBusinessFunction": "gr:Sell",
  "gr:hasPriceSpecification": {
    "gr:hasCurrency": "USD",
    "gr:hasCurrencyValue": "1350"
  },
```

```
  "gr:includes": {
    "@type": [
      "gr:Individual",
      "pto:Racing_bicycle"
    ],
    "gr:name": "Giant TCR Advanced 1",
    "schema:url": "https://www.giant-bicycles.com/enus/bikes/model/tcr.advanced.1.force/ ↵
      14797/66271/"
  },
  "gr:name": "Used Giant Road Bike"
}
```

To add structured data to your HTML5 markup about your local business, you can use the LocalBusiness vocabulary from Schema.org. Make sure that you use the most specific type for your business (http://schema.org/Library for libraries, http://schema.org/ShoppingCenter for shopping centers, http://schema.org/AutomotiveBusiness for garages, http://schema.org/FinancialService for financial planners and banks, etc.). A school or a sports club should use http://schema.org/Organization instead, while http://schema.org/Corporation is more suitable for enterprises. The most commonly used LocalBusiness properties are name, description, address, and telephone (see Listing 8-4). The physical address details can be embedded to PostalAddress.

Listing 8-4. LocalBusiness Annotated with Microdata

```
<div itemscope="itemscope" itemtype="http://schema.org/LocalBusiness">
  <h1><span itemprop="name">The Blue Cafe</span></h1>
  <span itemprop="description">A nice cafe on the beach with a friendly atmosphere.</span>
  <div itemprop="address" itemscope="itemscope" itemtype="http://schema.org/PostalAddress">
    <span itemprop="streetAddress">123 Esplanade</span>
    <span itemprop="addressLocality">Nice Beach</span>,
    <span itemprop="addressRegion">CA</span>
  </div>
  <p>
  Phone: <span itemprop="telephone">123-456-7890</span>
  </p>
</div>
```

Depending on what you want to display as human-readable data on your site and what you want to add as machine-readable only, you can use different markup elements and style sheets. For those data you add for software agents only, use the attribute values on the meta element.

Social Media Applications

Excellent examples for Big Data implementations on the Semantic Web are the social media graphs, such as the Facebook Social Graph, the Twitter Interest Graph, the Twitter Follow Graph, the LinkedIn Professional Graph, or the LinkedIn Economic Graph.

Facebook Social Graph

The Facebook Social Graph is the largest social graph in the world, containing tens of petabytes of structured data about approximately 1 billion users. Because every object is a graph node, and every relationship is a graph edge on the Facebook Social Graph (see Figure 8-4), any object can easily be accessed directly in the browser as a user and programmatically from Facebook apps.

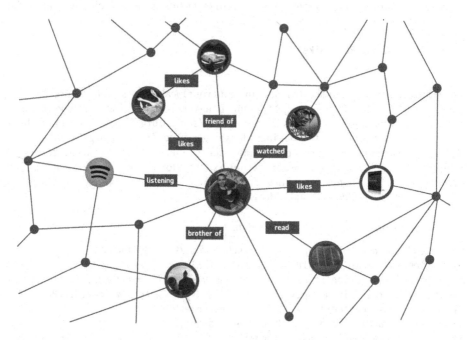

Figure 8-4. *On the Facebook Social Graph, every object is a node and every connection is an edge*

In fact, the easy access of this vast user data is exploited well beyond Facebook, as the social connections and links of the Facebook Social Graph are also used by other social networking portals, such as Pinterest and Last.fm (*social bootstrapping*).

Have you ever wondered how Facebook recommends friends? Using the edges of the Facebook Social Graph, it is straightforward to identify those people who have at least one friend in common (see Figure 8-5).

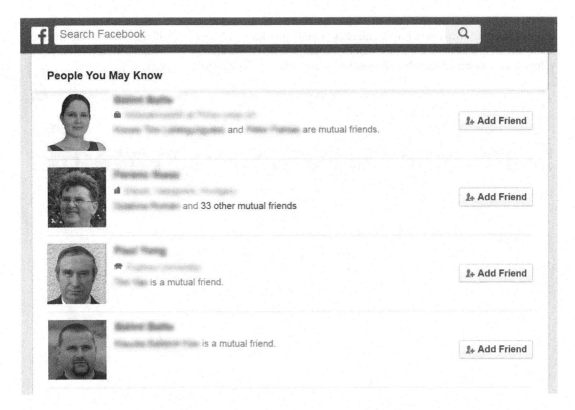

Figure 8-5. *The edges of the Facebook Social Graph make it possible to suggest people you may know*

The Facebook Graph API

The *Facebook Graph API* is the core of the Facebook Platform, enabling developers to read data from and write data into Facebook user profiles. The Graph API represents the current state of the Facebook Social Graph through graph objects such as people, photos, events, and pages, as well as the connections between them, such as friend relationships, shared content, and photo tags. In other words, the Graph API makes it possible to programmatically access user objects and connections from the Facebook Social Graph, which can be used for Facebook apps.

The Graph API can not only query data but also post new stories, publish Open Graph stories, read information about a Facebook user, upload photos, update information in the Social Graph, and perform similar tasks used by Facebook apps. All the objects of the Facebook Social Graph (users, photo albums, photos, status messages, pages, etc.) have a unique identifier, which is a positive integer and makes it possible to refer to any node or edge.

Originally, the Graph API provided data to applications exclusively in JSON. The two different key/value pair sets of JSON are the objects (where keys are strings) and arrays (which represent the set of keys as a finite, counting sequence of nonnegative integers). The values can be JSON objects, arrays, or primitives (strings, numbers, Boolean values, and null).

Because the Graph API is a RESTful JSON API, you can access it in your browser. The web interface of the Graph API is called the *Graph API Explorer*, which is available at https://developers.facebook.com/tools/explorer/. With this tool, you can use and traverse the Facebook Social Graph. You have to have a Facebook account and log in to use the Graph API Explorer. Once you are logged in and visit the Graph API Explorer, you can see a JSON object on the right, with two properties, the identifier and the name of the current user, because these are the two fields selected by default (displayed under the me node on the left). If you unselect the two check boxes, and click Submit, the Graph API Explorer will reveal more information about the user (see Figure 8-6). How much detail is provided depends on your privacy settings. These field values are the default data to be returned when no fields are specified in your query.

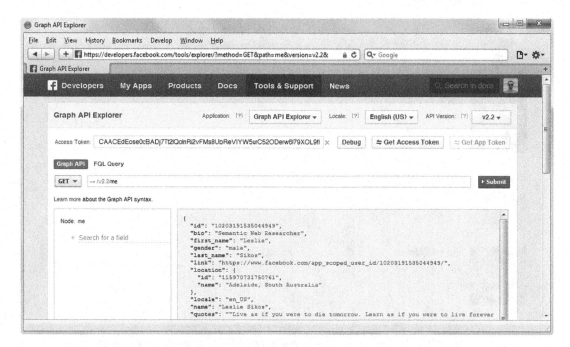

Figure 8-6. *With the Graph API Explorer, you can access fields of a node in the Facebook Social Graph*

If you need more data about the node, you might have to generate an access token (Get Access Token), select the additional fields of your choice, and give permission to the Graph API to access those data. The Graph API Explorer performs simple HTTP GET requests in the background, as demonstrated in Listing 8-5, and provides a drop-down on the left, with the GET, POST, and DELETE choices. The default value is GET. To initiate a new request, you have to click Submit on the right.

Listing 8-5. HTTP GET Request Through the Graph API Explorer

```
GET /v2.2/me HTTP/1.1
Host: graph.facebook.com
```

While every node in the Facebook Social Graph has an identifier, you can refer to any node either by the numeric ID or the username (if the object has one). For example, if you change the request after GET from the default me value to your user ID or your username and hit Submit, you get the same results for your queries. This works even for Facebook pages.

Due to the HTTP GET requests used under the hood, every query can also be performed directly. For instance, to get information about the Facebook page of this book (http://facebook.com/SemanticWebBook), you can directly open http://graph.facebook.com/SemanticWebBook in your browser to retrieve the JSON output. This makes it possible to access any node or edge of the Facebook Social Graph programmatically, with software libraries that handle HTTP requests and the JSON format. To make it even easier, Facebook provides SDKs for popular languages and platforms such as PHP (see Listing 8-6), JavaScript (see Listing 8-7), iOS (see Listing 8-8), and Android (see Listing 8-9).

Listing 8-6. Make an API Call from PHP

```
$request = new FacebookRequest(
  $session,
  'GET',
  '/me'
);
$response = $request->execute();
$graphObject = $response->getGraphObject();
/* result handler */
```

Listing 8-7. Make an API Call from JavaScript

```
FB.api(
    "/me",
    function (response) {
      if (response && !response.error) {
        /* result handler */
      }
    }
);
```

Listing 8-8. Make an API Call from iOS

```
[FBRequestConnection startWithGraphPath:@"/me"
                     completionHandler:^(
                           FBRequestConnection *connection,
                           id result,
                           NSError *error
                     ) {
                           /* result handler */
                     }];
```

Listing 8-9. Make an API Call from Android

```
new Request(
    session,
    "/me",
    null,
    HttpMethod.GET,
    new Request.Callback() {
        public void onCompleted(Response response) {
            /* result handler */
        }
    }
).executeAsync();
```

Since 2011, Facebook provides data retrieved from the Social Graph, not only in JSON, but also in a semantically enriched RDF serialization format, to include Linked Data URIs. The implementation is meant to be flexible and robust, so the Turtle format has been chosen, although JSON-LD has also been considered. The JSON output to Turtle translation is accessible via HTTP content negotiation. A URI or blank node is assigned to a JSON object or array as the subject of RDF triples. The predicate and object of RDF triples are derived from the key-value pairs of JSON objects and arrays. The JSON key is translated into a URI, while the value is converted to an RDF term, such as a meaningful literal, a URI, or a blank node.

The primitive values correspond to RDF literals, and the conversion is made by applying heuristics to determine the most suitable RDF datatype URI for literals. The JSON strings that form URIs are translated to URIs. The most frequently used datatype URIs of the JSON-Turtle conversions are `xsd:Boolean`, `xsd:dateTime`, `xsd:decimal`, `xsd:double`, and `xsd:integer`. The object identifiers remain strings, even if they seem to be integers. Facebook implemented the RDF 1.1 convention for strings, namely that regular strings are left as plain literals (implicitly handled as `xsd:string`) rather than explicitly typing them as `xsd:string`. To comply with httpRange-14 (to ensure that HTTP GET requests won't lead to an undefined domain), fragment identifiers are preferred over slash URIs. Because the output represents an isolated graph that is not connected to external resources, the resulting Linked Data is four-star Linked Data only (see Chapter 3). Still, the RDF/Turtle output is semantically richer than the JSON output, due to explicit semantics accessible as ontologies utilizing the RDFS and OWL vocabularies.

The Linked Data can be accessed the same way you perform an HTTP GET request directly, i.e., using the `http://graph.facebook.com` or `https://graph.facebook.com` base URI, followed by a slash and the Facebook username or Facebook page name. As an example, the Linked Data URIs can be used to augment a person's FOAF profile, as shown in Listing 8-10.

Listing 8-10. FOAF Profile Augmentation

```
@base <http://graph.facebook.com/> .
<http://www.lesliesikos.com/datasets/sikos.rdf#sikos>
owl:sameAs </1105249544#> ;
rdfs:seeAlso </1105249544?metadata=1> ;
foaf:depiction </1105249544/picture> ;
foaf:account <http://www.facebook.com/sikos> .
```

Facebook Module of Apache Marmotta's LDClient Library

The Facebook Module of Apache Marmotta's LDClient library represents the Facebook Graph API objects and connections as RDF triples using Schema.org, Dublin Core, FOAF, SIOC, and SKOS terms. Whenever feasible, the mapping will use Schema.org terms. The Facebook Module of Marmotta (ldclient-provider-facebook) registers an endpoint to handle all URIs starting with `http://graph.facebook.com` and `http://www.facebook.com`. The Facebook Module can be used in your Apache Maven project by adding a dependency, as demonstrated in Listing 8-11.

Listing 8-11. Dependency for the Facebook Module in Maven

```
<dependency>
   <groupId>org.apache.marmotta</groupId>
   <artifactId>ldclient-provider-facebook</artifactId>
   <version>3.3.0</version>
</dependency>
```

Each Facebook object has at least a category (mapped to Schema.org terms using `rdf:type` whenever possible), an identifier (mapped to `dcterms:id`), a name (mapped to `schema:name`), a description (mapped to `schema:description`), and a Facebook web page (mapped to `foaf:homepage`). This allows programmatic access to Facebook objects from Maven projects.

Facebook Open Graph Protocol

Inspired by Microformats and RDFa, the *Open Graph Protocol* makes it possible for developers to integrate their pages into the Facebook Social Graph.

The Open Graph vocabulary can be used to annotate your web site markup with metadata that can be associated with Facebook properties. For example, a book can be described as shown in Listing 8-12. The namespace of Open Graph is http://opengraphprotocol.org/schema/.

Listing 8-12. Open Graph Annotation in the Markup

```
<meta property="og:title" content="Web Standards: Mastering HTML5, CSS3, and XML" />
<meta property="og:type" content="book" />
<meta property="og:url" content="http://www.masteringhtml5css3.com" />
<meta property="og:image" content="http://www.masteringhtml5css3.com/img/ ↩
 webstandardsbook.jpg " />
<meta property="og:site_name" content="Web Site of the Book Web Standards: ↩
 Mastering HTML5, CSS3, and XML" />
<meta property="og:description" content="A book describing web standardization to create ↩
 optimized, device-independent web sites with cutting-edge technologies." />
```

Twitter Cards

Similar to Facebook's Open Graph annotation, Twitter provides the so-called *Twitter Cards* annotation to add structured data to your markup about Twitter objects [2]. Because the Twitter Cards are based on the same conventions as the Open Graph protocol, the tags are similar, and you can generate a Twitter Card intermixing Open Graph and Twitter Card annotation without tag or data duplication. While it is recommended that users specify the og RDFa Core 1.1 CURIE prefix mapping for Open Graph on the html element (<html prefix="og: http://ogp.me/ns#">), Twitter Cards do not require similar markup; however, they can use the twitter: prefix as the value of the name attribute of the meta element. Another difference is that while the Open Graph protocol specifies the use of property and content attributes for markup (e.g., <meta property="og:image" content="http://example.com/ ogimg.jpg"/>), Twitter Cards use name and content. The parser of Twitter will understand the property and content attributes of existing Open Graph markup. To define a summary card (the default Twitter Card type), you can mix Twitter Card and Open Graph annotation on the meta element, as shown in Listing 8-13.

Listing 8-13. Twitter Card Annotation in the Markup

```
<meta name="twitter:card" content="summary" />
<meta name="twitter:site" content="@lesliesikos" />
<meta name="twitter:creator" content="@lesliesikos" />
<meta property="og:url" content="http://www.lesliesikos.com/linked-data-platform-1-0 ↩
 standardized/" />
<meta property="og:title" content="Linked Data Platform 1.0 Standardized" />
<meta property="og:description" content="The Linked Data Platform 1.0 is now a W3C ↩
 Recommendation, covering a set of rules for HTTP operations on Web resources, including ↩
 RDF-based Linked Data, to provide an architecture for read-write Linked Data on the ↩
 Semantic Web." />
<meta property="og:image" content="http://www.lesliesikos.com/img/LOD.svg" />
```

IBM Watson

IBM Watson's *DeepQA* system is a question-answering system originally designed to compete with contestants of the *Jeopardy!* quiz show, where three contestants compete against one another in answering open-domain questions. While the system famously won the contest against human grand champions, it has applications well beyond *Jeopardy!*, namely, natural language content analysis in both questions and knowledge sources in general [3]. Watson's cognitive computing algorithms are used in health care, to provide insight and decision support, and give personalized and instant responses to any inquiry or service issue in customer service. Developers can use the *IBM Watson Developers Cloud*, a collection of REST APIs and SDKs for cognitive computing tasks, such as natural language classification, concept expansion, machine translation, relationship extraction, speech to text, and visual recognition.

Among other technologies, Watson uses triplestores such as Sesame, ontologies, and inference. The information resources of DeepQA consist of unstructured, semistructured, and structured data, of which the last one plays an important role, mainly by implementing RDF in IBM's DB2 database platform [4]. DeepQA uses three types of structured data, including online structured data repositories such as DBpedia, GeoNames, YAGO, and movie datasets; structured data extracted from unstructured data; and curated data that provide additional information to be stored in the triplestore, such as question-and-answer types. Watson performs reasoning over the data, using Semantic Web technologies [5]. DeepQA uses a variety of technologies to produce candidate answers to each question. The subsequent candidate answer ranking components are primarily powered by Semantic Web technologies. In particular, Linked Data sources are used to provide typing evidence for potential answers [6]. Linked Open Data plays a crucial role in the DeepQA architecture, not only in generating candidate answers, but also to score the answers while considering multiple points of view, such as type coercion and geographic proximity [7]. The data extracted from DBpedia also supports entity disambiguation and relation detection. YAGO is used for entity type identification, wherein disjointness properties are manually assigned to higher level types in the YAGO taxonomy. To be able to answer questions from a variety of domains, Watson implements relation detection and entity recognition on top of the Natural Language Processing (NLP) algorithms that process factual data from Wikipedia [8].

BBC's Dynamic Semantic Publishing

The British Broadcasting Corporation (BBC) has implemented RDF since 2010 [9] in web sites such as the World Cup 2010 web site [10] and the London 2012 Olympics web site [11]. Today, BBC News [12], BBC Sport [13], and many other web sites across the BBC are authored and published using Semantic Web technologies. The BBC News articles use automatic metadata tagging and interlinking, and the different BBC domains (brands, locations, people, and general subjects) are integrated by a hierarchy categorizing the terms expressed in the Simple Knowledge Organization System (SKOS) [14]. The identifiers of the content categorization system (CIS) of the BBC Programmes web site [15] are mapped to DBpedia concepts. The BBC Music web site [16] is also built on Linked Data, and each artist is represented in RDF. The BBC Earth web site [17] is powered by RDF and its own Wildlife Ontology.

The publishing platform of the BBC curates and publishes XHTML and RDF aggregations based on embedded Linked Data identifiers, ontologies, and inference. The in-house content management system of the BBC (called the Content Management/Production System, or CPS, for short) supports static metadata entry through a WYSIWYG (What You See Is What You Get) editor. The manual content administration processes are completed by dynamic semantic annotations, yielding automated metadata, rich content relationships, and semantic navigation. The publishing platform automatically aggregates and renders links to relevant stories and assets [18].

The Library of Congress Linked Data Service

The US Library of Congress, the largest library in the world, featuring more than 160 million items [19], publishes subject heading taxonomies as Linked Data for cataloging. It provides the LC Linked Data Service to present data in RDF [20], and where appropriate, in SKOS, as well as using its own ontology for accurate description of classification resources and relationships. All records of the Library of Congress are available individually via content negotiation as XHTML+RDFa, RDF/XML, N-Triples, and JSON [21]. To address the limitations of MAchine-Readable Cataloging (MARC), a standard initiated by the Library of Congress, MARC records have been mapped to BIBFRAME vocabulary terms [22] to leverage Linked Data benefits. Other controlled vocabularies used by the library are Dublin Core and MARC Relator Terms (which uses the marcrel prefix). For example, the contributor term of the Dublin Core vocabulary has been refined using the correspondent term of the MARC Relator Terms vocabulary, which allows catalogers to specify the role that an individual played in the creation of a resource, such as illustrator, calligrapher, or editor, in RDF [23].

High-Performance Storage: The One Trillion Triples Mark

AllegroGraph (http://franz.com/agraph/allegrograph/), the industry-leading graph database discussed in Chapter 6, constantly sets new records in loading and querying huge amounts of RDF triples. In 2004, the first version of AllegroGraph was the first graph database that loaded and indexed 1 billion triples using standard x86 64-bit architecture. In 2008, 10 billion quads were loaded with AllegroGraph on the Amazon EC2 service. In June 2011, it successfully loaded 310 billion RDF triples in just over 78 hours, using an eight-socket Intel Xeon E7-8870 processor-based server system configured with 2TB RAM and 22TB physical disk space [24]. Two months later, AllegroGraph was the first graph database in the world to load, infer, and query more than 1 trillion (!) triples. This mind-blowing, unmatched performance would be enough to store [25]

- 6,350 facts about each of 158 million items in the Library of Congress, the largest library in the world

- 1000 tweets for every one of the 1 billion Twitter users

- 770 facts about every one of the 1.3 billion Facebook users

- 12 facts about every one of the 86 billion neurons in the human brain.

- 400 metabolic readings for each of the 2.5 billion heartbeats over an average human lifetime

- Five facts about every one of the 200 billion stars in the Milky Way

AllegroGraph is designed for maximum loading speed and query speed. Loading triples and quads through its highly optimized RDF/XML and N-Quads parsers is very powerful, particularly with large files. The 1,009,690,381,946 triples were loaded in just over 338 hours, with an average rate above 800,000 triples per second (see Table 8-1).

Table 8-1. *AllegroGraph's Performance in Triple Loading and Indexing*

Configuration	Triple Count	Time	Load Rate (T/s)
2×4-core Intel E5520@2.26 GHz, 48GB RAM, CentOS 5.3	1.106 billion	48 m 30 s	379,947
32-core Intel E5520@2.0 GHz, 1TB RAM, Red Hat Enterprise Linux 6.1	1.106 billion	36 m 49 s	500,679
32-core Intel E5520@2.0 GHz, 1TB RAM, Red Hat Enterprise Linux 6.1	22.120 billion	12 h 18 m 16 s	499,188
64-core Intel x7560@2.27 GHz, 2TB RAM, 22TB disk, Red Hat Enterprise Linux 6.1	310.269 billion	78 h 9 m 23 s	1,102,737
240-core Intel x5650, 2.66GHz, 1.28TB RAM, 88TB disk, Red Hat Enterprise Linux 6.1	1.009 trillion	338 h 5 m	829,556

Oracle Spatial and Graph with Oracle Database 12c reached the 1 trillion triples mark in processing and indexing RDF triples in September 2014. Oracle has a maximum load rate of 1,420,000 quads loaded and indexed per second (see Table 8-2).

Table 8-2. *Oracle Spatial and Graph's Performance in Triple and Quad Loading and Indexing*

Configuration	Count	Time	Load Rate*
64-core SPARC64 VII+@3GHz, 512GB RAM, 160 drives in dual F5100 flash arrays, Oracle Database 11.2.0.2.0	1.1 billion triples	28 m 11 s	650,500 TLIPS
64-core SPARC64 VII+@3GHz, 512GB RAM, 160 drives in dual F5100 flash arrays, Oracle Database 11.2.0.2.0	3.4 billion triples	105 m	539,700 TLIPS
40-Core Intel E7-4870@ 2.4GHz with 1TB RAM on one Sun Server X2-4 node, dual node Sun ZFS 7420 storage	27.4 billion quads	13 h 11 min	273,000 QLIPS
192-core Oracle Exadata Database Machine X4-2 High Capacity full rack, 2TB RAM, 44.8TB flash cache, eight-tray dual controller ZS3-2 storage, Oracle Database 12.1.0.1	605.4 billion quads	115.2 h	1,420,000 QLIPS

*TLIPS: Triples Loaded and Indexed Per Second; QLIPS: Quads Loaded and Indexed Per Second

Summary

In this chapter, you saw Big Data applications using Semantic Web technologies in search engines, social media, and high-performance storage. You learned how to add structured data to your web site, to be considered by Google for inclusion in the Knowledge Graph, whose data will be used to show additional data on the Knowledge Panel and Knowledge Carousel. You know by now how to write semantic annotation for Facebook and Twitter objects in the markup.

The final chapter will demonstrate step-by-step use cases for a variety of real-life situations.

References

1. Google (2015) Introducing the Knowledge Graph. www.google.co.uk/insidesearch/features/search/knowledge.html. Accessed 9 March 2015.

2. Twitter (2015) Getting Started with Cards. https://dev.twitter.com/cards/. Accessed 12 March 2015.

3. Gliozzo, A., Patwardhan, S., Biran, O., McKeown, K. (2013) Semantic Technologies in IBM Watson. www.cs.columbia.edu/nlp/papers/2013/watson_class_acl_tnlp_2013.pdf. Accessed 23 April 2015.

4. Gucer, V. (2013) IBM is embracing Semantic technologies in its products. In: 5 Things To Know About Semantic Technologies. www.ibm.com/developerworks/community/blogs/5things/entry/5_things_to_know_about_the_semantic_technologies?lang=en. Accessed 23 April 2015.

5. Le Hors, A. (2012) Interview: IBM on the Linked Data Platform. www.w3.org/blog/2012/05/interview-ibm-on-a-linked-data/. Accessed 23 April 2015.

6. Welty, C. (2013) Semantic Web and Best Practice in Watson. In: Proceedings of the Workshop on Semantic Web Enterprise Adoption and Best Practice (WaSABi 2013), Sydney, Australia, 22 October, 2013. http://ceur-ws.org/Vol-1106/keynote2.pdf. Accessed 23 April 2015.

7. Unger, C., Freitas, A., Cimiano, P. (2014) An Introduction to Question Answering over Linked Data. In: Reasoning Web: Reasoning on the Web in the Big Data Era. Lecture Notes in Computer Science 2014, 8714:128–130, http://dx.doi.org/10.1007/978-3-319-10587-1. Accessed 23 April 2015.

8. Gliozzo, A. M., Kalyanpur, A., Welty, C. (2011) Semantic Web Technology in Watson. Tutorial at the 10th International Semantic Web Conference, Bonn, Germany, 23-27 October 2011. http://iswc2011.semanticweb.org/tutorials/semantic-web-technology-in-watson/. Accessed 23 April 2015.

9. Shotton, D. (2012) A major user of RDF linked data—the BBC. http://jats.nlm.nih.gov/jats-con/2012/presentations/shotton_jatscon2012.pdf. Accessed 24 April 2015.

10. BBC (2010) World Cup 2010. http://news.bbc.co.uk/sport2/hi/football/world_cup_2010/. Accessed 24 April 2015.

11. BBC (2012) London 2012 Olympics. www.bbc.com/sport/0/olympics/2012/. Accessed 24 April 2015.

12. BBC (2015) BBC News. www.bbc.co.uk/news/. Accessed 24 April 2015.

13. BBC (2015) BBC Sport. www.bbc.co.uk/sport. Accessed 24 April 2015.

14. Kobilarov, G., Scott, T., Raimond, Y., Oliver, S., Sizemore, C., Smethurst, M., Bizer, C., Lee, R. (2009) Media Meets Semantic Web—How the BBC Uses DBpedia and Linked Data to Make Connections. Lecture Notes in Computer Science 2009, 5554:723–737, http://dx.doi.org/10.1007/978-3-642-02121-3_53. Accessed 24 April 2015.

15. BBC (2015) BBC Programmes. www.bbc.co.uk/programmes. Accessed 24 April 2015.

16. BBC (2015) BBC Music. www.bbc.co.uk/music. Accessed 24 April 2015.

17. BBC (2015) BBC Earth. www.bbc.com/earth/uk. Accessed 24 April 2015.

18. BBC (2012) Sports Refresh: Dynamic Semantic Publishing. www.bbc.co.uk/blogs/legacy/bbcinternet/2012/04/sports_dynamic_semantic.html. Accessed 24 April 2015.

19. Library of Congress (2015) Fascinating Facts. www.loc.gov/about/fascinating-facts/. Accessed 24 April 2015.

20. Library of Congress (2015) LC Linked Data Service. http://id.loc.gov/. Accessed 24 April 2015.

21. Ford, K. (2010) ID.LOC.GOV, 1½ Years: Review, Changes, Future Plans, MADS/RDF. http://id.loc.gov/static/presentations/kefo_dlf_id.pdf. Accessed 24 April 2015.

22. Library of Congress (2015) Vocabulary (Bibliographic Framework Initiative Technical Site). http://bibframe.org/vocab/. Accessed 24 April 2015.

23. Harper, C. A., Tillett, B. B. (2007) Library of Congress Controlled Vocabularies and Their Application to the Semantic Web. Cataloging & Classification Quarterly 2007, 43(3-4):47–68. http://dx.doi.org/10.1300/J104v43n03_03. Accessed 24 April 2015.

24. Franz Inc. (2011) Franz's AllegroGraph Sets New Record on Intel Xeon E7 Platform. http://franz.com/about/press_room/Franz-Intel_6-7-11.lhtml. Accessed 12 March 2015.

25. Oracle (2014) Oracle Spatial and Graph: Benchmarking a Trillion Edges RDF Graph. http://download.oracle.com/otndocs/tech/semantic_web/pdf/OracleSpatialGraph_RDFgraph_1_trillion_Benchmark.pdf. Accessed 3 February 2015.

■ ■ ■

## CHAPTER 9

Use Cases

By reading the book, you learned how to write HTML5 Microdata and JSON-LD annotations in the markup, develop Semantic Web applications, describe web services in standardized languages, run powerful queries on Linked Open Data (LOD) datasets, and develop Semantic Web applications. Now that you have become familiar with Semantic Web technologies, let's analyze four complex examples, to get ready for real-life implementations!

RDB to RDF Direct Mapping

Using the R2RML language for expressing customized mappings from relational database (RDB) to Resource Description Framework (RDF) datasets, you refer to logical tables to retrieve data from an input database. A logical table can be either a base table, a view, or an SQL query [1]. Assume you have a relational database about the staff members in your enterprise and would like to map it to RDF. Each staff member is identified by a unique identifier (ID), which is used as the primary key (see Table 9-1).

Table 9-1. *The Employee Database Table*

ID	FirstName	LastName
INTEGER	VARCHAR(50)	VARCHAR(50)
10	John	Smith
11	Sarah	Williams
12	Peter	Jones

The employee projects are described by the employee identifiers (ID_Employee) and the project identifiers (ID_Project), both of which are primary foreign keys (see Table 9-2).

Table 9-2. *The Employee_Project Database Table*

ID_Employee	ID_Project
INTEGER	INTEGER
10	110
11	111
11	112
12	111

The projects use an integer identifier (ID), which is a primary key featured by the description of a maximum of 50 characters (Table 9-3).

Table 9-3. *The Project Database Table*

ID	Description
INTEGER	VARCHAR(50)
110	WebDesign
111	CloudComputing
112	DomainRegistration

The *direct mapping* defines an RDF graph representation of the data from the relational database [2]. The direct mapping takes the relational database (data and schema) as input, and generates an RDF graph called the *direct graph*. During the mapping process, the staff members, the projects, and the relationship between them are expressed in RDF using the Turtle syntax (see Listing 9-1). The rule for translating each row of a logical table to zero or more RDF triples is specified as a *triples map*. All RDF triples generated from one row in the logical table share the same subject. A triples map is represented by a resource that references other resources. Each triples map has exactly one rr:logicalTable property with a value representing the logical table that specifies a Structured Query Language (SQL) query result to be mapped to RDF triples. A triples map also has exactly one *subject map* that specifies the technique to use for generating a subject for each row of the logical table, using the rr:subjectMap property,[1] whose value is the subject map. The triples map may have optional rr:predicateObjectMap properties, whose values are *predicate-object maps* that create the predicate-object pairs for each logical table row of the logical table. The predicate map-object map pairs specified by predicate-object maps can be used together with the subjects generated by the subject map for creating RDF triples for each row.

Listing 9-1. Direct Mapping from RDB to RDF

```
@prefix foaf: <http://xmlns.com/foaf/0.1/> .
@prefix ex: <http://example.com> .
@prefix xsd: <http://www.w3.org/2001/XMLSchema#> .
@base <http://example.com/base/> .

<TriplesMap1>
  a rr:TriplesMap;

  rr:logicalTable [ rr:tableName "\"Employee\""; ] ;

  rr:subjectMap [ rr:template "http://example.com/employee/{\"\ID\"}"; ];

  rr:predicateObjectMap
  [
    rr:preficate        ex:firstName ;
        rr:objectMap    [ rr:column "\"FirstName\"" ]
  ];
```

---

[1]Alternatively, the rr:subject constant shortcut property can also be used.

```
  rr:predicateObjectMap
  [
    rr:predicate        ex:lastName ;
        rr:objectMap    [ rr:column "\"LastName\"" ]
  ]
  .

<TripleMap2>
  a rr:TriplesMap;

  rr:logicalTable [ rr:tableName "\"Project\""; ] ;

  rr:subjectMap [ rr:template "http://example.com/project/{\"\ID\"}"; ];

  rr:predicateObjectMap
  [
    rr:preficate        ex:id ;
        rr:objectMap    [ rr:column "\"ID\"" ]
  ];

  rr:predicateObjectMap
  [
    rr:predicate        ex:description ;
        rr:objectMap    [ rr:column "\"Description\"" ]
  ]
  .

<linkMap_1_2>
  a rr:TriplesMap;

  rr:logicalTable [ rr:tableName "\"Employee_Project\""; ] ;

  rr:subjectMap [ rr:template "http://example.com/employee/{\"\ID_Employee\"}"; ];

  rr:predicateObjectMap
  [
    rr:preficate        ex:involvedIn ;
        rr:objectMap    [ rr:template "http://example.com/project/{\"ID_Project\"}" ];
  ] .
```

The R2RML mapping is supported by software tools such as the db2triples software library [3], OpenLink Virtuoso [4], RDF-RDB2RDF [5], morph [6], and Ultrawrap [7]. In this example, the result is a set of RDF triples that describe the staff members and the projects they are involved in (Table 9-4).

Table 9-4. *The RDF Triples of the Output*

Subject	Predicate	Object
<http://example.com/ employee/10>	<http://example.com/lastName>	"Smith"
<http://example.com/ employee/10>	<http://example.com/firstName>	"John"
<http://example.com/ employee/12>	<http://example.com/lastName>	"Jones"
<http://example.com/ employee/12>	<http://example.com/firstName>	"Peter"
<http://example.com/ employee/11>	<http://example.com/lastName>	"Williams"
<http://example.com/ employee/11>	<http://example.com/firstName>	"Sarah"
<http://example.com/ project/110>	<http://example.com/description>	"WebDesign"
<http://example.com/ project/110>	<http://example.com/id>	"110"^^<http://www/w3/org/2001/ XMLSchema#integer>
<http://example.com/ project/111>	<http://example.com/description>	"CloudComputing"
<http://example.com/ project/111>	<http://example.com/id>	"111"^^<http://www/w3/org/2001/ XMLSchema#integer>
<http://example.com/ project/112>	<http://example.com/description>	"DomainRegistration"
<http://example.com/ project/112>	<http://example.com/id>	"112"^^<http://www/w3/org/2001/ XMLSchema#integer>
<http://example.com/ employee/10>	<http://example.com/involvedIn>	<http://example.com/ project/110>
<http://example.com/ employee/12>	<http://example.com/involvedIn>	<http://example.com/ project/111>
<http://example.com/ employee/11>	<http://example.com/involvedIn>	<http://example.com/ project/112>
<http://example.com/ employee/11>	<http://example.com/involvedIn>	<http://example.com/ project/111>

By default, all RDF triples are in the default graph of the output dataset. However, a triples map can contain graph maps that place some or all of the triples into named graphs instead.

A Semantic Web Service Process in OWL-S to Charge a Credit Card

Assume a Web service that charges a valid credit card. In OWL-S, Web services can be modeled as *processes* that specify how clients can interact with the service. There can be any number of *preconditions*, which must all hold in order for the process to be successfully invoked. A process has zero or more *inputs*, representing information required, under some *conditions*, for the performance of the process. A process might have any number of *outputs* that represent information provided by the process to the requester. *Effects* describe real-world conditions the process relies on. To describe the credit card charging process in OWL-S, we have to check whether the card is overdrawn or not, which can be defined as an *atomic process* (a description of a service that expects one message and returns one message in response). If the card is overdrawn, a failure should be displayed. Otherwise, if the card can be charged, the process has to be executed. Hence, the description of a process includes two `result` elements: one for charging the card and another for the error handler (see Listing 9-2).

Listing 9-2. OWL-S Description of Charging a Credit Card [8]

```
<process:AtomicProcess rdf:ID="Purchase">
    <process:hasInput>
        <process:Input rdf:ID="ObjectPurchased" />
    </process:hasInput>
    <process:hasInput>
        <process:Input rdf:ID="PurchaseAmt" />
    </process:hasInput>
    <process:hasInput>
        <process:Input rdf:ID="CreditCard" />
    </process:hasInput>
    <process:hasOutput>
        <process:Output rdf:ID="ConfirmationNum" />
    </process:hasOutput>
    <process:hasResult>
      <process:Result>
        <process:hasResultVar>
            <process:ResultVar rdf:ID="CreditLimH">
                <process:parameterType rdf:resource="&ecom;#Dollars" />
            </process:ResultVar>
        </process:hasResultVar>
        <process:inCondition>
          <expr:KIF-Condition>
            <expr:expressionBody>
            (and (current-value (credit-limit ?CreditCard)
                                ?CreditLimH)
                 (>= ?CreditLimH ?purchaseAmt))
            </expr:expressionBody>
          </expr:KIF-Condition>
        </process:inCondition>
        <process:withOutput>
            <process:OutputBinding>
                <process:toParam rdf:resource="#ConfirmationNum" />
                <process:valueFunction rdf:parseType="Literal">
                   <cc:ConfirmationNum xsd:datatype="&xsd;#string" />
```

```
                </process:valueFunction>
              </process:OutputBinding>
          </process:withOutput>
          <process:hasEffect>
            <expr:KIF-Condition>
              <expr:expressionBody>
                (and (confirmed (purchase ?purchaseAmt) ?ConfirmationNum)
                     (own ?objectPurchased)
                     (decrease (credit-limit ?CreditCard)
                               ?purchaseAmt))
              </expr:expressionBody>
            </expr:KIF-Condition>
          </process:hasEffect>
        </process:Result>
        <process:Result>
          <process:hasResultVar>
            <process:ResultVar rdf:ID="CreditLimL">
              <process:parameterType rdf:resource="&ecom;#Dollars" />
            </process:ResultVar>
          </process:hasResultVar>
          <process:inCondition>
            <expr:KIF-Condition>
              <expr:expressionBody>
                (and (current-value (credit-limit ?CreditCard)
                                    ?CreditLimL)
                     (< ?CreditLimL ?purchaseAmt))
              </expr:expressionBody>
            </expr:KIF-Condition>
          </process:inCondition>
          <process:withOutput rdf:resource="&ecom;failureNotice" />
            <process:OutputBinding>
              <process:toParam rdf:resource="#ConfirmationNum" />
              <process:valueData rdf:parseType="Literal">
                <drs:Literal>
                  <drs:litdefn xsd:datatype="&xsd;#string">00000000</drs:litdefn>
                </drs:Literal>
              </process:valueData>
            </process:OutputBinding>
          </process:withOutput>
        </process:Result>
      </process:hasResult>
</process:AtomicProcess>
```

The data transformation produced by the process is specified by the inputs and outputs (hasInput, hasOutput). Atomic processes always receive the inputs specifying the information required for the execution of the process from the client. The result of the process execution is that the credit card is charged, and the money is withdrawn from the account. The effect in this example describes that the customer now owns the object (own ?objectPurchased) and that the amount of money in the credit card account has been reduced (decrease (credit-limit ?CreditCard) ?purchaseAmt). In real-life applications, such services typically send an invoice with or without a notification about the success of the transaction. Credit card transactions have two results: one for the case in which there was sufficient balance to pay the bill, and one for when there wasn't. Each result can be augmented with a further binding.

Modeling a Travel Agency Web Service with WSMO

Assume the following scenario. Leslie wants to book a flight and a hotel for a tropical holiday. The fictional Dream Holidays Travel Agency provides recreational and business travel services based on Semantic Web Service technologies. The travel agency arranges the flight booking and the hotel booking under the contract with the service providers (Figure 9-1).

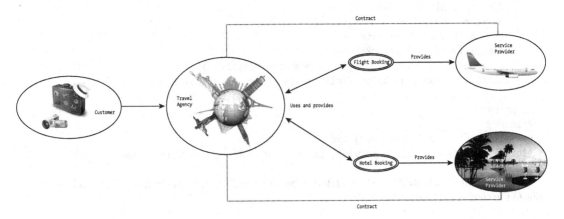

Figure 9-1. *Travel agency modeling*

The goal of the service can be described as "book a flight and hotel room for a tropical holiday for Leslie." The post-condition is to get a trip reservation by providing the current location, the destination, the payment method, and the name of the hotel (see Listing 9-3).

Listing 9-3. Defining the Service Goal

```
goal _"http://www.example.com/successfulBooking"
  capability
    postcondition
      definedBy
        ?tripReservation memberOf tr#reservation[
            customer hasValue fof#Leslie,
            origin hasValue loc#adelaide,
            destination hasValue loc#bali,
            travel hasValue ?flight,
            accommodation hasValue ?Hotel
            payment hasValue tr#creditcard
        ] and
        ?flight[airline hasValue tr#staralliance] memberOf tr#flight and
        ?hotel[name hasValue "Tropical Paradise Hotel"] memberOf tr#hotel .
```

The DREAMHOLIDAYS service description should contain the tickets, hotels, amenities, and so on. The pre-state capability description includes the reservation request and the prerequisites, such as a valid credit card (see Listing 9-4).

Listing 9-4. Pre-State Capability Description

```
capability DREAMHOLIDAYScapability
 sharedVariables {?creditCard, ?initialBalance, ?item, ?passenger}
 precondition
  definedBy
   ?reservationRequest[
        reservationItem hasValue ?item,
        passenger hasValue ?passenger,
        payment hasValue ?creditcard,
      ] memberOf tr#reservationRequest and
      ((?item memberOf tr#trip) or (?item memberOf tr#ticket)) and
      ?creditCard[balance hasValue ?initialBalance] memberOf po#creditCard.

 assumption
  definedBy
   po#validCreditCard(?creditCard) and
   (?creditCard[type hasValue po#visa] or ?creditCard[type hasValue po#mastercard]).
```

The post-state capability description includes the post-conditions, the reservation price, and the final value of the credit card (see Listing 9-5).

Listing 9-5. Post-State Capability Description

```
postcondition
        definedBy
            ?reservation[
                reservationItem hasValue ?item,
                customer hasValue ?passenger,
                payment hasValue ?creditcard
            ] memberOf tr#reservation .

    assumption
        definedBy
          reservationPrice(?reservation, "AUD", ?tripPrice) and
          ?finalBalance= (?initialBalance - ?ticketPrice) and
          ?creditCard[po#balance  hasValue  ?finalBalance] .
```

Querying DBpedia Using the RDF API of Jena

As mentioned earlier, Apache Jena uses the ARQ engine for the processing SPARQL queries. The ARQ API classes are found in com.hp.hpl.jena.query. The core classes of ARQ are Query, which represents a single SPARQL query; the Dataset, where the queries are executed; QueryFactory, used for generating Query objects from SPARQL strings; QueryExecution, which provides methods for query execution; ResultSet, which contains the results obtained from an executed query; and QuerySolution, which represents a row of query results. If there are multiple answers to the query, a ResultSet will be returned, containing the QuerySolutions.

To query DBpedia from Jena, you can use QueryFactory and QueryExecutionFactory. QueryFactory has create() methods to read a textual query and return a Query object with the parsed query. QueryExecutionFactory creates a QueryExecution to access a SPARQL service over HTTP in the form QueryExecutionFactory.sparqlService(String service,Query query), where service is a string representing a SPARQL service. You can create a test connection to DBpedia's SPARQL service, as shown in Listing 9-6.

Listing 9-6. Test Connection to DBpedia's SPARQL Endpoint

```java
import com.hp.hpl.jena.query.QueryExecution;
import com.hp.hpl.jena.query.QueryExecutionFactory;
import com.hp.hpl.jena.sparql.engine.http.QueryExceptionHTTP;

public class QueryTest {
  public static void main(String[] args) {
    String service = "http://dbpedia.org/sparql";
    String query = "ASK { }";
    QueryExecution qe = QueryExecutionFactory.sparqlService(service, query);
    try {
      if (qe.execAsk()) {
        System.out.println(service + " is UP");
      }
    } catch (QueryExceptionHTTP e) {
      System.out.println(service + " is DOWN");
    } finally {
      qe.close();
    }
  }
}
```

As you can see, the `service` string contains the SPARQL endpoint of DBpedia. Now, run a query to retrieve people who were born in Eisenach. To achieve this, you need a SELECT SPARQL query that searches the person objects for dbo:birthPlace: Eisenach, as shown in Listing 9-7.

Listing 9-7. A SPARQL Query to Run on DBpedia from Jena

```java
String service="http://dbpedia.org/sparql";
String query="PREFIX dbo:<http://dbpedia.org/ontology/>"
 + "PREFIX : <http://dbpedia.org/resource/>"
 + "PREFIX foaf:<http://xmlns.com/foaf/0.1/>"
 + "select ?person ?name where {?person dbo:birthPlace : Eisenach."
 + "?person foaf:name ?name}";
QueryExecution qe=QueryExecutionFactory.sparqlService(service, query);
ResultSet rs=qe.execSelect();
while (rs.hasNext()){
  QuerySolution s=rs.nextSolution();
  Resource r=s.getResource("?person");
  Literal name=s.getLiteral("?name");
  System.out.println(s.getResource("?person").toString());
  System.out.println(s.getLiteral("?name").getString());
}
```

The result should contain the people who were born in Eisenach, such as Johann Sebastian Bach.

Summary

In this chapter, you analyzed four complex Semantic Web examples. You saw how to map a relational database table to RDF, describe a process in OWL-S, model a Semantic Web Service in WSMO, and, finally, query an LOD dataset programmatically from Apache Jena.

By having read this book, you now understand the core Semantic Web concepts and mathematical background based on graph theory and Knowledge Representation. You learned how to annotate your web site markup with machine-readable metadata from Schema.org, DBpedia, GeoNames, and Wikidata to boost site performance on Search Engine Result Pages. By now, you can write advanced machine-readable personal descriptions, using vCard-based hCard, FOAF, Schema.org, and DBpedia. You have seen how to publish your organization's data with semantics, to reach wider audiences, including HTML5 Microdata or JSON-LD annotations for your company, products, services, and events to be considered by Google for inclusion in the Knowledge Graph. You know how to serialize structured data as HTML5 Microdata, RDF/XML, Turtle, Notation3, and JSON-LD and create machine-readable vocabularies and ontologies in RDFS and OWL. You have learned to contribute to the Open Data and Open Knowledge initiatives and know how to publish your own LOD datasets. You know how to set up your programming environment for Semantic Web application development and write programs in Java, Ruby, and JavaScript using popular APIs and software libraries such as Apache Jena and Sesame. You also learned how to store and manipulate data in triplestores and quadstores and became familiar with the most popular graph databases, such as AllegroGraph and Neo4j. You are capable of describing and modeling Semantic Web Services with OWL-S, WSDL, WSML, and WS-BPEL. You can run complex SPARQL queries on large LOD datasets, such as DBpedia and Wikidata, and even encourage data reuse with your own easy-to-access OpenLink Virtuoso, Fuseki, or 4store SPARQL endpoint. Finally, you learned about Big Data applications leveraging Semantic Web technologies, such as the Google Knowledge Vault, the Facebook Social Graph, IBM Watson, and the Linked Data Service of the largest library in the world.

References

1. Das, S., Sundara, S., Cyganiak, R. (eds.) (2012) R2RML Processors and Mapping Documents. In: R2RML: RDB to RDF Mapping Language. www.w3.org/TR/r2rml/#dfn-r2rml-mapping. Accessed 1 May 2015.

2. Arenas, A., Bertails, A., Prud'hommeaux, E., Sequeda, J. (eds.) (2012) Direct Mapping of Relational Data to RDF. www.w3.org/TR/rdb-direct-mapping/. Accessed 1 May 2015.

3. Antidot (2015) db2triples. https://github.com/antidot/db2triples. Accessed 1 May 2015.

4. OpenLink Software (2015) Virtuoso Universal Server. http://virtuoso.openlinksw.com. Accessed 1 May 2015.

5. Inkster, T. (2015) RDF-RDB2RDF—map relational database to RDF declaratively. https://metacpan.org/release/RDF-RDB2RDF. Accessed 1 May 2015.

6. Calbimonte, J.-P. (2015) morph. https://github.com/jpcik/morph. Accessed 1 May 2015.

7. Capsenta (2015) Ultrawrap. http://capsenta.com. Accessed 1 May 2015.

8. Martin, D. et al. (2004) Service Profiles. In: OWL-S: Semantic Markup for Web Services. www.w3.org/Submission/OWL-S/. Accessed 1 May 2015.

Index

Get the eBook for only $5!

Why limit yourself?

Now you can take the weightless companion with you wherever you go and access your content on your PC, phone, tablet, or reader.

Since you've purchased this print book, we're happy to offer you the eBook in all 3 formats for just $5.

Convenient and fully searchable, the PDF version enables you to easily find and copy code—or perform examples by quickly toggling between instructions and applications. The MOBI format is ideal for your Kindle, while the ePUB can be utilized on a variety of mobile devices.

To learn more, go to www.apress.com/companion or contact support@apress.com.